PETER CAPSTICK'S
AFRICA
A RETURN TO THE LONG GRASS

Victoria Falls.

PETER CAPSTICK'S AFRICA
A RETURN TO THE LONG GRASS

Peter Hathaway Capstick

photographs by
Paul Kimble and Richard van Niekerk

St. Martin's Press
New York

Paul Kimble: *iv, xxii,* 5, 6, 11, 12, 13, 15, 16, 20, 23, 26, 29,
31, 33, 39, 41, 43, 45, 46, 47, 49, 52, 53, 55,
59, 61, 63, 67, 70–71, 74, 77, 80, 85, 88, 89, 92,
97, 106, 107, 111, 112, 114, 116, 118, 119, 121,
125, 131, 132, 133, 137, 138, 140, 142, 143, 147,
149, 150–51, 152, 154, 159, 161, 162–63, 164, 165,
166, 169, 209, 211

Richard van Niekerk: 171, 175, 178, 181, 184, 187, 189, 190, 191,
192, 195, 196–97, 198, 200, 201, 202, 203, 205

Peter Capstick: 82

Fiona Capstick: 96

Library of Congress Cataloging-in-Publication Data

Capstick, Peter Hathaway.
Peter Capstick's Africa.

1. Hunting—Africa.   2. Safaris—Africa.   I. Title.
SK251.C274   1987   799.296   87–4484
ISBN 0–312–00670–5

First Edition

10 9 8 7 6 5 4 3 2 1

THIS BOOK IS DEDICATED TO GORDON JAMES PETCH CUNDILL
AND
LEWIS STURDEE GAMES,
BOTH PROFESSIONAL HUNTERS WORTHY OF THE TITLE WHO RISKED THEIR LIVES
FOR THE AUTHOR IN THE COURSE OF THIS ADVENTURE,
TAKING TWENTY POUNDS OFF HIS WAIST AND FORTY YEARS OFF HIS LIFE.
THANK YOU, GENTLEMEN.

Africa with her mystery, her freedom, her untrammeled spaces, and her barbarism had become my mistress. . . . Those shackles so subtly forged are not fetters that easily are cast aside for all time. . . .

For what did I return? Perhaps the spirit of this book may answer. If this dedication to a land that holds men enraptured through the cheerless dawn of a fever bed in the wilderness, and beckons them away from all that culture and enlightenment proclaim as the joy of living, be dumb, then must I shake my head in the knowledge that no words of mine can ever frame a reply. . . .

Thus I have learned my Africa.

—Owen Letcher, The Bonds of Africa, 1913

CONTENTS

FOREWORD

Perhaps once in every generation Africa is blessed or cursed, according to the lights of the hunting cadre, with a writer who can grip the essence of the hunting experience. Baldwin, Cornwallis Harris, Selous, Hemingway, and Ruark have been read avidly to this day, never to be judged by the reactions of their contemporaries but by the lasting attraction of their writings to later generations. To this generation, Peter Hathaway Capstick holds undoubted claim as being the most successful writer on the modern African hunting scene.

From the writers of those early journals with their records of vast bags and unacceptable ethics by our standards, through the great era of the sportsman-hunter between the wars, right down to the antihero standards of the eighties, the common denominator and prerequisite for the writers' success has been that they have written about what they have known. In my view, no fiction based on the ethic and adventure of the hunt can ever grip as does the raw product written from experience.

I have shared a small part of the epic of Peter Hathaway Capstick. I first met him through the medium of his writings, and have seen this acquaintance mature through all the vagaries of Africa to the point where I have the privilege of intimacy borne of things shared. It is an intimacy which grows out of that unique sporting experience—a hunt shared. In our case, even unto a Nitro-Express that malfunctioned four times on a charging lion as Peter stood his ground and kept shooting.

Few men of success are not blessed with a special partner, and it is my hope and wish that the years before Fiona and Peter will be, as in the ancient Zulu pronouncement to friends, an *Ndlela enHlope* —an open road.

Whether you, the reader, seek information or perhaps a sense of participation, you have at hand the work of a writer worthy of the traditions of the honourable African hunting heritage. You share here the heat, the sweat, the frustrations and disappointments, as well as the moments that make all hunters hunt again! Capstick's books are filled with the verve of an accomplished craftsman and are spiced with the unique flavour of experience and of spurs won according to the only criterion that matters to a hunter—personal achievement.

Writing redolent of the smell of woodsmoke and the bite of a strong whisky (with little soda and less ice) but still part of the primeval past—that is the great asset of the *present* which the hunter, naturalist, photographer, and traveller seek to make a part of their own and yet to share and to preserve.

To the lure of primitive Africa must be drawn the interest—nay, the dedication—of the present to ensure its future.

There is no more potent tool than the pen, especially in the hands of a writer who binds the interest and whets the appetite, as Peter truly does. The *zing* of the cicada at midday, the *quank* of the yellow-billed hornbill in the hot sun of the open *mopane* forest, the chirp of the Scops owl at the periphery of the camp fire, and the wailing, whooping hunting call of the midnight hyena pack—all reach deep into the soul of any man who has once felt the strange magic of Africa, which reaches across oceans and across years to draw him back once more. Through the writings of the Capsticks, the Ruarks, and the Hemingways—and all those who went before them—new seekers are attracted who come to prove themselves to themselves and who leave with a considerable sense of being beholden to Africa for an experience that lives indelibly in their memories, even in the face of the vast attractions of the rest of this small world of ours. Perhaps the most important of these memories lies in the making of new friends, the establishing of relationships, and the accomplishment of deeds, however small, by yourself.

There is no more worthy advocate for the cause of hunting and the role it plays in the conservation of wildlife in Africa than Peter Hathaway Capstick. I fear to bore the reader, but I must make this point: hunting today, with its high costs and its hugely complex organizational infrastructure, is probably the surest method of preserving wild animals for the future. In modern Africa, this is the reality which governments are beginning to understand and to which they can relate their own economics. The greatest justification for the setting aside of vast areas for the enjoyment of the sportsman lies firmly embedded in the commercial development of hunting as a form of land utilization and as a vital element in the industries and foreign currency earning capacities of the African states where the sadly depleted herds still survive.

—Gordon James Petch Cundill
Chairman of the Board, Hunters Africa
King's Pool, Botswana.
June 1985.

INTRODUCTION

That truth is indeed stranger than fiction is more than a simple platitude considering the events of this book.

The concept of this opus was spawned during a transatlantic call to Lincoln Child, my good friend and editor at St. Martin's Press, in November 1984 to discuss future projects. As the most recent of my five books, *Safari: The Last Adventure,* had been completed and was enjoying excellent sales, Linc sweetly suggested, "Why don't you go back to your old haunts and try to get yourself killed again?"

Having quit professional hunting in the mid-1970s, except for taking the odd cattle-killing lion or leopard on friends' ranches, I had not really been back in the bush as a pro for some years. I considered the idea as Linc continued: "Just make it close. No seegar. We need the manuscript."

Had this been a novel, I would not have dared write an outline that included the absolute mayhem which in fact came to pass when I took Linc up on it. Nobody would have believed it anyway. Still, I went on safari in the winter of that year, was charged by a record-book lion that took ten shots to discourage, lost a wounded leopard to a second party, was very nearly nailed by a bull hippo, burned myself, almost broke both legs in a bad fall, had my photographer badly bitten by a very poisonous spider, and enjoyed a generally marvelous time.

I very much pushed my luck in not ending up in a couple of local slammers, courtesy of indigenous gentlemen most anxious to oblige with reservations and free board. In any case, *A Return to the Long Grass* is not a casual part of the title of this book.

Having pondered and accepted Linc's suggestion that I go back, I next considered the when, how, with whom, and how much of the project. As I had recently completed the research and writing of my previous book, *Safari,* I knew that Hunters Africa was the answer: the company had so many operations in so many different areas and offered such a tremendous variety of species. That meant contacting one Gordon Cundill, the African managing director and full partner in the old and revered firm, which had been started in East Africa and that had gone through a variety of acquisitions, these, however, not really being the point of this book. Suffice it to observe that Mr. Cundill and his partners control a rough 200,000 square miles of Africa. That seemed to me to be enough elbowroom.

I approached Gordon at a prearranged meeting at Jan Smuts Airport, near Johannesburg. My wife Fiona and I met him in front of twin statues of the two earliest South African aviation pioneers,

and we spoke for about an hour on the pending project.

Initially, my idea had been to take a big jumbo in one of Gordon's Tanzanian concessions in memory of my years as a professional hunter and cropping officer. Gordon, however, seemed to see things on a larger scale, and he immediately suggested that it would make for a far more interesting book were I to trace my old spoor through Zambia, Botswana, and Zimbabwe (the former Rhodesia) in an effort to find my old pals and bush staff who had shared many of my earlier adventures. (Ethiopia, however, was out, as I have developed an advanced allergy to incoming automatic rifle fire.)

Gordon's enthusiasm was enormous and his subsequent follow-through typical of his firm's efficiency. As matters turned out, the elephant concept in Tanzania did not materialize: several of Gordon's employees had reportedly been grabbed by the Red element up there and forwarded to Mozambique (as supposed members of, variously, the CIA, South African Intelligence, and RENAMO, the Mozambican national resistance movement). Huge complications resulted from this incident, but it does not mean that safari in Tanzania is in any way over. As this is being written, Julius Nyerere has stepped down as head of state. What posture the future regime will adopt toward the safari-induced inflow of foreign exchange into the country remains to be seen and will probably be evident by the time this book is in print.

It was both painful (owing to bad luck physically) and a great source of renewed self-confidence to return to the long grass (which, if anything, turned out to be longer than I remembered). Gordon Cundill, as chief, was invaluable to the entire undertaking and has become a close personal friend. So have people such as Lew Games and his wife Dale, Steve Liversedge and Bruce Riggs, Paul Kimble and Dick van Niekerk, all of whom, together with many other people, are recognized in the acknowledgments at the end of this book.

In an attempt to collect these aberrant observations, I should like to point out that probably nothing in my life holds quite the value of this multiple trip to the places I hold so dear. I wondered if I still had "it" and was delighted to be personally satisfied that I do.

I must, with unspeakable sadness, tell those of you who have read my previous books that Silent, my gun bearer of so many years, is dead; gone in 1983. This information was conveyed to me through the great courtesy of Andre de Kock, who currently has my old camp at Nyampala on the Luangwa River. Andre searched the ancient villages until he determined that Silent was dead, and that Invisible was still alive but moved to parts unknown.

The overall conclusion I have gained from wandering back through the long grass is that the Old Africa is still there. One must simply turn over a few flat rocks to find it.

Peter H. Capstick

—Peter Hathaway Capstick
Zambia, Botswana, and Zimbabwe
January 1986

PETER CAPSTICK'S
AFRICA
A RETURN TO THE LONG GRASS

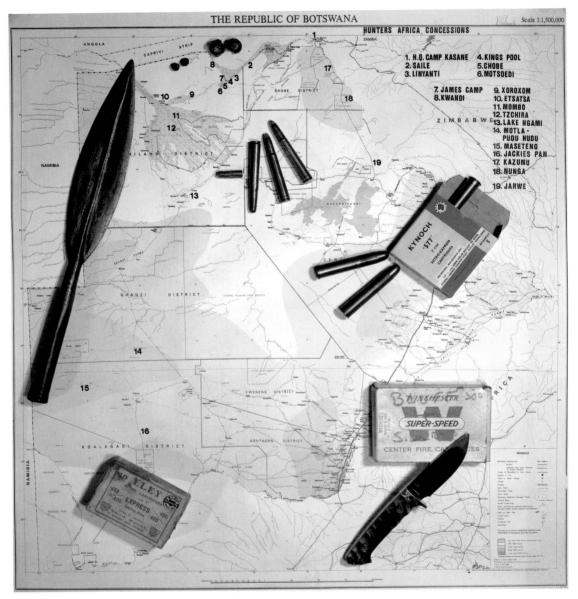

Map of Botswana, showing all camp locations.

PART ONE

Saile

"Through the back of the head," whispered Gordon Cundill in the tiniest of tones.

Keeping my eyes locked on the hazy outline of the huge lion, I eased the .375 H&H Magnum to my shoulder. Even through the low setting of the variable scope, his head looked like a small townhouse with excess shrubbery, just a peripheral halo of mane and mass, facing nearly away from me. With an imperceptible *snick,* I flipped the magnetic scope post into position, held as best I could through the heat waves reflected by the searing Botswana sun that would have staggered a Venetian glass-blower, and leveled at the spot where I reckoned his head met his neck. High, I would take the base of the skull; low, and the spine would be shattered. Either way, a record-book lion for the wall.

If I pulled the shot aside on a horizontal angle, however, both Gordon and I knew what would happen.

It did.

After five and a half days of tracking and two close encounters of the worst kind, I could only see a long, grass-shielded impression of the *Tau entunanyana*—as he is so pronounced in Tswana—just his head; one ear and the curve of his skull. I knew he was accompanied by a female, with whom he had been doing what came naturally but at a rate and frequency that would astonish any human. (How's about a roll in the hay every twenty minutes? Maybe you, brother, are up to such acrobatics but I have had back problems recently.) I lined up the sights, knowing the 300-grain Winchester Silvertip would have to bull through considerable bush and grass, and aware that a deflection was not only possible but probable. I eased off the trigger of the custom Mauser anyway.

That was a major and very nearly fatal error.

Whether through bush deflection, lousy shooting (for which I am not especially known), or simple bad luck, the tremendous lion jumped fifteen feet into the air, swapped ends, and came down in what was most certainly our direction. I believe that he charged the sound of the shot, rather than Gordon, Karonda the gun bearer, and me, as our cover was as good as his. With more than five hundred pounds of male lion coming at us as quickly as he could manage, however, the matter was academic and fast becoming immediate. Unfortunately, he had to clear some heavy cover, mostly *mopane* scrub, before we could take a second whack at him and have, even in African terms, a relatively clear shot.

He broke around a clump of *mopane* some ten yards from where he had been lying with his paramour, in company with two fully grown but nontrophy-sized lions. When I tell you that he charged, I use the term not lightly. He wanted us. Badly. Later, we were to discover one of several good reasons was that he contained a not inconsiderable amount of buckshot in his guts, about the American equivalent of a Double-0. They were old wounds but had still made a clear impression on his future attitude toward humans.

As he rounded the clump of bush, you can absolutely bet that I had one thing on my mind: putting as many 300-grain bullets into that bastard as soon as possible and before our acquaintance became any more intimate. I had been knocked down by lions seriously intent on biting me on a couple of previous occasions and was not especially eager to repeat the scenario.

I found out later (although I do not

remember hearing it at the time, so intense was my concentration in trying to kill the goddamn thing) that he was roaring fit to blow the leaves off the trees and the calluses off your right foot. Lord, but that was one *awfully* angry lion. (I suppose that had I just caught a .375 Silvertip at the base of the neck, I would have shared his sentiments.)

I shall never forget the gleam of his amber and anthracite eyes through the scope when he got into thinner cover only a few yards away. They glistened and glimmered in the hot sun above the crosshairs and post of the Bushnell scope like uncut gems, radioactive orbs centered on one thing:

Me.

I have no idea why everything tries to eat me. Maybe it's my breath. In any case, this was becoming a rather serious matter, especially when I heard a very strange sound just off to my left: a *click,* followed after perhaps a second and a half by a tremendous *boom!* I knew, of course, that it was Gordon firing his .500 Westley Richards Nitro-Express double rifle in a rather fervent attempt to keep the lot of us alive.

The only problem was that his ammo was defective and, after four attempts, Gordon had had three hangfires and one complete dud. It was a rifle worth more than a fine sports car (one of three he owns by noted craftsmen/manufactur-ers), and it had to be just our luck that when our lives were on the absolute line, his big bore—which should have been the precise item required to keep us all paying taxes—failed. Or, to be fair, at least the ammo did.

I shifted my sight to adjust to the fact that the lion was coming in at a five-degree angle and smashed a bullet right where it should have counted, smack in the middle of the chest. Okay, I knew that a .375 H&H Silvertip right through the engine room of anything less than a Tyrannosaurus rex was going to have a very negative effect on the chances of your becoming a grandfather. Gordon and Karonda knew the same thing.

The lion didn't.

He at least swerved at a few yards, and, with a dexterity I thought long gone, I worked the bolt and got a fresh round up the spout. As he turned, I thought, Aha! Gotcha!

Wrong again.

I have not yet had the chance to examine the skull of that grand beast, but I can tell you with a dozen witnesses, three of whom were on the spot when the incident occurred, that I shot that bloody lion exactly behind the base of the left ear. Precisely what the damage was has not yet been determined, but it sure as hell wasn't enough. He spun and came straight for us—and when a lion does that from a few yards, you had better have the ammo belt in the Maxim if you want to see the home airfield again.

Gordon's .500 Nitro slapped me again as I heard a peripheral *click—boom!* Another hangfire!

To say that this lion had me highly motivated would be an extreme understatement. There have probably been men who have worked a Mauser bolt-action faster, but I am inclined to at least give myself the benefit of a tie. I claim not the record, but I *will* tell you that there was a fourth round in my chamber in an astonishing hurry. As the lion continued his spin, I smacked him up the butt in an attempt to smash the pelvic girdle. Although the bullet hole was not more than an inch from his evacuating mechanism, I might as well have missed the bastard completely. It just made him madder and, trust me, he was mad enough to start with after my first shot.

I heard the snap of Gordon's striker on the .500 again, but this time there was no report at all. Meanwhile, the bloody thing was damned near on us, so old Karonda, the eighty-year-old Subiya gun bearer, decided to have a go at him with the spare .375 he was carrying. I saw it blow a clump of turf into the air some six feet behind the lion, though he later swore he had shot it through the hips. (There was no such bullet mark, more to our bad luck, as Karonda had once saved Gordon's life from a highly imminent lioness under very similar circumstances.)

I believe high-school boys have a term for the position we were now in but it is not for family reading.

I was carrying nine cartridges, all 300-grain Silvertips, and had thus far shot that cat twice through the head, once through the chest, and again up the arse. Gordon, through what I consider magnificent shooting, considering his hangfires, had to date placed at least one big soft-point through his guts. It's not the kind of shot that does much to break a lion down but, let's face it, it must be to *some* degree discouraging.

Negative.

Having by now clearly seen us, the brute finished his turn and came straight for us. He was one hell of a lot bigger than the lions you see on television, at the circus, or in the zoo, and I want to tell you he was most definitely on a kamikaze mission. I slammed him again in the chest, which, according to all the textbooks as well as my own work and experience, should have cooled him down considerably. This was, however, not a cooperative lion. I don't think he could read.

You must understand that all this sort of thing goes on in a matter of seconds—if you're that lucky—and it is pure reflex that keeps you alive or gets you killed with amazing rapidity. You just don't

Zebra were plentiful near the camp.

fool around with wounded, charging, re-cord-book lions. Not very often, you don't.

I had now shot him four times, as I said; twice through the noggin, once in the chest, and once more in unspeakable places. Gordon had by that point gotten at least one 570-grain soft-point into him and—it all happened so fast—perhaps a second. (Hitting a running lion at that speed with three hangfires and a dud and connecting with two of the three rounds that actually fired is an amazing feat of marksmanship and shows the kind of, shall we say, intestinal fortitude with which Gordon Cundill is gifted.)

I carry a custom Mauser-action, Blin-dee-barreled, bolt-action .375 by the

Continental Arms Corporation of New York. I had it made to hold six cartridges. If one loads directly from the action, however, there is always the risk of breaking the extractor, which is precisely what you don't need in the middle of a safari, let alone a lion charge. I therefore carry four rounds in the magazine and one in the chamber with the hammer down. My last shot was in the chamber of the barrel.

The lion finished his spin and resumed his charge. Gordon was off to my left and Karonda just to my right. As the beast whirled around, I stuck the last round in the rifle into his shoulder and aimed for his spine. It was the only lousy shot I made, just an inch high. It could have cost us our lives. No two ways: I blew it.

My rifle was now empty. Gordon's insurance gun, his dinosaur-stopping .500 Nitro-Express double, didn't work. It very much appeared that my career at the typewriter and the Mauser would both be coming to rather dramatic ends in the next few seconds. . . .

The tarmac of Jan Smuts Airport turned from coarse pavement to flowing black velvet as our plane gathered speed. I was sitting on the aisle, my wife Fiona in the middle, and Paul Kimble next to the window. One of the better-known South African photographers, I had "engaged"

.500 Nitro dud.

him for the trip. There would be others to follow.

Our destination was the Smoke That Thunders, the magnificent Victoria Falls in Zimbabwe, where SAA flight #40 landed in fine style. Paul, Fiona, and I were met on the dot by Keith Essen, representing Hunters Africa, who whisked us through Customs despite our guns and the other paraphernalia sometimes queried by authorities in any country.

Our final destination was not Zimbabwe, however—where I had spent time in the Matetsi region as a professional hunter during the bush war in the bloody days of the seventies—but Botswana, and this was the easiest route.

Curiously, while at Vic Falls Airport, I ran into Eric Wagner, whom we were shortly to visit. Eric was, at the time, the head of the Safari Club International Conservation Fund. He had, as Fate would have it, acquired the rights to Matetsi Unit #4, precisely my old stamping ground, and promptly invited our party down for a stay, provided the lion Gordon and I were about to assault did not do me first. Fair enough. I accepted, especially when I discovered that Eric had employed Stuart Campbell, my friend of some seventeen years, as his general manager.

We drove from Victoria Falls Airport (which I could barely leave with a dry eye, having met so many wonderful friends and clients there in the past) and turned off onto the old hunters' road to Pandamatenga. Our destination was Kasane, in Botswana, where we would take a flight by light aircraft to Saile airfield, only a few hundred yards from Saile Camp.

It seemed as if nothing had changed on the old Pandamatenga Road I had traveled so many times before. As Keith Essen expertly maneuvered us along, I even recognized individual trees. We had, however, a slight problem looming ahead.

Not many hours before, the South African Defence Force had carried out a preemptive strike against several strongholds harboring African National Congress terrorists in the capital city of Gaberone, way to the south. Now two of my party were holding South African passports, and I was wondering if there would be an international incident at Kasane that could possibly sabotage my safari plans.

I think that what is about to come is technically called a digression, but I shall do my best to deliver it accurately. Should you be going on safari, I hope you will take it as gospel. Africa today is not that of Robert Ruark in the early days. To highly (but not inaccurately) simplify matters, it seems there is now just one element that matters, especially in so-called emerging nations: *power!* Individually or on any other basis, it is the cornerstone of all black African society. When you enter Customs, as I shall vividly demonstrate later in this book, you may or may not understand precisely what I am saying but you will soon catch on. My observations are not intended as racial slurs but, as I have said in previous works, are a function of culture and of my personal experience.

The immense majority of Customs and Immigration officials are charmingly helpful in most emerging black African countries, especially those I visited for the purposes of this book. One does, however, run across the "new man" who is most anxious to obtain promotion by putting somebody in jail. That was bloody nearly me, and I have a low threshold for incarceration, especially in countries where the man on the street doesn't do very well feeding himself, let alone the poor bugger in the slammer. Spare me Third World slammers. . . .

With all this chasing through my mind. we were promptly and without incident delivered at Kasane, which is the border post between Zimbabwe and Botswana in the far northeast of Botswana. I was sweating blood as well as more urgent juices as we approached the tiny concrete-and-corrugated-steel hut that housed the formalities of Customs.

No problem. My American passport as well as the South African documents were hardly glanced at. Honestly, in retrospect, I don't think that word of the strike on parts of Gaberone had reached Kasane yet.

After a brief stop at the Hunters Africa office in Kasane, we were then driven to the airstrip, accompanied by Peter Hepburn, Hunters Africa's manager there. Our pilot, a Frenchman called Luc, was already on hand, and it was less than an hour later that we landed as smoothly as pancake batter at the airstrip close to Saile Camp after a delightful flight in perfect weather.

Gordon was there in person to meet us, along with his entire African safari staff —the damndest collection of charm and talent I've ever run across. Well, that's Gordon. If you're not the best, you don't work for him. Not for long you don't.

If you have spent any time in Africa, you may flatter yourself that you have a feeling for the people of the more remote tribes. In my case, considering the years I have spent in several African countries, my self-flattery is probably accurate. I have always had a rather indefinable affinity for the men I worked with, especially for those to whom I owe my life.

Gordon's personal crew consists of Mack, a Masarwa Bushman with classic peppercorn hair; Jehosephat, also a Masarwa and a very handsome, slenderly built man; Otesetswe, a member of the baYei people from the Maun area, farther to the south, and a fellow who could, I am sure, track a leopard up the vertical side of a basalt cliff; and Karonda, who truly has one of the most outstandingly striking faces of the "Old Africa" I have ever seen. He is a Subiya from a village north of Maun but whose ancestors lived in the Caprivi Strip for generations. (The Caprivi Strip is a slender tongue of land on the northern border of Botswana, facing Angola and part of Zambia, which was obtained as a concession by the Germans in 1880 when the present South-West Africa/Namibia was German South West Africa. Germany's idea at the time was to find access to the sea.) I would have been proud to have had these men on my safari team anywhere.

The really interesting personality, however, was Karonda, the man who later stood his ground when the lion charged and proved that there was more between his legs than his loincloth. Nobody really knows how old Karonda is, including Karonda. Rural Africans often tend not to reckon age in the manner of whites, but are inclined to relate their births to one or another well-known happening. Karonda appears to be old enough that nothing of any particular import came to pass during the year he was born, so the exact date is lost. Gordon, who has spent his entire life among black Americans, reckons that Karonda is probably a shade over eighty, yet he can walk you and me into the ground and carry both our carcasses home, one over each shoulder . . . an amazing man. (I was present once when Gordon asked Karonda if he remembered the First World War. The old man replied in dialect that as far as he was concerned, the whites were always fighting among themselves and he really couldn't keep their wars straight.)

If you spend any time at all with Karonda, you'll soon notice that he has but nine fingers; his left index is missing. Now there's a story worth telling.

During the mid–1970s, Karonda had a particularly good season as Gordon's gun bearer and one November he found himself with an exceptional amount of salary and clients' tips. Being a good hunter in every sense, he immediately concluded that he should dispose of such lucre in aid of the local economy, particularly in the acquisition of some cattle and a new wife, transactions he promptly went about securing.

He found and engendered the favor of a local lass, delivered the *lobola* of cattle, and went on his presumably merry way to his wedding bed. There was soon, however, some or other monumental difference of opinion, and the relationship was terminated when the new wife nearly severed Karonda's finger with the brilliant expediency of her teeth.

As I have observed elsewhere, everything in Africa bites. Karonda would agree.

You must understand that Karonda is not just another chap when it comes to the structure of his society. He is a senior headman in his home village, Shorobe, just north of Maun. This is no small position to hold in a culture as highly sensitive and ancient as his. You just don't bite the boss, and that point was made clear by Karonda with a large stick before driving his new ex-wife back home some two hundred miles on foot to her father. Once there, Karonda reclaimed the bride price cattle, promptly turned round, and then herded them back over the same two hundred-mile stretch—all told, about four hundred miles on foot.

It was then that Karonda noticed he had a slight problem with his finger, and that some sort of infection was in fact proceeding up his hand and into his arm. It turned out to be blood poisoning—and not an especially cheery case, at that. Doctors were able, after another hundred-plus-mile walk by Karonda, to save his life. His arm and hand, too. The finger? Forget it. It was only the old man's natural resistance to dying that pulled him through. Should you meet him one day, never ask about that missing finger. Point of honor, I suppose.

Gordon, after reciting the epic of Karonda to me, wandered off in search of a bourbon, muttering one of his usual Kiplingisms: "Which just goes to show that the female of the species is more deadly than the male. . . ."

We drove from the airstrip in spotless hunting vehicles the few minutes to Saile Camp (pronounced *Sigh-EEE-lay*) and arrived in grand fashion as Gordon sorted out Paul, Fiona, and myself as to the peculiarities of how he liked to run things in camp. Somebody would say something original like "knock-knock" at the most inconceivable hour of the morning, there being no walls or doors to actually knock on, since we were using classic safari double-fly tents. Upon arising, the choice was then coffee, tea, or in my case, a cold beer, since I take medication that dehydrates me and precludes caffeine. Beer's more fun, anyway.

Saile, while not being an especially attractive camp, nevertheless has great charm. It lies directly on the Linyanti River, which is heavily vegetated with tall reeds, and is northeast of the Linyanti Swamp and southwest of Lake Liambezi —not exactly Coney Island on the Fourth of July. Across this marshy, reed-filled river is the Caprivi Strip, which is controlled by South Africa. The camp itself, with its huge shady trees set amidst this wildly beautiful region's unthinkable variety of fauna, made the spot one of the most pleasant places I have hunted—had it not been for that bloody lion.

We spent the first afternoon outside the camp, rechecking the zero of the scope of my custom Mauser. At one hundred yards it shot five rounds within a half-dollar, whereas it normally placed as many within the diameter of a dime. Well, I put it down to inflation and decided to charge on.

Satisfied that the rifle was doing what it was supposed to do, and with evening falling fast, we headed back to camp. I normally keep the scope at about 3½X- to 4X-power, but when we saw a very big boar warthog jogging across the plain at a distance so great and in cover so thick that I will not relate it here lest I be accused of literary perfidy—and when Gordon said, "Take him. We need camp meat"—I switched to 8X-power.

I swallowed twice, stalked some three hundred yards from the vehicle, and caught a glimpse of the boar as he put things into overdrive. It's all automatic anyway, but I suppose, given his speed and distance, I held my sight a couple of warthogs ahead and across the level of his back. The sear of the Mauser broke and the firing pin fell. To the astonishment of everybody (including, I am positive, the warthog), he crashed into everything but flames, nailed just behind the ear.

Saile Camp, on the banks of the Linyanti River.

Zeroing in is immensely important to the performance of a rifle and its shooter. It can keep you alive.

When we got up to him and I saw the perfect running shot, I lost nothing in my reaction at Gordon's slap on the back. Mack was so excited at the prospect of meat that he put his lit cigarette backward into his mouth, reacting as might be imagined. Gordon and the whole crew collapsed with laughter.

"Sonofabitch," said I. "I was shooting for the earhole! The bloody shot's a good half-inch off." Disgusted, I stomped back to the vehicle with the flash of at least a few eye whites from a couple of the crew who knew some English. In any case, we had dinner.

If you have ever been on safari, you are aware that your status in the bloodshot eyes of the staff depends largely on the result of that first shot. If you luck

into a spectacular performance, such as I had with that warthog, you're made. If you bugger up that first shot, however, through nerves, booze, or carelessness, it won't matter a damn to the gun bearers and trackers what you do afterward. You're a loser. If you can't shoot, you can't perform what to them is the essential function: putting meat on their table. You may, in their full sight thereafter, brain-shoot fleeing humming birds offhand at five hundred yards, but it will never be the same. Whether you can shoot or not, in their opinion, depends entirely on the initial results. That is, *nyama*—meat. The fact that I later had to shoot my big lion so frequently and quickly meant nothing. It was the single round behind the warthog's ear that really got their attention.

Perhaps the essential reason that I chose Cundill to hunt with was his sense of ethics. Neither he nor I believe in shooting from cars or carrying on a safari in any manner other than traditionally. Dangerous game is taken up close and personally or it ceases to *be* dangerous game. It sounds hambone, but we both believe that honor comes before all. In sentiments such as these lie our personal and professional reputations and the maintenance of such. If you don't do it honorably, or if you take a step backward, you're no better than a bullfighter who runs or a kamikaze pilot with ninety-seven missions. One can *hunt* dangerous game or one can *kill* dangerous game. Both arrive at the same conclusion of the adventure, but the gulf in morality is immense.

When one considers a man of Gordon's cut, one must be careful not to let personal impressions color the actual man to anything but the true hue. I can simplify that by saying he is one of the three best professionals I have ever been in the field with, either professionally or as an amateur. When it comes to lions, I know of nobody better; and, as extraordinary company around a campfire, you would be hard-pressed to match him.

I had known Gordon for months before I learned that he was a Rhodes scholar with a degree in international law from Oxford University, so modest is the man. And this trait carries over into his business. Cundill is the "quietest" of the really good professional safari operators. He runs an absolute empire yet is as unassuming as you can imagine, despite being chairman of the board of the largest safari conglomerate in Africa. He is a hard but totally fair man whom I am proud to call my personal friend.

Gordon, as you can see from the photographs in this book, is well over six feet tall, stronger than a couple of Cape buffaloes, and able to walk your arse off from here to northern Ethiopia and back (if that's what they're still calling the place). He shot his first lion on what I secretly believe to have been his fiftieth birthday, which would have been some time in 1948. He is reputed to have been involved in the taking of another simba sometime in 1957, but this remains unconfirmed.

The curious thing, for such an "intrepid" lion hunter—an adjective much favored by earlier writers—is that he actually has people who care for him, despite his constant state of disarray. His sartorial splendor in the bush is—to say the least—highly individualistic, typified by his ever-present monocle. A glance at his lovely wife, Leslie, would knock out your master eye, and his three kids are straight out of Central Casting. Considering Gordon, it really is phenomenal the abberations that genes will cause.

Gordon Cundill and his safari staff.

As you will likely guess, Gordon and I are *very* good friends, which is also why I worry about him. He is far too casual around dangerous game, a trick few get away with for very long. I shall elaborate on this later, but it is my most fervent hope that he doesn't get what will most obviously come to him in a great rush if he continues to follow, unarmed, the tracks and spoor of the stuff that gets even. You see, Gordon has a habit of leaning out of his vehicle, noticing something interesting, and setting off for half a mile or more with nothing but his canine teeth as cover. If he keeps this up, he's going to get nailed. Lion, leopard, buff, hippo . . . whatever. Sooner or later he will bump into something that will bite him. That he is very good is verified by the fact that he took his first license as a professional at the age of seventeen in what was then Tanganyika, and has in fact never gotten caught by one of the bad ones. Gordon bears no scars, which is more than I can say of myself.

I will baldly state that Gordon Cundill, though the odds of your getting him as your professional hunter are virtually nonexistent, is one of the absolutely most competent men in the field and, as the British say, full stop.

The lead-lined curtain of the African night dropped like a fisherman's cast net, leaving nothing but the sequined sky, as bright as any I have seen since my old British Honduras days. Satellites and falling stars lazed by, and the hippos, in obvious proximity, made their territory apparent. The primordial fire glowed dully, and the smell of *mopane* and leadwood smoke mixed with the aroma of Gordon's Old Granddad to summon up a whole smoldering pile of emotion that I had been yearning to experience again since 1975, when I quit shooting for active safari to concentrate on my writing. I had a frosty beer at hand, as did Paul, and Fiona seemed pleased with her medium sherry. I spoke to the horrid parasite that lives in one of my bush jacket pockets, my voice-activated microcassette tape recorder, having walked away from the party to record the events of our departure and arrival while taking great care not to fall into the croc-infested river. Short, the headwaiter, resplendent in his *Jaegermeister* uniform with its crimson sash and fez, was so kind as to reaccommodate me, when I rejoined the group around the fire.

We finished our drinks reasonably close to eight o'clock, and were then summoned to dinner, where we attacked a succulent proliferation of roast chicken, preceded by a hearty buffalo tail soup and trailed by a gourmet's delight of vegetables (obtained and transported at no slight trouble), and culminating—in the literal middle of the bush, goddamn—in

Cundill and author.

a feast of genuine ice cream. As we went back out for something to settle our spirits around the fire, I had a chance to speak with Gordon about his own background as well as to inquire about the status of the local lion population and conditions in Botswana in general.

African campfires are generally memorable, and this one was no exception. We had a brandy and a couple of beers while Gordon told me, as a Botswana citizen, of the local state of affairs. Off to our left, the hyenas had pulled down an impala or some other luckless beast whose time had come, and they were having a hell of a wonderful time processing its essential salts and protein into whatever makes the grass grow. It was cold—very cold—and we were all wearing down jackets. (One of the basic and uniquely crazy enjoyments of the African campfire lies in the fact that your shins roast like well-basted

The quintessential Africa: sunset over the Linyanti.

spare ribs while your back freezes.) It all centers around the campfire: the arguments, the compliments, and the lies. Every now and then a dribble of truth seeps in, but it is, as a rule, largely avoided.

A giant fruit bat practically skimmed my ear as Gordon assumed the classic bum-warming position before the yellow tongues of flame. I had the .375 with solid 300-grainers close by in case of the uninvited appearance of hippo, several of which were demonstrating loudly a bare fifty yards away in the reeds. As I have espoused elsewhere, I hate hippos and would have ample opportunity to reinforce my dislike during this trip. The moon was not yet up but promised to be reasonably full. The beer we were drinking was equipped with the now standard flip-top container, which caused Gordon, upon picking one off the ground with a muffled curse—under no circumstances having been dropped by me, I might add—to utter what I have come to consider as a "Cundillism": "The canned container is the most ubiquitous evidence of man, particularly of the ubiquitous Albion and all his descendants."

Gordon actually speaks in this fashion, and, in this observation, I agreed with him.

The moon appeared at the propitious moment, and Paul Kimble went into raptures as he trapped the fool thing between reeds and through trees, like a small boy with his Double Nitro-Express camera in Paradise. His excitement was so intense I thought we would need an extra washing of his shorts, but in fact he took a truly lovely sequence of the essence of safari—the campfire, one's companions, and that essential but indefinable substance of the African night.

Night in Africa is not like night elsewhere, especially not while you're on safari. There really *are* things that can and joyfully will eat you. No kidding. After an American TV diet of Joy Adamson and so much of the crud that has been spread around about dangerous game,

one is no less than a pure, undiluted idiot if he or she goes on safari without learning the true facts of life in the bush. You, my dear boy or girl, are nothing but protein, which will be happily ingested by anything that eats meat. You *are* meat. I shall shortly tell you of some who learned the errors of their ways without opportunity for correction.

The Botswana night is now a miasma of shadow and sound. Hyenas. A damned big lion off to the right. An answering call from a lioness. Hippos—soon to become far more evident—and the trumpet of an elephant that has somehow escaped the AK-47 automatic fire on the other side of the river, where his cousins' bones lie stacked in homage to the dubious skill of clumsy but efficient poachers.

Fiona has long since gone to bed, soon to be accompanied by me and the .375. Gordon, his bum presumably warmed to the proper temperature, is preparing to quit the scene. Paul has toddled off to whatever photographers dream about. Gordon, armed with a weak flashlight, paraphrases Kipling half under his breath as he wanders into the night: "Send me somewhere east of Suez where a man can raise a thirst. . . ."

My thoughts could only revert to my own slim knowledge of Kipling: "They're 'angin' Danny Deever in the morning, You can hear the quick-step play. . . ." I wonder, listening to the carnivora in the immediate background, if there were any Deevers swinging from the branches of my *own* family tree.

It is now nearly two in the morning, and my soul has at last burst free of the bondage of commercial writing. Again, at last, I have the smells, sounds, and actual *vibrations* of the Long Grass, the Africa I have loved for so many years. I have the fire, dying in a blaze of blue glory; the smell of fresh biltong drying on the white man's wires; still the soft Tswana gabble of sleepy conversation; the sluggish gurgle of the river; the swirl of a croc or hippo; and the cold caress of the relentless Botswana winter night wind.

I am home.

Actually, it was a damned lucky thing that I chose that night to sit out until four in the morning, since the following evening was not quite as cheerful. I must, however, tell you of the following day. . . .

The verbal "knock-knock" came at a quarter to six, as predicted by Gordon, so, after less than two hours sleep, I was something less than "bushy-tailed." The hours alone, however, had been worth the loss of sleep, even had they been paid back in solid platinum. I had relocated my spirit. It had been missing for about a decade, so far as I know, but it had come back with a grand rush the night

before. And it was further cemented when I smelled breakfast: *mealiemeal,* ground corn mush, which is the staff of life in most of the southern part of Africa and which is one of my favorite dishes.

In celebration of my resurrection, I even ate a couple of fried eggs, probably the first two in over a year. Hell, but it was pure *muti* to smell the early mist of the swamp, the incredible carryings-on of the doves echoing in my muzzle-blast-deafened ears.

The evening before, Gordon and I had discussed his most pressing thought: that of the future of game in Africa in general and in Botswana in particular (although he has operations in many other areas). I was highly impressed by his knowledge of the ecological situation in Botswana as well as with his practical field skills. He's good—possibly because he has so much to lose. In any case, before the lot of slackers went to bed, I had the chance to discuss the situation with him.

The key is cows. As in cattle. And Gordon obviously knew his stuff. He pointed out that the basis of all currency from Roman times (and certainly considerably earlier) was cattle. The Latin word *pecu* meant cattle, money. This developed into the concept of *pecunia,* money, originally "riches in cattle." It all went back to the value of a relationship of cattle to people and the relative perception of such.

The curious thing about the status of cattle in Botswana, as in much of Africa, is the fact that the quality of cattle owned has no relevance to others' views of the owner's wealth or status. Sheer volume is what counts. This fact, along with the indiscriminate spraying of nonbiodegradable insecticides in Botswana, is really at the root of the problem.

That cattle and game are clearly at odds, because they both take up space, is well illustrated by the fate of the tsetse fly. When I was hunting in Botswana some sixteen years ago, the tsetse would grab your carcass and then argue about whether to eat it on the spot or take it home to their young.

No more.

The point is that where there are tsetse there is no domestic stock—no chickens, goats, sheep, or, more importantly, cattle, which are in direct competition with game for grass, browse, and sheer acreage of habitat. The absence of tsetse implies an absence of game. Or, as Gordon put it to me in his Oxfordian English, "Cattle has status, game does not. Further, there is no thoroughgoing educational program to clarify the value of game to the Botswana economy."

He took a healthy slug of Granddad, stared into the fingers of fire as a Scops owl played his tune in the tree above, and continued. "The survival of wildlife in this and other African countries depends entirely upon its economic relevance to the country involved. Operations like Hunters Africa *must* survive because they are economic private enterprise and produce the foreign exchange absolutely vital for imports. Botswana, which is roughly the size of France or Texas, yet is the most thinly populated of the emerging African countries, needs food, fuel, vehicles, and the rest of the imports that proper utilization of game can provide. Through firms like ours, and under careful biological supervision, game *can* provide the American dollars, deutsche marks, and Swiss francs needed so desperately to keep the economy viable."

He stood up, backed up to the fire, and tossed off the rest of the bourbon. I killed my beer deader than a hand-wrought nail. Pouring a replacement, I listened to Gordon continue over the honk of hippos, which sounded as close as if they were in my back pocket.

"Take, for example, a zebra. A guy can buy a zebra license for the Botswana equivalent of about fifty dollars and resell the license for about a hundred and eighty. That's a lot of money in the Okavango Swamps. Of course, he must be a Botswana citizen to do so, the basis of said transaction being that the Botswana citizen feels he has a traditional, hereditary *right* to kill a zebra—or divest himself of the license at highly capitalistic rates. In fact, despite the concession fees we pay, some seventy percent of the game is allocated to local hunters."

I knew he was right, since, at the time when I was there, a general license, which would literally include tons of meat, was available to citizens for not more than the equivalent of $1.50. Huge flatbed trucks would pull up with a load of local people and one or two professional hunters, who would shoot out their licenses for them. Exactly what the percentage arrangement on the sale of the dried meat or biltong was, I never knew, but it was generally embarrassing when one had clients in the field who were under the impression they were on the edge of a firefight.

"Now," said Gordon, "Botswana is a capitalist country. But consider, however, the American or German safari client who comes here for a minimum of twenty-one days, unless he's just fishing or bird shooting. At the moment, this would cost him one thousand American dollars a day. Now that doesn't count the additional game licenses and other fees, all of which are put directly back into the rural economy. I must have fifteen men working in this camp alone, and it's one of our smallest. How could they earn a living beyond mere subsistence, were it not for us? Hell, Peter, we have two cooks, two waiters, men who make up beds and tents, people who do nothing but carry firewood and water, people who wash the clients' clothes and iron

them fresh every day, skinners, trackers, gun bearers, mechanics, drivers, and—most importantly—the barman. Which reminds me. . . ."

It would be my own observation after my years of exposure to the more remote areas of central Africa, that if game is to

The author standing in a cavity of a Baobab tree, which was eaten away by elephants.

survive, it will only be through the economic expediency of their value in international currency. Even Gordon, who is actually a Botswana citizen, must pay all fees generated by his firm in foreign currency, not in *pula,* the local denomination. Bear in mind that a warthog only costs a local citizen about seven and a half *pula*—less than four American dollars. Perhaps it is indeed morally true that the citizen of a country such as Botswana *does* have the innate right to take game at ridiculous prices. But then, why are times so tough? Why all the international foreign aid when the country is quite capable of generating huge amounts of exchange merely through the intelligent use of its wildlife as an asset?

Well, I for one can do nicely without being persona non grata in Botswana and have no personal interest in any interference in the official policy of any country. My intention is simply to bring to the forefront the economic value of wildlife to Africa.

Perhaps political expediency is the same in all countries. Whatever the case, I wish to make it immaculately clear that the views I express above are purely my own and certainly not those of any other party. I believe they are accurate and, in fact, financially valid. I want game to survive, but it will not unless a more realistic attitude toward it is adopted throughout Africa—and *fast.*

Obviously, this can best be achieved with the cooperation of the African governments themselves and the applicable agencies. With equal obviousness, this includes the various game departments, parks boards, and such, as well as the rural inhabitants of game areas. This is not a book about ecology, but the relationship between domestic stock and game cannot be underestimated. You can have goats or game. Take your choice.

I am very strongly reminded of an incident that took place a couple of years ago in which I was asked by an old colleague to visit him in his bush camp. It seemed he had a break between safaris and thought it would be a good time to test our elbow tendons. This was not in Botswana; in fact, I shall not mention where the incident took place for fear of some reprisal on my pal's memory (he was killed in an aircraft accident in America not too long ago).

It was a particularly rude dawn, my atmospheric observations possibly being linked to the fact that we had indeed tested our fortitude until about three that morning. I was half-awake, trying to come up with some excellent ornithological logic why we should not venture off bird shooting at such an unsporting hour when I was levitated six feet above the camp bed by a burst of automatic fire not more than three hundred yards down the road from camp. I instantly recognized it as coming from a Soviet-bloc AK-47 assault rifle. I grabbed the shotgun and, wrapped in a *kikoy,* dashed in the direction of my pal's tent. He was standing at the camp entrance next to a dirt road as a battered Land Rover pulled up in an angry cloud of dust.

Yup. Here we go again, I thought, as four ragtag locals piled out and demanded some beer. Since one was carrying the AK with a fresh banana magazine, another had an old Cogswell and Harrison .375 H&H Magnum, and one of the remaining two was toting a .458 Brno bolt-action, they got their beer. Good and cold it was, too. The fourth member of this merry band was unarmed but wore the remnants of an olive-drab uniform.

"And how are the valiant members of the game department faring?" asked my pal. "Why don't you gentlemen have a smoke with us as you finish your beer?" A pack was produced and depleted.

So far so good, thought I, as I saw the AK resting on a piece of firewood. I eased the shotgun full of five loads of buckshot against my chair but kept it within easy reach. Then I noticed that the man in the tattered uniform was looking at me— and had been all this time. I was most definitely beginning to wonder what he had on his mind.

"I know you," he said flatly, in the tone (it seemed to me at that moment) a survivor of Auschwitz would have used if he had bumped into Adolph Hitler at a cocktail party. I looked at him hard. There *was* something about him that seemed familiar. But what? He answered the question by breaking into a tremendous grin and stepping across to embrace me.

"I am George. I worked for you fourteen years ago. You advanced me some wages for a bride price. I will never forget that. I now have many children by that woman."

In fact, I did remember the incident from my professional hunting days and it certainly was the same man. Considering that his initial purpose in visiting our camp was extortion, I breathed a mental sigh of relief.

His armed pals looked confused, but a scowl from George showed pretty clearly who was in charge. We exchanged the usual pleasantries until my friend had a chance to interject that he was going to have a "slash." I reckoned that to be a capital suggestion. We excused ourselves effusively and went to the cliff at the edge of his camp, where peeing was as much fun as drinking what caused it.

"Listen chum," said the professional, "we've got to get rid of these guys. They're motherless on palm wine already and although you and George are some kind of red Indian blood brothers, if we don't bribe them off, they may well strip

The grand stand of trees surrounding Saile with the Linyanti Swamp to the front.

this place down to the contents of your underwear. I know George. He's very heavy in this district. You seem to have a romantic rapport, so see what he wants or sure as the Lord made elephant droppings, a lot of items are going to turn up missing."

I didn't answer beyond a casual nod as we walked back to the fire, which had now blazed up pleasantly from the previous night's coals.

"George, old friend," I asked him in dialect, "where are you off to now?"

"Hau!" he replied in delighted exclamation. "I am going to see a certain lady with some meat. By luck, there was a large herd of impala just outside your camp. As chief game officer of this area, I decided to crop some, since they are far too numerous for the good of all."

That explained the automatic fire that had given me the heart attack earlier. But I knew they were a dead tame herd that always hung around camp, and George knew it, too. He, of course, wanted the meat to purchase the extended favors of a local tart. "Meat for meat" is one of the oldest African expressions, which led me in an earlier book to observe that prostitution is most definitely not the oldest profession: hunting is.

"Ah," said I, with a knowing wink, "then you will want to be on your way before your meat, taken for the good of the people, spoils. Might ten liters of petrol not bring you and this comely lass to a practical agreement, with more time for you to bargain before the sun is high? It is how I would handle such a matter, old friend." My pal stifled a smile despite his pet herd having been machine-gunned.

"Twenty liters would get me there even more quickly. There might even be time for a buffalo. Could you let me have some .458 cartridges? I am rather low."

I apologized, explaining that I was only shooting birds and that I didn't have a .458 or the wealth of Solomon in ammo would be his for his selfless duty among the savage beasts of the *bundu.*

We warily haggled among ourselves and finally settled on a gift of twelve liters of petrol, worth its weight in bonded bourbon. At last, the rickety vehicle rolled off to pick up what was presumably an extra man keeping the vultures off the impala they had sprayed with the AK. (Later, the camp staff found the pools of blood where five of the by then literally dead tame impala had lain. There were several more blood spoors, but though we followed up as best we could, only one animal could be found. The others were either lightly wounded or else something had got to them before we could.)

As we settled down to a light breakfast, far off in the distance came another roll of automatic fire from the AK. I guess they had no .375 ammo either.

The preceding is by no means an indictment of the game department of any African country where I have spent time. It is merely the recitation of an incident that impressed me, because if this sort of thing continues, not only will you and I be the poorer, but more immediately so will those subsistence-level nations who so badly need correct utilization of their hereditary natural resources.

Dawn seemed to me to resemble the candlelit curtain-raising of a Shakespearean first performance. I eventually found myself at the delightful breakfast. We left late that first day, as one must appreciate the stowing of rifles, ammo, Paul's photographic equipment, and the determining of just who would sit where. As it turned out, I had Fiona and Paul sit on top of the open rear, since there was a raised seat and they would enjoy observing from that vantage point better than I would (I don't shoot from vehicles). Anyway, I wanted to get to know Gordon, who would be driving, a lot better.

Besides we *mlungu*, there was old Karonda, Jehosephat, Mack, and Ottie, as well as chop boxes, axs, high-lift jacks, ropes, towing cables, and what seemed like enough stuff to outfit an Italian regiment in the field. Gordon's rifle—the perfidious Westley Richards, or at least the rifle with what would prove to be bum ammo—was stowed in a special rack behind the cab roof. I sat in the front left-hand seat with my rifle butt balanced against the top of my instep. It was not particularly comfortable this way, but I had always given some consideration to the thoughts of old friend and international pistol and rifle shot Bill Jordan, who believes that resting the butt of a rifle on the floorboards of a hunting vehicle will sooner or later knock the scope out of zero simply through constant thumping.

We were after lion. The news that one of Gordon's pros, who had had no client with him at the time, had seen sixteen of the bastards on his way past a waterhole some fifteen kilometers from camp came as a rather mixed blessing. I wanted a nice lion of my very own, despite the number I had shot on previous official duties, but

I had been fouled up with big prides before and never left the scene of combat with more joy than terror. A lot of lions can do a lot of damage, especially if one has to stop them in one or another mass charge. Not recommended.

We soon found out why they had been watering so early in the morning: not far off was the recently killed carcass of an eland, a pretty fair meal even for sixteen lions. A big bull eland can weigh nigh on a ton.

We were essentially reconnoitering, and we eventually came to the conclusion from the various spoors we covered that the big pride had moved off but that there was still no shortage of lions in the area. There were at least two "satellite" males in the area with paws the size of tennis racquet heads, big chaps that would, through their very size and intimidatory capacity, stay on their own and only visit prides when a female was in season (which can be any time of year, depending on where you are).

We shot a zebra later that day, the skin going to Paul as a gift, and then decided which of the big gentlemen lions we would follow. We settled on one that ranged a territory about ten miles away, through thick thorn and low to medium *mopane* scrub. Since we did not have the personnel right there to load the carcass of the zebra, we took the hind legs as well as the skin and then pushed off in full

dark, back to camp. It would prove to be a most interesting night.

We dined on the warthog and, despite my usual tenacity at the campfire, I decided on this occasion to sack in at about midnight. I had the .375 stoked with solids lying along my leg, keeping in mind that there was just a single layer of green canvas between me and the rest of Africa. At two in the morning, it would prove to have been good judgment.

I had heard the hippos tearing and munching at the grass along the Linyanti River. Having very nearly cashed in all my chips with that species on several previous occasions, I was on my guard. Fiona is my guard: unlike yours truly, she is not nerve deaf from years of muzzle blast. Of course, you would had to have been completely without hearing, considering what began a little after the small hours of two. First, there was the goddamndest uproar of bellows, grunts, bass screams, and curses since Wall Street crashed. Gordon boiled out of his tent on the far side of ours as the camp seemed to go completely beserk. Not unwisely were the indigenous upset: two mature hippos, one certainly a big bull, had burst upon the scene in hot pursuit of either a reluctant female or another bull concentrating on the same favors. It was pure bedlam or the Houses of Parliament, depending on how you viewed matters. The second thing that happened, as Gordon would

A zebra kill.

say, in the fullness of time—a couple of seconds—was that the big bull stepped with geometric precision into the huge pot of scalding water kept for mixing with the cooler stuff for the clients' showers. Apparently, he did not like this, since he then attacked the campfire with no less accuracy. Standing about in the coals just worsened his general attitude, which he articulated with remarkable vocal ability. Even I could hear him—all two and a half tons, and just twenty yards away.

As I stepped out of the velcro-sealed tent dressed as originally issued, I heard the thunder of the two hippos turn toward the sound of Gordon starting his Toyota Land Cruiser. This pleased me half to death as I had no intention of repeating my several personal although memorable relationships with hippos, especially at night, when I knew that if I flicked on my flashlight it would probably provoke an immediate charge.

Gordon, unbeknownst to him at the time, was armed with the defective .500 ammo. Thanks above he didn't get into a jam, as he could well have had the course. Badly.

Cundill, madman that he is, actually bumped one of the hippos as they headed at top speed—and that ain't slow—toward the quarters of the crew. Later, we found tracks smack over the middle of Ottie's blanket (he having been busy inspecting the night-blooming aspects of certain substantial upper foliage at the time). With a stomach-turning crunch, one of the animals slammed into the employees' *chimbuzi,* or drop-hole toilet. Happily, it was unoccupied, or a dead man would for sure have been fished out next morning.

Most things, if you give them long enough, do go away. So did our hippos, and we returned to bed. All in all, it was a most unsuccessful raid on their part, but they just as easily could have come through Gordon, Paul's, or our own tent with a lot less trouble than it took to demolish that outhouse. What if Gordon had been forced to try to stop a determined charge—or share his front seat

with a love-lorn bull hippo—and found that he had lousy ammo? The mind boggles. All I could think of was, "Christ, but what happens to my safari deposit?"

I was by now bloody tired for reasons of my own doing, and recalcitrant hippos didn't help matters. Yet I felt that although staying up late certainly made the going in the morning a lot tougher, I still could not resist that inexplicable campfire mystique. I could live forever in a house, but there were only so many days of true safari and I was getting younger in not much of a hurry. How many of these nights were left to me? I knew not, nor did I want to seriously speculate. I just knew that however many there were, not a possible, physical instant of such a magic time and place should be wasted. . . .

We picked up the spoor of the big lone male where he had crossed the dirt track about eight miles from camp. I had been up since well before dawn, walking silently with Gordon to what might remain of the previous day's zebra carcass, left where it was as baiting is illegal in Botswana and this certainly was not our point. Flesh, nevertheless, brings flesh eaters, and we could have walked into just what we were looking for, however coincidentally. Curiously, not even a hyena had touched what we had left, let alone a lion. The wind was very funny, though, as it so often is in the Botswana winter. This would be further confirmed as we sought the big *Tau* after breakfast.

Mack and Jehosephat started off on the spoor, but a sideways glance from Gordon spoke volumes of frustration. One second the breeze would peel the Vitalis off what was left of my hair, and the next it would blast our scent over most of southern central Africa. It was most definitely not lion-hunting weather, and the lion had realized this and put about four area codes between us.

We never even saw him, although his spoor was still so warm you could light a soggy cigar off it.

It was hot. If you think Botswana gets cold at night, just try to follow some fool lion around at midday. The humidity was so low you didn't notice yourself sweating, just a thickening layer of dried salt on your light bush shirt. Only then did you realize that you were oozing precious body fluids at a scary rate. After six and a half hours of this nonsense I realized I was in trouble.

I'm not *Death in the Long Grass* age anymore and, as I said, I take two prescriptions daily, both diuretics. These, together with the charming combination of scalding sun and nonstop walking, suddenly gave me the poignant realization that unless I got rehydrated in a reasonable hurry, it might be me that was carried back lashed to a hardwood pole.

Thankfully, the lion had cut a three-quarter circle that drew us back quite close to the hunting car. I drank the warm Cokes and swallowed the remaining beer. Of water there was none, since I had drunk most of it myself during our hike. (That Gordon does not suffer from such physical inconveniences is well demonstrated by the fact that he once followed a lion for fifty-four miles over twenty-four hours without a break. Got him, too.)

As many of the staff in camp were of the Zionist faith (not related to the Jewish religion) and wore a badge backed by a small piece of forest green cloth, they would not eat pork. This automatically dealt out the warthog, so something else had to get the deep six or our people would be mighty hungry. That "something else" appeared to be a wildebeest standing in the relative open, facing me.

The distance was a hundred and ninety paces, and I held just above the eyes with the .375 on full 8X power and resting on a low antheap. I stuck a round precisely between the nostril holes, and he went down like Judgment Day, never twitching as the bullet passed smack through his thinker. There followed great rejoicing in the land as the men butchered him, and we proceeded on our merry way.

Camp was a dull glow through the bush as we pulled in. We were all tired but I was the only one not in the least

How to pick up hot spoor and move in on it before it moves first. Here, I am covering Gordon from the rear.

hungry, my main sentiment being the imminence and frank hope of a quick death. Whew! But I was as sick to my stomach as I can ever remember. It was apparently part of the dehydration I had experienced during the long tracking and all the liquid I had taken to try to correct the situation. In any case, it will give some idea of the acuteness of the situation when I

advise you that a full hour passed before I could keep down a beer. I did, however, get the hang of it and the local breweries would have awarded me with their Order of Merit. Around the campfire that evening, we discussed the latest developments. Gordon thought the lion we had been spooring was the same one he had seen four times before, a huge bugger badly in need of a haircut. Unfortunately, as he was one of the two satellite lions in the area, he was extremely used to being hunted. The closest Gordon ever viewed him was at a range of about four hundred and fifty yards as the beast watched him and his client from the relative obscurity of a termite heap. It was far, far too distant for a shot, but there was, on the other hand, a helluva big male in company with a lady lion and, at various times, one or two fully grown but not well-maned lions. We were to find out just how true this was that night, in fact, in the early morning hours when the lions reversed the roles of the hunters and the hunted.

The roar was one of those things that are never forgotten. It was instantly picked up by the female and the younger chap until Saile reverberated as if it were the inside of a bass drum. I could hear the classic challenge of the lions overwashing every other sound, but the one that interested me most, given a certain poetic license, was the deepest in tone, the one about ten feet outside my tent flap. I think the Crusaders had the right idea when they built their walls thick and high. A green canvas tent is not much in the way of a psychological reassurance, particularly if you happen to be inside it.

As was the case with the hippo invasion the night before, I again wondered what the hell to do. I didn't want to walk into one of Gordon's .500 slugs and I didn't want to get in his way either, since I could hear him shouting things I doubt he had learned in the hallowed halls of Oxford—or perhaps that's exactly where he picked them up. They may not have impressed the lions but they certainly astonished my sense of the impressive use of forceful language. The man really has vocal talent when it comes to lions and perhaps his finest performance was that one, in the bush of Saile that night.

Well, I reckoned that although I had a very large male lion a few yards away, it was probably better not to press matters. If the damned thing tried to come into the tent, I had in immediate stock enough buckshot to stall a panzer regiment. I would be able to tell where he was trying to enter and could nail him more easily than I could wandering around au naturel in the dark with a torch—or, as I have almost forgotten to call it, a flashlight. So, I stood in between the beds and listened to this chap perform. What had happened was that the big male, which had been playing the dating game with his true love, had apparently caught the smell of fresh meat from the local quarters and had figured on a bit of shoplifting. This may well have included one or more of the staff, as throughout the country Botswana lions appear to be particularly aggressive. The following quote from the *Durban Daily News* of October 23, 1985, bears this out:

It had been at least the third attack in the Moremi area by lions in the past year or so. Two of the attacks had proved fatal.

The track of a huge lion that the author, Gordon, and Paul, with staff, followed for several days.

And it was precisely the area where I used to operate.

As I was to learn at breakfast, Gordon had again put on the Disaster Drill, still without knowing he was carrying dud ammo. He burst out of his tent with a suitably genteel oath that reflected heavily on the heritage and general upbringing of lions, tucked his .500 Westley Richards against his leg, jammed himself against the car door, and started to break up the party.

His first major action on the way to the Toyota was to nearly fall over the very big but especially well-tonsured *Tau*. This had the effect of scaring the religion still clinging to Gordon's rather scared soul somewhere to the far west. Happily, it did the same to the big male in front of my tent, as well as to the female that remained in the murk.

The younger male ran at top speed through the dark and disappeared into the papyrus of the swamp while the big male who was considering me as a potential midnight snack also wandered off. Lions don't especially like horns and lights, but you never know. There had been several killings not that far south in the past few months, and nobody ever knew who was who in the lion department, especially on a moonless night in the middle of camp.

Gordon was plenty red-eyed that dawn and I assure you the cause was most certainly not Granddad. "Let's go and get that big bastard," he said, emphasizing *bastard* as if he really meant it. The spoor was obvious, and I took particular interest in the fact that the large male had been lying something short of nine paces from our tent. So obvious were signs of the threesome that we even took time for breakfast, Paul stuffing down enough assorted eggs, toast, orange juice, milk, muffins, and whatever to keep a small Yugoslav partisan unit in the field for a month, while Gordon forked in enough to maintain a full regiment of the same, including their guard dogs. (If you want lessons in the art of volume eating, by all means consult Cundill. For a man of even his considerable but certainly not over-weight size, he puts away more *skafu* than anybody I know.)

Meanwhile, I looked over the spoor and determined that there were only three lions; Gordon reckoned on four. I'm not certain I agree with him entirely, but he may well have been right in thinking that there was another younger but larger male that had hung back on the periphery of camp.

As we were finishing breakfast, Gordon and I got wandering through the subject of lions and lion hunting and how it is done honorably. That Cundill, after a night of chasing lions around in the dark on the edge of a swamp, could still be retrospectively accurate is an indication of his nature. Few things perturb him, except for Brewster's patent, the disposable beer or soft drink can top aluminum ring, the playing of a radio in camp on a commercial band, or the perfidy of absolutely anybody.

I felt I was back in college as I listened to his views on the species.

"The attitude towards lions remains the same as it did in the time of the Greeks, Romans, and anybody else who kept cattle. If anything, the lion is even more prized now as a trophy than he was in those days."

He paused to shovel—with great relish—another measure of eggs into his maw.

Giraffe. Near Saile Camp.

"Lions are successful because they educate their young in the same way the leopard does. Young lions are taught not only *how* to hunt but *what* to hunt. In this matter is included the Tsavo bunch as well as the gang George Rushby had to sort out in Njombe that took several thousand people in the years they operated.

"Don't tell me that people are not natural prey for lions, taught by their mothers to hunt man as normal prey; there are just too many precedents to counteract this notion. And let us never forget the unique relationship between predator and predator, as exists between man and lion."

As I said, Cundill actually speaks this way.

I was also to later find that the same relationship, in practical terms, exists between leopard and lion. The hyena, of course, fills every other notch. It's just like Wall Street. All predators eat other predators.

Cundill also told me of the time Karonda saved his life, or at least his complexion, and the tale is good enough to go down as one of the first lion tales in this book. . . .

The incident took place during the safari of the first man to fly the Messerschmitt 262, the first jet fighter produced by the Germans during World War II. At the time, it was the gentleman's seventieth birthday, and although Gordon reports that he shot a damned fine male lion, and shot it well, the thing didn't fall dead. For reasons that will never be known, he simply took off into the long grass, crossing a small river on his way, and slunk into an impossible tangle of scrub, where he remained, obviously waiting for his pursuers.

Mack, Cundill's other gun bearer, spotted the lion after climbing a tree and signaled to Gordon where he was lying up. The lion charged from the grass almost instantly and Gordon pasted it in the chest. But it was so hyped it didn't waver an inch.

Gordon got down on one knee to get a good raking shot with the second barrel from the Wilkes .500 Nitro and let the cat come. As he fired, he noticed with not inconsiderable interest that a four- to five-inch thick *Longicartus* tree sagged over, blown practically in half by a 570-grain slug. He was now empty and the lion almost on top of him.

As Gordon himself said of the incident, "When the animal comes in a full charge, the shooter is not aware of obstructions in the immediate foreground. Thus, I partially defoliated the area. The charge," he continued, slicing off a chunk of biltong before the orange light of the fire, "was a touch oblique. It was, however, no longer so when I hit him with that first barrel and he located me."

There was no possible chance for Gordon to reload the double. Karonda, who was no kid at the time, was not in the least fazed and promptly shot the creature through the brain with a spare .375 just before it was on Gordon's immaculate body.

Cundill has since had a lot of time for nine-fingered Karonda. . . .

Breakfast over, we took off on the tracks of what had now become a threesome. If, in fact, there had been a fourth lion, he had left the proceedings and wandered elsewhere. We had the whole team in tow: Gordon, Paul, Fiona, Ottie, Jehosephat, Karonda, and Mack, all tearing our shins to shreds through the low thorn bush.

The track meandered for some miles, but we kept up until the cover thickened and we got into more mature *mopane* forest, made very difficult by an underscrub of thorn and lower growth. After about four hours of trekking, we were close enough to be able to practically smell them: the big male, which was stopping frequently to mate with the female, and a lone, younger chap that was surely the one Gordon had damned near kicked the night before.

Finally, in the scalding heat of midday,

we came upon an obvious lying-up place for lions, a termite heap with two trees growing from it, a large one roughly in the middle and a smaller one off to the right, the side we were on. The tracks seemed to lead behind the large heap and we all presumed that the big boy and his lady were mating while Junior stood by at a respectable distance, possibly picking up some technical points.

To say that we tiptoed would be a huge understatement. Maybe we should have made a bit more noise, though, as the first thing I was aware of was the rear end of a lion sticking out from behind the smaller tree. I instantly covered it with the .375 and noticed that it was standing almost broadside to us, its chest covered by the tree but its eyes looking right into mine from about five yards, which is uncomfortably close when speaking of lions.

We could all see that it was a young male, and one that would be a good trophy in another year or two; but there was no way we were going to pat him on the head and saunter around that antheap where the other two were presumably procreating. Keeping him covered, we were able to back off without a point-blank charge. Gordon and I figured on going around the left side of the heap, where we hoped to find the big boy and his tootsie. No such. We got another ten yards away from the younger—I do not say "little"—lion and tried to edge around the mound, knowing that it would be a direct confrontation.

I didn't have a chance to count the white knuckles, but you can bet there were plenty. The young lion, realizing what we were and what we might represent, buggered off into the shadow of *mopane* in a highly creditable disappearing act. Still expecting to rub noses with the mating pair on the other side of the hill, we sleuthed around the corner without the benefit of tracks, all of which came in from the right. That the pair had in fact slipped away and were doing their thing about eighty yards away behind impenetrable cover and under the shade of another big *mopane* was impossible to detect from where we were standing.

When suddenly there was a thunderous thumping of rapid exodus from the area coming from a cloud of dust and dirt that obscured the pair of lions, I thought we had startled a herd of buffalo that had been lying up in the shade. There was no way for a shot.

Never, in all my years of taking lions, have I heard a couple make so much noise! The ground in the Saile region is generally part of the Gussu Shield, which is the northern limit of the Kalahari ground structure. Yet this bloody lion was so big and heavy that he literally could be heard galloping off for several hundred yards, despite the muffling cover.

Cundill, with his usual charm, cushioned his head on the nearest large elephant dropping and, with the casual comment that we ought to give them a while to calm down and get their act in order, promptly went to sleep.

We tracked those lions for miles through snagging, barbed-wire wait-a-bit thorn, getting almost into range before the damned wind would shift. Dejected, we finally had to turn for home. On the return trip I shot an impala, if for no other reason than we needed camp meat and our morale was at stake.

With the fire greeting us, along with a cold Lion Lager—I did not miss the irony—I reflected on our companion for the day: a single fork-tailed *drongo,* a coal-black flycatcher that takes his prey in flight. We had flushed most of it for him —grasshoppers and other assorted *goggas* —which he nailed with the accuracy of the tail gunner of a Belfast milk truck. He had become so tame in following us around over the course of a couple of days of lion hunting that he would almost sit on your finger and let you touch him. Another few days and I believe you could have stuck him in your breast pocket. He was a great added charm to the venture, and we marveled at his increasing tameness. I have always loved flycatchers and bee-eaters of all species, their aerobatics never ceasing to astonish me. At a leopard bait, you will always get a collection of *drongos* and, especially, Little bee-eaters feeding on the flies and other insects attracted to the bait. Their performances always remind me of an aerial Bolshoi as they flash, chandelle, split-ess, and soar, generally appearing to be the most mobile birds in the air.

Gordon and I discussed the events of the day over the fire and a few rounds of those additives created to give lion hunters strength and courage. The best we could do, we decided, was to play it by ear. How else could it be handled? Lions could not be baited—not that I would have under any circumstances wished to have hunted them that way. True lion hunting is a matter of man and lion. Gordon certainly feels the same.

Our chance came on the fifth day, largely owing to Gordon's sense of timing. There was a strip of land, probably not fifty yards across at its widest point, which ran between the parallel roads of the Chobe National Park and the Saile Concession, controlled by Gordon. Fire and the anticipatory control of the same is a major factor in the modern perception of African ecology, although I've not yet determined that I agree with the conclusions reached by people with impressive American and British doctoral degrees. To me, fire and its relatively light aftermath, depending on the bush

and grass, can be highly beneficial; on the other hand, when areas are badly damaged by Old Jumbo, fire can be a great threat to the general ecology, since the flora cannot be reestablished as it used to be. But then, Africa is always changing, this being the great lesson I took away from this exercise, which also nearly took my life with it.

In any case, the strip between these roads had to be burned, and under supervision. Since one of the tenets of my deal with Gordon was that I would largely be working with permanent employees of Hunters Africa in order to avoid the additional cost of professional hunters, who were paid by the day (and who would have to have been paid by me), this was just nifty. Right. We go and burn a road strip. My lions could wait.

We pulled out of camp at a purely disrespectable hour, my having spent the small hours of the morning inspecting the heavens, the state of the fire, and the timbre of the hyenas until such time as I could not read my wristwatch. Knowing I would catch a fine collection of used buckshot from Fiona if I arrived unannounced at our tent, I had to signal my presence in low terms before the inside brass hooks were released. Fiona is very handy with buckshot and not very shy about using it, either.

It took four grown men and a boy to get me out of bed, but I was finally roused by Gordon's promise of a cold beer if I came along quietly. That's an offer I find hard to pass up. I had a quick shower that froze me to death and actually shaved before witnesses. In fact, I felt pretty reasonable—but nobody could ever have felt sufficiently decent for what was to come that day.

I had heard the tractor-pulled flatbed truck go by at dawn, carrying the men who would be stationed for a few days at the twin roads to the west in order to supervise the burning of the strip between the roads as a firebreak. Africans are noted for a great many talents but quietude at reasonable hours is not one of them. As they were moving slowly, we caught up with them and passed them about eight miles out of camp. It was then that we noticed steaming, fresh lion spoor in the road—the same bunch that had come by a couple of nights before and which we had spent the previous day tracking. There was the clear spoor of the big male's track as well as the female's, accompanied by Junior. There was also another track, that of a male—the fourth —that had also apparently joined the blue-movie cast. They must surely have heard our vehicle a few hundred yards away, as the recentness of their departure into the dense cover lining the track was obvious. Lions are a relatively soft-footed animal and love to travel along sandy hunting tracks. Not that they

won't hang around rocky places, but there is a lot to Gordon's observation: "If you want to find lions, take off your shoes. They don't like thorns any more than we do when traveling a territory."

Clearly, they were close. But they knew we were, too. We inspected the tracks and decided to give them a couple of hours to settle down. After five minutes, noting which way they seemed to have gone, we resumed our drive toward the strip to be burned. Gordon left one of his men behind to warn the lagging flatbed of thirty pyromaniacs, as Gordon called them, not to disturb the area and to just keep going, which they did.

It was about ten in the morning by the time we arrived at the burning zone and got everybody squared away with torches and shovels. At about eleven we headed back along the track to follow the lions. We pulled up roughly a mile short of the point where the spoor had left the road, and Gordon, Karonda, Jehosephat, and I pushed into the really hairy stuff, knowing that there were four lions ahead just waiting for us.

I badly wanted pictures of the hunt, but the bush was simply so thick it would have been criminally negligent to have brought Paul or Fiona along. Paul probably wouldn't have gotten a frame off anyway, since he would have had no field of view at all, judging by the way things were looking right off. In fact, it was a wise decision; the smaller the party, the less noise we were likely to make, and the better our odds of collecting the big boy.

The question of the female was also not one to be considered lightly. Traditionally, the female will charge either before or alongside the male, especially if he is hurt. There was just no way that I was going to permit Fiona to be exposed to such danger. In heavy or even relatively light cover, there's no telling which member of a hunting party a lion or lioness will choose, as many cameramen have found out to their everlasting woe.

The tracking was magnificent, not the least of which was by Cundill, through a thick amalgam of *mopane* in all its degrees of height and development—big ones, shady and dull sea green, shorter stuff, and the scrub that prevented a hunter from getting down low in the event of a lion charge. It was one of the finest stalks I have ever been on. How can a sportsman achieve anything more classic in hunting than a big Botswana lion in heavy cover? Give me an answer and I'll send you an ice-cream cone by parcel post.

We had left Fiona, Paul, and Ottie in the Toyota Land Cruiser pulled off into a shady grove, giving them an extra rifle just in case. Following Gordon and our trackers, I took the right, rather unusual for me, as I'm right-handed and prefer the left position so my muzzle is always

pointed away from the party at port arms. We went at least two miles through the thick stuff, the tracks of the lions wandering oddly, as if they knew we were on their spoor. We followed them in semicircles and came across short lie-ups and other kinds of rather unusual behavior, but for a change we had one definite advantage: the wind. It was blowing directly in our faces, which was rather odd, since lions will normally move across or downwind when they suspect they're being shadowed. Well, sex has gotten the better of many a chap less ardent than that big lion, and such would ultimately prove to be the case.

When I tell you it was thick, you will just have to trust me. We knew they were there, although I don't think the reverse was true. Brother, it was simply one bush to the next, never having the slightest

The perils of the bush: a piece of hardwood that pierced straight through a tire.

idea when the tracks would end at the bottom of a lion's paws. It was one of the greatest compliments to Cundill that when the trackers lost the spoor, it was he who recovered it: just the tiniest scratch in the hard, drought-stricken earth; Gordon, in a small whisper, tearing the collective tails off the trackers.

Not that I would in any way intimate that I am in Cundill's class as a tracker, but there was a time when I was considered reasonably competent. He, however, is really outstanding. But then, Gordon is really a white Zulu, having been raised among those people and having obviously learned a great many of their skills in the bush.

We walked in the classic stalking manner, putting the outside edges of our feet down first in a sliding motion so we would be sure not to break a twig or small stick. The spoor was not twenty minutes old, as we could tell by the erosion of the edge of the spoor in the softer patches of sand. These chaps were close.

Very close.

I was not tracking, but rather covering the other three with my rifle in case of the Big Surprise. Yet I happened to be looking to the left when Gordon, before the trackers, saw the outline of a lion in the shade of a fully-grown *mopane* off to our right and gave me the *hisssss* that started the artillery.

. . .

I have an old habit from my .470 Nitro double rifle days of always carrying extra rounds between the fingers of my left hand. As I have written elsewhere, I'm so used to it that I can eat a sandwich without even noticing they are there. When my .470 Evans was stolen in the States, I felt half-naked without extra rounds between my fingers and continued the habit when using the .375, despite its much larger magazine capacity. Damned good thing I did.

As Gordon said later, that bloody lion was dead eight times over and just didn't realize it. Small consolation.

Let's pick up the charge where we left it in the book's opening pages. When I left you, I was down to an empty rifle with four rounds of ammo left, three in my left hand, with which I was performing minor miracles trying to get them into the magazine. Happily, I had hit the lion badly enough with what Gordon later termed "the same sustained fire that saved the day at Omdurman" to slow him down.

Gordon had another hangfire, which missed the target, and then he was down to solid ammo meant for elephant and buff, which was not his idea of the ideal load for lion. To the great joy of us both, he never had to fire another round. I got lucky.

I jammed the three rounds from my left fist into the magazine—unquestiona-

The author with lion.

bly breaking the Olympic record—jacked one up the chamber, and continued to belt the lion as frequently as I could. I stuck the first two in his chest as he charged again. The last of my eight shots had made him turn, taking out both his shoulders and his major pipes, which is why I'm probably writing this and Gordon is still in the safari business. There was one cartridge left in the ammo holder in my belt, but I had decided that unless the sonofabitch was actually chewing my shoelaces, I would not fire it. Once I did . . . well chum, that was it, and I am very poor at thumbing lions in the eyes. (I know. I've tried it. It's murder on the cuticles up to about your elbows.)

The lion swerved at my eighth shot and fell a few yards away, behind a scrub *mopane* tree, not dead but unable to eat us. As he already had more holes than a spaghetti strainer, and as I was down to my last cartridge, I was not anxious to further increase his extensive ventilation. It took him twelve minutes before he finally died. (As I nearly did, with the scope tipped off and pointed at the base of his skull for the same amount of time. Try holding a rifle of that weight in position for that span of time and under that stress and you'll get my point.) Finally, he gave a sigh and relegated himself to my wall.

Observing the end of our lion hunt from a nearby tangle of *mopane* scrub was the *drongo*.

I was instantly mobbed by back-slapping trackers shouting all sorts of indecipherable congratulations at the Great Slayer of *Tau*. Hell, yes, boy. I was hot stuff!

Actually, it had been a *very* close item. Let me give you a few examples of how Murphy might have interfered and how things, as usual, might have gone wrong.

First, it took all our firepower combined to stop that grand beast, and for Gordon's .500 to choose the middle of a lion charge to pack up is nearly too incredible to write. But it happened. If the female or one of the younger males had come with him, we all would have "had our chips," as they say hither, because there was no possible way we could have stopped the pair, and somebody—perhaps me—might have had an acute attack of dying.

I've spent forty-six years avoiding that eventuality and things seem to get less promising as they proceed. There was also the technical matter of Cundill's semi-antique ammo. When he pulled or squeezed the trigger, he didn't know if the goddamn round would go off at all, let alone when. This meant that he had no indication, especially in the case of the dud, if it would fire when the action of the double rifle was open. If his head was in the way—the laws of physics being rather immutable—the heavy brass case might have been driven through his face or head had it been in line with the breech. That would have been purely charming, on top of everything else rather close at hand.

This was not the first time I had had firefights with lions, which are reputed to be light-boned and fairly easy to kill. I have written to this same conclusion myself, but I'm changing my opinion as I get to know lions under field circumstances over more and more years. The sheer quantity of punishment they can take is simply astonishing. This particular chap, which went most comfortably in *Rowland Ward's*, weighed over 500 pounds, and I suspect that most of it was heart. He took eight .375 H&H Magnums, all but one of which was correctly placed, plus two 570-grain .500 Nitros in the guts and did not quit until I broke his shoulders with my last shot. That computes into just about 42,000 foot-pounds of bullet energy expended on a 500-pound lion. Tell me more.

Tell me *no* more of lions that drop to a single shot from a light caliber rifle, unless its bullet is precisely placed. If a lion has been mating or otherwise has his blood up, you'd better watch the back end of your navel, my friend, or it may not be there when you get back to camp for dinner. To quote Carl E. Akeley, the Father of American taxidermy, who, in one way or another, got stuck into something like fifty lions, as well as killing a leopard unarmed:

Another test of a lion's strength is his ability to stand punishment. I have seen a lion charge with seven lead bullets from an old .577 Express rifle through his shoulder, and only finally succumb to the eighth bullet in his head.

Hell, I had shot this one *three* times through the head with a lot more modern stuff than the old black powder .577 with no better results. There was no problem with bullet performance, since, as you can see by the photographs, each mushroomed with textbook precision. I have no idea why these shots were not more effective, except that the lion had deter-mined he wasn't about to cash it in without taking at least one of us with him. Had his lady come along for the trip, he *would* have, too.

Lord above. Imagine paying money to do this!

We examined him closely before loading him into the back of the Toyota (a feat rather akin to carrying a 500-pound plastic bag full of water). Fiona, Paul, and Jehosephat, who had led the hunting car toward the spot of the kill, had by this time arrived with Ottie at the wheel.

The fangs that nearly got us all.

Actually, the goings-on at the car had been interesting enough in themselves. When things had calmed down and we had had a chance for a smoke without the very good possibility of a lioness charging out of the thickies, I heard what had gone on a couple of miles back at the car. Paul and Fiona were half-asleep at the beginning of the war, dozing in the shade. Ottie was completely out, as only a bush African or a medical student can be by merely closing his eyes. As the barrage of .375 and .500 fire opened up, Paul swears that Ottie came four feet off his blanket. Fiona, a professionally trained linguist with a feast of languages at her command, asked him what in hell he reckoned was going on. The best he could guess was that we had run into a major pride and were in the process of shooting our way out.

When the firing—eleven shots, including Karonda's valiant attempt to stem the leonine tide—had died, Ottie rightly figured it was about time to see if there were any walking wounded. Only, the car wouldn't start.

Dutifully and happily, Ottie, who had some remote idea of what made a hunting car go in the first place, figured out that either the plugs had somehow become fouled or that the points needed replacing. I never got into it with him, nor did Paul, who is no mean mechanic. In any case, the peanut gallery was *in situ* after meeting up with the unarmed Jehosephat, who had come to show them the way.

I was as pleased as double rum punch, even though we had missed a chance at some charge pictures. It was not the sort of situation that was worth a photograph in any book at the cost of a man's life—and it could have very damned well been any of ours. At least we were prepared to defend ourselves. Paul was not.

After a cold beer, we examined the waterline of that bull lion. How he stayed afloat for so long and got so close is to this day—not that long afterward—quite unbelievable. He was shot almost between the eyes, a bit high by me over the right eyebrow, behind the left ear, through the back of the head, three times in the chest, again the poor spine attempt (but he was really rolling along), and again by my rifle just a *touch* high over the heart proper, which is exactly where I wanted to break him down. He also had my shot a postage stamp in width from his bum, as well as the relatively accurate results of Gordon's fusillade with the .500 Nitro. Both these slugs had torn through his guts as he had spun after catching some of my hardware at the very second Gordon's rifle decided to fire.

We went through the usual photo sequences and walked Paul and Fiona through the scenario. At one point, Gordon and I stopped and gave each other a sidelong look that would have filled volumes. Mmmmm. Very close.

We were now both worried, considering the blowtorch heat of midday, that the bloody thing might slip some hair before it was skinned. We had to get it

The entire party (less Paul).

back to camp, which we promptly did, and although I have not yet seen the pelt, I believe it will be fine. I want Peter Becker, my old friend at Botswana Game Industries in Francistown, to just tan and felt-back the hide without sewing up the marvelous and quite interesting collection of bullet holes. They're really what that lion hunt was all about, and I am far more interested in them than in the cosmetic appearance of the cat.

We drove into Saile, refusing offers of sainthood and senatorship, past the hippo-ravaged *chimbuzi,* and into the skinners' camp. Skinners occupy rather the same social status as do head cooks or senior gun bearers like Karonda. They are the elite. But who, of all bloody people in Africa, should have stepped out of a grass *kaia* at that moment but Stomach, of whom I have written before in other books and who was my skinner when I had the camp Daryll Dandridge and I built in 1970 on the edge of the Oka-vango, now called "Splash." Stomach, so named because of the intestinal growlings his body was constantly making, was one of the best men with a knife in Botswana. When he saw me, he actually embraced me.

Quite possibly only God has any idea of Stomach's age, and, if so, He's not telling. What that man can do with a knife, however, would make a butcher blush. He was the skinner chosen by the Denver Museum on a fairly recent expe-dition to collect rare birds for their gall-eries. Stomach, I'm told, did an abso-lutely first-rate job on this immensely delicate task. With that in mind, I called for three chairs, and Fiona, Paul, and the Great Slayer of *Tau* sat for a couple of hours and watched the art of skinning at its best.

Essentially, I am an economic idiot. He was the fattest damned lion I ever saw, absolutely layered in lard, which alone would have almost paid the cost of that safari. Lion fat is considered to be great *muti* (black magic medicine) throughout central and southern Africa,

The author with Stomach, my old skinner from Okavango days seventeen years ago.

among other things reputed to be a cure for gonorrhea, syphilis, and arthritis. Had I had it rendered down, I could have sold it to one of the many *muti* shops in Pre-toria and Johannesburg, where you can buy just about every item seen in the first scene of *Macbeth.* Ah well, financial con-siderations have never been my forte.

Stomach, actually, is most likely par-tially demented. As I remember him in that old camp on the fringes of the Oka-vango, he spent most of his time actually growling at people. Whether this was some sort of mental aberration or just pure fun, I have never been able to de-cide.

As Stomach skinned out that huge lion, I made him the offer of one *pula,* the local currency, for every bullet he found. I was most interested to know what those Silvertips had done and how they had performed. As it turned out, he came up with a considerable amount of scrap metal, consisting essentially of my own rounds and a dose—possibly both barrels —of buckshot that, judging by their penetration, had been fired broadside into him as a youngster from some forty-odd yards (there was no obvious external evidence of the wounds). Perhaps he had wandered by somebody's tent and put on the same performance as he had for me not long before he reached his quietus.

In any case, by the time we were through with him and he with us, he would have never gotten through an airport security metal detector.

I salute for all time the gallantry of that marvelous animal, as I am sure does Gordon. It was him or us. Period. Yes, we started it, but he damned near ended it. And if, things had gone his way, I would rather have been killed by that Saile lion, I think, than by any other animal I have ever confronted.

We only found a couple of the mushroomed Winchester Silvertip slugs; exactly why so few were found I am not sure, since at the rate of one *pula* each, you can bet old Stomach was digging around in guts until the moon went down. Gordon's rounds that went off bulled completely through the lower body cavity and were not recoverable, although they made one hell of a pair of holes.

The twilight dropped and the riverine papyrus turned from green to dark amber. A rather unusual invitation was issued to my wife, Paul, and me to visit the staff campfire, which we did forthwith with a congratulatory stipend of *tshwala* in hand. A hell of a lot more than a merry time was had, as everybody who had been on the scene acted out the hunt and the immense prowess of the hunter and *Morena* Cundill. It was as charming as imaginable and a great honor to be asked to visit. I was hugely flattered, since, after all, most of the participants were not armed, except for Karonda, who couldn't hit a barn with the doors locked from the inside, anyway.

At the staff camp, where the author was invited for smokes and perhaps a touch of beer after the killing of the lion. A rare honor.

Well, maybe not so, according to the story Gordon told me later. We were partaking of something a bit more potent and distilled by a far northern race when Gordon mentioned the item I brought to your attention earlier, that of the lion that had tried to eat him, and damned well would have, had it not been for Karonda and his highly skilled or very lucky shot.

I might note at this juncture that Cundill is purely an African. He took the last vertebra from our lion and threw away the same of the previous one—always kept in his pocket—in whose killing he had been involved. Everyone has their personal talismans, as, indeed, I do. Gordon's is especially unusual. Don't ask me why he does it; I didn't ask him.

In fact, come to think of it, I did.

"I just do, old boy," quoth he, and the matter was laid to rest.

"Out of the sack, mighty slayer of lions! Here's a cold beer to hold body and soul amalgamated. *Ina! Vuka wena! Manje!*" I suppose it is not polyglot Fiona's fault when she says "move" and one is inclined to do so.

My head didn't really feel like the prize pumpkin at a world's fair exhibition, but I suspect it might have taken third prize. Fiona, who does not drink, smoke, or do anything else reasonably disreputable, had been up before dawn,

watched the sunrise, and eaten an amount of bacon and eggs that would have shamed the Green Bay Packers. It was almost campfire time on my Tahitian paradise, but not before Gordon and I did very rude things to some francolin and guinea fowl along the edge of the swamp.

During our absence, Fiona and Paul packed up and got things ready for the trip down the Linyanti River to Linyanti Camp, there to enjoy more assorted goodies.

And goodies they were. Run by Mike Hissey and his incredibly competent wife, Daphne, Linyanti is more of a sight-seeing camp than one for hunters, and I have never in all my years seen one so "jacked-up" as it was. Great Deities! Flush toilets! Unlimited hot water! The bloody place even had an expansive lawn in immaculate condition!

But it is with huge sadness, as this is being typed in January of 1986, that I must inform you that Mike died of a heart attack earlier this month. With his demise passes a hunting era. I am indeed grateful, however, that I had the chance to spend several memorable days with him and Daphne on safari.

Soon after we had settled into camp, Cundill was, as mildly as I can put this in a book intended for a general audience, highly disturbed by the electronic presence of a raucous shortwave radio receiver—locally known as a "wireless"—

The fire/cocktail area at Linyanti Camp, with a client hut at far right.

that was blasting out British cricket scores. Now Gordon, at something around six feet two inches and a hundred and ninety pounds, is nobody to fool with. Take it from me. I have seen him in the field. Why he did not hit the proverbial grass roof, I don't know, but he is not without wile in camp politics either, so whoever was playing the set was spared what might have been a ferocious scene.

I happen to agree with Gordon. Clients don't come all that way and spend all that money to listen to some bloody shortwave cricket scores when they might be listening to hyenas, lions, and leopards. I have never permitted a radio in camp unless the owner agreed to listen to it with an earplug; my sentiments remain the same to this day.

People come on safari only peripherally to hunt. Safari is the pure experience of itself. The wood smoke of seasoned *mopane,* the sweating beers and other revivers, the soft chatter of the staff, the hyenas in the background, the white ants or termites around the Cadac pressure lamps, the brilliant clarity of the night sky as one may never have seen it, the distant roaring of a pride of lions—hopefully *quite* distant—the smell of cordite and the aroma of freshly shot guinea fowl or francolin for lunch in the bush—these are what safari is really about: hardly the killing of animals which, with a true sportsman, is at least tertiary.

I can remember coming back to the States after a season of standing around leadwood and *mopane* fires and opening my suitcase. The residual smell of the bushveld smoke, so alien to America, was actually enough to dampen my eyes with nostalgia and make me wonder what in hell I was doing away from there.

In camp with Mike and Daphne were Daph's brother, the well-known East African and Botswana professional John Northcote, as well as two of his clients who were soon to figure in something of a reasonable drama involving Gordon.

Mike, who had earlier been the manager of the Galana Scheme in Kenya before everything shattered hunting-wise there, had been the famous Elmer Keith's favorite professional hunter, and I seem to recall that Elmer dedicated a book to Mike. Elmer, a dear old pal of mine, also wrote for the Petersen Publishing Company in Los Angeles and contributed to *Guns & Ammo,* as do I from time to time.

In any case, we were a happy crew who, among ourselves, knew just about every man—or woman—who had held professional hunting licenses in our rather extended times. In comparison with the modern crop of professional hunters, we had between us decades devoted to the bush. Hissey? Don't ask me. He had been out there hunting when black rhino was a common feature on a hunting license. Today, most of the young professionals have not even *seen* a black rhino in the wild, let alone have a client take one.

The first night in camp at Linyanti there was an amazing confrontation between Gordon and his company's clients, who were due to fly out at the crack of dawn the following day. One of the gentlemen was a French-speaking white Senegalese, the other a Sicilian, who was as charming as the Senegalese was rude. They had been hunting with John Northcote and apparently couldn't hit the proverbial bull in the butt with a bass fiddle. Oh, yes, they got some stuff, especially the Italian, who took a very fine buffalo—which irritated his *compadre* into the first sentiments of a hunting "accident"—that dropped as dead as the Rock of Gibraltar with his first shot, further stirring the ire of his companion.

Protocol, being what it is, is rarely

aimed and fired. The Senegalese jumped on Gordon as soon as he had figured out who he was. His French was full-cocked and loaded with invective of the Double-O variety. Gordon, not speaking any French or Italian, roped in Fiona to interpret the tirade around the table, and she ate them alive. Interpreting exactly what was being said, as is demanded by the interpreter's credo, Fiona conveyed the following statement from the Senegalese to an astounded Gordon:

"In any safari camp with any self-respect, there are always fresh lemons. Why are there no more fresh lemons in this camp? How can you run safaris without fresh lemons? We grow lemons all over the place in Senegal."

"Lemons?" asked Gordon.

"Lemons," answered Fiona in English.

"Fiona," said Cundill, "please indicate to our guest that this is Botswana, and a remote corner of Botswana at that. We supply enough lemons for a British sailing ship for each safari. They are transported at great cost from hundreds of miles away. If our guest has priced fuel in this country recently, he'll have greater clarity as to what I am saying. And please inform the gentleman that, my being little conversant with the agricultural potential of Botswana from the lemon point of view, I am at a loss as to why lemons are not being grown all over this country

too. It would ease our logistics problems. Now ask our guest if he would, in conclusion, join me in having one of our truly superior Cape brandies."

The Senegalese pouted at the prospect of a substitute for "the real thing," cognac—from France, of course. He was being a plain and simple garden-variety bastard, but such was Cundill's grasp of the man's mood that it was not long before we were all being showered with invitations to Senegal, where life was *really* plump and the proper wines and brandies could always be found—as well as lemons.

This, of course, is a précis of the conversation, the Sicilian sitting and looking on, rather like a nicely tanned version of Kermit the Frog.

The next morning, the two hunters had gone, proving that we do have a Fairy Godmother—at least as far as the Senegalese was concerned.

Essentially, we had gone to Linyanti because we had already taken the lion, and Gordon now wanted me to enjoy some bird-viewing and fishing on the Linyanti River from Mike's special pontoon boat. An added attraction was the table set by Daphne, surely one of the best in Africa.

Paul was using an 800mm lens, and he got some really good shots of bee-eaters and monitor lizards. As we cruised along

The Linyanti Camp pontoon at its mooring, just outside camp.

for some hours, coming within arm's-length of exotic birds on numerous occasions, a rather fascinating thing came (as one would say in biblical parlance) to pass.

There was a piece of flotsam a couple of feet wide floating down the river, and perched upon it was a francolin, or crested quail, chick only a couple of weeks old. Cundill immediately called the boat to a halt—to the astonishment of the driver who, I think, had foreseen great joy in swamping the little thing with the boat's wash but did as he was bloody well told.

When John, the driver, mismaneuvered the pontoon boat, I don't think I've *ever* heard such a skinning of anybody.

He came back upstream and put Gordon into position to try and catch the little bugger with a landing net. Unfortunately, the chick was more frightened of us than of the crocs, of which there were plenty in the Linyanti, and swam the few yards to shore. Naturally, it chose the thickest wait-a-bit thorn bush and tried to hide in the middle of it, with no small degree of success.

Oh well, once Cundill gets motivated there's little that can stop him. He more than likely picked up more scars in the next fifteen minutes than in fifteen years of lion hunting, but he caught the chick, his forearms and legs pouring with blood. Gordon then had John put him ashore, where he walked a full hundred and fifty yards into the bush—thick stuff—unarmed and tucked the chick into the bottom of a leafy bush, safe from hawks in a place where his mum might hear him cheeping.

Not that I wouldn't have done it too, but I had to ask Cundill his motives. "Why the hell did you go to the trouble and blood of saving that little bastard when you shot five of the same species last evening?" I inquired, seeing that he was still mightily irritated at the boatman.

I got a Cundillism: "In the first instance, by no method of ours, this little thing was stranded in the middle of the river and had no chance to survive; and

Cundill saving the francolin chick.

in the second instance, it then took itself off to what little security it did have. I don't know, just a matter of fair play. Probably the same reason we track lions rather than poison or trap them."

Fair play. Get the drift?

This is probably the appropriate time to mention that baboons, for some reason absolutely unknown to this writer, are completely protected in Botswana. That's why there are so few game birds—all the eggs and nestlings are eaten. There is nothing remotely like the numbers of game birds I knew when I was a professional hunter there. What would prompt the authorities to completely protect the baboon, whose depredations are infamous, and to declare the various subspecies as protected, is well beyond my understanding. In areas like Linyanti, they are rife . . . and bloody cheeky, too. They are a positive menace not only to children and local crops but even to adults, especially women. I am not speaking of old wives' tales, but of the genuine danger that has arisen in places like Kenya, Zimbabwe, and South Africa.

A bit later, I shall describe in greater detail my personal campaign against the Vlackfontein baboons. But before leaving the subject, I would mention the huge lone baboon written of by Pretorius that killed a number of local people in Central Africa and then ate their brains; a remarkable creature that caused entire villages to be deserted in the Ruvuma region of what is now Tanzania.

Paul (right) and Gordon Cundill (left) on pontoon houseboat at Linyanti. (Photograph: Peter Capstick)

It was the twenty-fourth of June, my having shot the impala for camp meat for the "pyromaniacs" burning the strip that morning. Before we arrived at Linyanti, we drove past the turnoff to see King's Pool, the camp where the current King and Queen of Sweden had enjoyed their honeymoon. It was now Gordon's personal camp for himself and his family (and later to become mine on a return visit for back-up photographs with Dick van Niekerk, another excellent professional who filled in when Paul was unable to continue with us).

The track goes through some eight kilometers of a finger of the Chobe National Park. We pitched up to inspect the construction of Gordon's camp. It was a perfectly beautiful spot, a comma in the Linyanti River that curled back, filled with a hippo herd that appeared oddly docile and, for some reason or another, didn't invade the camp at night. I immediately liked it. Not that I liked the black mamba that swam ashore from the Caprivi, but the shotgun was packed away and it was in the grass before anybody could do anything.

We didn't stay at King's Pool that night or on any other during the trip, but went on, as mentioned earlier, to Linyanti a few miles away to hang our bags with Mike, Daphne, and John, who were about to have an empty camp for a few days after the memorable departure of the Senegalese and his companion. The cruise up the Linyanti and then down to the papyrus and rush dam some distance downstream revealed magnificent riverine life and provided a welcome break from the dusty conditions of lion hunting. It was also pleasant not to be losing pints of blood every day, so to speak, struggling after lions. Far more enjoyable to be adding cold beer to one's system. And Paul found a soul mate in Mike Hissey when it came to fishing. The sun, peace, and clean air were further perks, on top of the grand company and superb surroundings of Linyanti.

It was the same day, June 24, 1985, that we heard heavy-bore fire from across the Linyanti in the Caprivi Strip. In fact, through my Trinovid binoculars, I could clearly see the dying smoke from the fire of the hereditary chiefs' professional hunters on the other side. Many wounded hippo, as Gordon told me, had come to the Botswana side before now to die, as had elephant in similar condition.

Each Caprivi chief is granted six hippo and eight elephant. As Gordon put it in his uniquely succinct way: "The tragedy stems from the attitude in the mind of the rural African people that wildlife is just food. . . . Now, if wildlife is to survive in Africa, these people, especially their leaders, must be led to understand that wildlife is one of their resources, no less valuable than the diamonds at Orapa or gold. More so, wildlife is a *replenishable*

resource, a net foreign-currency earner if properly utilized.

"The aspect that is so often lost sight of is that sport hunting has already solidly proved itself in Europe and the U.S. as a superior form of conservation, and in Botswana, certainly, hunting companies provide the income that goes toward the maintenance of the national parks and their staff. They also, through their concessions, provide the reservoir area in which animals can survive, this also being true of Zambia and other game-rich areas.

"It is my opinion that when education will have reached down through several decades and generations to determine local attitude toward wild animals, there will be no more time to further educate rural Africans in this sense. At the moment, we can only deal with the contingencies of convincing his *leaders* of the

The late Mike Hissey.

importance of utilizing wildlife as a foreign-currency resource."

Cundill is dead right. While this is an adventure book about hunting big game, the foregoing subject is so inextricably tied to the sport itself as to be obvious. If all the animals disappear through poaching and agricultural overexpansion, and the accelerated introduction of goats, cattle, and donkeys into game habitat, what do you expect?

Where I used to hunt in Botswana, Zambia, and Zimbabwe, the tsetse were rife. They're largely gone now, and so is one hell of a lot of the game. There's still plenty, but not in the same places. We can get into the elephant situation and enhance any conclusions, based upon my lengthy campfire conversations with damned near everybody from the chief conservation Officer of Botswana to the man in the field.

"Get your posterior out of that rack, Capstick!" bellowed Cundill in Oxfordian tones. Only Gordon would say "posterior."

I did.

"The good lady at breakfast as well as your host have demanded a Cape buffalo. We have a meat crisis and the sepoys are upon us. *Nyama,* Capstick. Now! You will place a large hole in a *narri* as soon as possible." More's the loss that Cundill was born too late for the Indian army.

I inquired with my usual politeness what they would want with such a smelly thing, Paul echoing my sentiments while hiding behind a Lion Lager.

"The gentlemen up at King's Pool haven't seen meat since the original Bastille Day," intoned a clear-eyed Cundill, a rare enough sight to get my attention.

"Why don't you go shoot one while I get my notes together?" I asked.

"I'm afraid of them. They bite," said Cundill. "Anyway, I want to see if that lion was an accident."

"You're goddamn right it was an accident. Yours. *They* bite, too. Listen," said I, turning to Paul, "don't forget to get plenty of pictures. This light won't be right for my profile for at least another two hours."

Slamming Paul's instep, I gently suggested that he would have no chance of decent footage until the sun as well as our spirits were considerably higher.

He happily agreed.

"Right. Into the truck!" You don't argue with Gordon when you have a hangover and he is pure. A rare state of circumstances; in fact, I can't think of another instance. . . .

Gordon's grandfather was a transport rider between the coast and the diamond diggings during the last century when it was one of the toughest and most dangerous occupations in early Africa, and where things tended to bite even more than they do today. Apparently, there is some sort of residual gene passed on to transport riders' grandsons.

I stoked the Mauser with 300-grain Remington solids (meant to penetrate rather than mushroom), gave a hand up to Fiona to the rear of the hunting car, and off we went, looking for buffalo spoor.

Actually, there are a hell of a lot of buff in the Linyanti area, and they tend to be less than truly spooky, since there is not too much poaching. Typical of Botswana buffalo, they tend to stay in large herds, with bunches of up to a dozen bachelors on the periphery. Some of these are real whoppers, and to my eternal regret, I didn't pop one I saw that went at least forty-nine inches across the spread, *Rowland Ward* manner—a real beauty. I had just shot a zebra—to have the skin around and perhaps to have some artifacts made from it—before spotting a bunch of bull buff, including this really big chap.

Now, I've shot over a thousand of the blighters, either on a personal basis or on official duties with one or another game department, so I didn't spoil my shorts since I have seen better. I'm sorry now I didn't take him, but then, that's hunting. (The next day, second-thinking the matter with Paul, we went back. I might as well have tried to find the *Titanic*.)

In any case, I was expected to shoot a buffalo for the crew down the road who were refurbishing King's Pool, as well as for the staff at Linyanti and ourselves. I had no great desire for a buff as a trophy, because they tend to dominate a room by their very size when shoulder mounted.

We came across a herd of bulls the next day, however, and it was decided— by whom, I'm not sure—that I should take a shot. (After all, our guys were *hungry*.) It was a very bad setup, and I almost could have predicted what would happen. And happen it did.

There was an old bull about a hundred yards from us, across a *relatively* open area (meaning scrub *mopane* only five feet high). I took a rest on my thumb and hand against a handy tree and sent an airmail .375 solid. Owing to the recoil and subsequent loss of the bull in my sight, I didn't know what had happened, but that bull was *hambile,* gone. Uh-oh. The hold was right, but the bush wasn't. Before I could get another round into the bastard, he had turned and fled.

This was still very thick stuff, mostly scrub *mopane* and *conbretum*. I was shooting at an outline that rather resembled a steer Angus in a field of corn. The slug had hit a branch, been thrown off course, and smashed through two *mopane* stems as thick as your wrist, wailing away in one direction as the buff bellowed off in the other. Because of the ringing of the shot in my ears and the recoil of the .375,

I had lost any reality with the situation. Yet the testimony of the gun bearers that they had clearly heard the bullet "singing" made me feel a hell of a lot better. Bush deflection. No thick stuff out of which we would have to root a sick and highly angry *Bos kaffir.* Hopefully no wounded buff at all. Still, because of the possible consequences if the bull *had* been hit, Gordon, Paul, and I combed the thickets so that nobody would walk into a wounded buff bull.

It took two hours during the hottest part of the day just to be sure. We, of course, had no idea whether the goddamn thing was waiting behind the next clump of crud, sick and mean, with us directly on his mind. There was no blood whatever, and we found where the bullet had struck a branch midway before tearing up the two *mopane* trees. Satisfied, we moved on. We still needed meat.

The sun, a molten orb in a cerulean sky, was sliding away when we found the next bunch. We were all parched, and even the prospect of taking on another buff was not as intimidating as it should have been.

It was rather a large herd, perhaps a hundred and fifty animals. I noticed, since I wasn't particularly interested in a trophy bull but more in some fresh red meat, that tail-end Charlie seemed eminently qualified for our needs. He was a big bull and brought up the very rear of the herd;

an old chap who would probably have worms in his liver as well as in his stomach, but who would taste just as good as any of the rest of them. Just as he spun and began to thunder away over the drought-parched earth, I decided it was getting too late to fool around. I stuck him.

He was going at an angle of about twenty degrees off to my left, so I didn't have to hold off much. I put the solid just in front of his right rear thigh, shooting to take the big pipes or lower lungs and perhaps break the left front foreleg. Even at sixty yards I could hear the hollow thump of the solid as it hit right where I wanted. I was trying to rake him, slow him up, so he would be sick enough to drop out of the herd and cooperate. Happily he did, and I waved Paul (who is an ex-combat photographer) forward as the buff turned sideways in an open area. Paul got the shots of my shoulder-shooting the wounded buff.

It is quite extraordinary in Africa the way vultures, marabous, and other scavengers assemble when they see meat. I have actually put out a pure red bandana and drawn a swarm of the critters. (The old-timers used to tie a white rag to the feet of an upended antelope to keep vultures *away.*) By the time that buff hit the ground, the air was nearly black with birds. They didn't have all that long to wait, either, since our trackers and gun

Chasing a herd of Cape buffalo in an attempt to get a clear shot.

bearers left mighty light pickings by the time we were finished.

I mentioned that I've shot four figures worth of buffalo, but I had never before seen one with such a collection of parasites. His paunch, full of fodder, contained at least an equal amount of red worms of a type I didn't happen to be

particularly familiar with. If Gordon knew what they were, he didn't mention it, either.

Jehosephat, Karonda, Mack, and Ottie made quick work of the carcass, leaving only a little guts and some well-stripped bones. I sent Paul off to get a few shots of the scavengers, which he did with a wild, screaming charge into the midst of them, camera clicking on motor drive. For a minute, I wondered just who was going to get whom, but a ragged Paul reappeared, nicely spotted with vulture —what's the polite term?—guano. (On the way back to camp he rode in the back. The far back.) In the meantime, we had lunch in the shade of a *mopane,* Gordon's old East African chopbox producing its usual wonders. I'd trade you something very dear to my soul to own that box. Solid teak, it almost seemed to exude the essence of the Old Africa. How many hundreds of thousands of miles it had done were unknown, as was its age. Even Gordon has forgotten where he originally picked it up, but bear in mind that he started his professional career as a kid of seventeen in Tanganyika and is now somewhat older! Knowing Gordon, I very much doubt that he purchased it new, either. Hell, the Sultan of Zanzibar might well have used it as his lunch box, as there was plenty of room for a loaf of bread, a jug of wine, and even thee.

I might add here that some slightly more exotic items than the simple tastes of Omar Khayyám were enclosed therein, among them a thing called "ice," which I saw so infrequently in Africa I almost always forgot how to spell it. There was cold francolin, a good jar of Dijon mustard, and various chilled meats from such ho-hum fare as warthog and impala. (You know, the sort of thing you regularly pick up at Burger King or the Explorers' Club Annual Dinner.) There was even—damn—ice cream. Vanilla.

Actually, it would be unfair and probably dastardly to infer that all of Hunters Africa's camps do not have ice. Hell, you could chill a hippo into a state of hibernation in the middle of the bush with the amount of ice the company's modern conveniences produced at their camps.

But back to the buffalo. I had noticed Jehosephat looking at the thing with a rather intense stare. When I mentioned this to Gordon in the Toyota, I got a pretty good answer.

It had been the year before, Gordon explained. Cundill had had his young son along with him as well as his usual crew and a good personal friend. It was *terminalia* country, very thick, and they came across a herd of some four to five hundred *narri.* I have been in that area and if there is a place you don't want to try to sort out a wounded buff from some half-thousand, that spot would rank pretty high. *Terminalia* is some five to seven feet tall and stops bullets like a regiment of sandbags.

In any case, the man shot and the buff was obviously hit, but not hard enough or in the right place. To make matters worse, there was no visible blood spoor because of the dust of the other five-hundred-odd *narri.*

Charming.

The bull disappeared into the herd before Gordon could break it down with his .500 Nitro (or, knowing him, a large stick). The hunting party skirted the heavy cover ahead and climbed a termite heap some hundred yards further on. Despite a lengthy search with binoculars, there was still no sign of that particular bull, and Gordon figured that, with so many animals, he'd better send for the vehicle to see if any blood could be picked up at the edges of the herd's spoor.

There was small clump of *terminalia* upwind past which the party had to go, the trackers/gun bearers leading the way as Gordon and his friend covered them. Oh, yes.

The trouble was that Mack and Jehosephat ran straight at Gordon with the wounded buffalo right behind them, narrowing the three-point gap to the extent that Gordon couldn't fire without hitting one of the men with a 570-grain solid. The buff had been shot too far back, through the guts, and was rapidly gaining ground on the fleeing men. Experienced as they were, they should have known enough to zigzag and offer their cover gun a field of fire, but the buff was so close they completely forgot their instructions. (Can't much blame them, personally. Charging buffaloes definitely scare me, and I carry a rifle.)

Mack finally pulled a J-turn, while Jehosephat completely lost his head and continued straight toward Gordon, the buffalo almost at his heels. Gordon's only impression in the seconds that a buff charge takes was of flashes through the bush. And there was still no way to get

Part of a motor-driven sequence in which the author, after shooting a buffalo in a raking fashion in front of the right-rear hip and breaking the off-front shoulder with a solid, pays the insurance.

off a shot without hitting Jehosephat, who was breaking all Olympic records for out-running wounded buffalo.

The buffalo, according to Gordon, actually caught Jehosephat just as he reached an elephant-damaged piece of bush, a *mopane* that had been knocked down but had survived to spend the rest of its life at a sixty-degree angle. Jehosephat went flying from a vicious thump of its horns, and there was a sickening smashing sound as the bull hit the tree at full speed. Jehosephat, either by luck or design, had managed to fall behind it. As Cundill ran forward at top speed there was one hell of a commotion as the buff tried to sort out Jehosephat. And try mightily he did.

As Gordon came up to the spot and the buffalo saw him, he immediately forgot Jehosephat and charged Cundill. Gordon gave the buff a permanent prenasal drip up the nostrils and got down on one knee with the thing only a few yards off. Sure that Jehosephat was dead, he saved his last barrel of the .500 Nitro-Express Wilkes for when it would really matter.

The buff took the second dose from a couple of feet away. He crashed at Cundill's feet and never twitched. As Cundill told me in his inimitable accent: "When you have an animal charging like that, you must let him come to the point that you are positive you can kill him."

Remember, by his own testimony, he was only able to see patches of the action through the heavy bush. Yet he made the additional comment that, "In open cover, as this was, when I shouted him off Jehosephat, this becomes very personal, especially with an animal as fast and as dangerous as a wounded buffalo."

Yes, I would agree it is highly personal, having had a couple of dead buff pulled off my carcass. They're very heavy.

"I went back to find what might be left of Jehosephat and discovered him behind the rather substantial root system of this tree. Although he had several cracked ribs from the initial impact, these were all the injuries he had sustained. This was my eight-year-old son's introduction to buffalo hunting."

Gordon continued in agreement with me that Jehosephat, who seemed to have no fear spooring lion or other dangerous game, was just too brave and would more likely sooner than later get permanently hammered, either by buff or lion.

We spent an Elysian week with Daphne, Mike, and John Northcote, which was, however, capped by an incident that might well have been deadly for all concerned. But before this, we photographed Mike's giant kingfishers, a very rare species, which were nesting downriver but would come to camp every day, where Mike would catch minnows to feed them. There were also two pairs of

The white-fronted bee-eater (Melittophagus Bullockoides) *on the bank of the Linyanti River.*

fish eagles, which look much like the North American bald eagle, their call even sounding similar: an eerie wail that seems to echo off any reasonably sized body of water. We were to see more and get better photographs on a later trip to the Okavango main channel, but these initial encounters were just further soul regenerators for me. Little bee-eaters, one of my favorite types of birds, swarmed the Linyanti, as did the white-fronted, another lovely member of that tribe. But birds were in fact the reason we damned near got somebody killed.

They were all professionals in that camp at Linyanti—Gordon, Mike, and John. There was also me, no longer holding a license in hopes of living a longer life. We had decided that, despite the depredations of the hordes of baboons, perhaps a bit of roast sand grouse might go nicely with the rest of Daph's Ritzian offerings, and had arranged to enjoy a spot of wing shooting one afternoon.

Mike told us about a waterhole, or "pan" (as such pools are locally called throughout most of central and southern Africa), nearby that was reputed to have more sand grouse drinking from it at dusk than businessmen at a Third Avenue bar. Conveniently, it was quite near the airstrip, probably not five hundred yards away. (Now, when I say airstrip, I mean a place where trees do not currently grow. Of course, that is not true of the internationally famous Capstick Airport, located in the strategic Mupamadzi Valley in Zambia, but sheer modesty prevents me from rendering the details concerning that huge honor until a later point. Trees *do* grow there, however, and you must dodge them a bit unless you want to bend the wings of your charter plane, a minor matter in any case.) We selected two vehicles, piled everybody in, and headed off toward the pan.

I have commented elsewhere that to my great personal loss as well as that of his family, Gordon *will* get nailed by

something ugly if he continues to climb off that hunting car and wander for hundreds of yards unarmed to follow lion spoor or buffalo tracks or heaven knows what else he discovers with his clever little nose. As I cannot emphasize enough, if it bites and you can't bite back, you're out of business. The gun back in the hunting car is not worth a goddamn if you're a hundred yards away and you've got a lion atop of you.

Well, I knew better but had gotten lulled into the pattern, too. We arrived at the site near the Linyanti airstrip, the pan being something around an acre and a half in size but apparently fairly deep. Gordon emerged from the cab as did I. Paul helped Fiona down as Karonda, Mack, and Jehosephat piled off. I presumed Ottie was in the other vehicle.

Gordon assumed his classic position, monocle wedged firmly in his eye socket, hands clasped behind his back, bent over looking at the spoor of the hundreds of buff and God-knows-what-else that had been drinking there. He muttered the occasional "ummm" and "ahhh" as one or another spoor came to eye. But he was unarmed. As was Fiona. As was Paul. As were, unfortunately, the rest of the men and I.

I, at least, knew better.

We had walked completely around the pan in, by my best guess, something like seventeen minutes, and were waiting for Mike, John Northcote, and Ottie to show up. (They had, it turned out, taken a few minutes to sort out some shotshells and were about ten minutes behind us. Just as well.) When they did—and it was a minor miracle, since Mike's driving made Mario Andretti look like a tricycle-driver—I had just finished making the following statement to Fiona: "You know, this is, in my experience, exactly the place a badly torn-up bull hippo that's been fighting would come to save his bacon. I've got an eerie feeling without a rifle."

I had no sooner got out the quotation marks when all hell broke loose. Or, to quote Gordon: "In the words of William Charles Baldwin, esquire, 'Behemoth appeared.'" Personally, I'm astonished he didn't quote Chaucer or, at the very least, Kipling. Maybe Kipling wasn't into hippos.

But we sure as hell were.

The middle of the pan absolutely erupted with the power of a depth charge, as probably nigh on three tons of bull hippo, bleeding and rampaging, burst upon us. And, nobody had a rifle. It was one of those moments that, in a lifetime of professional hunting, lasts less than a minute—if you are very lucky and clever. Better still to be fast on your feet.

I nabbed Fiona by the collar, stuck her face into mine, and simply said, *"Run! Now!"*

She couldn't see it, but she's no fool and was on top of the cab in a flash, passing me with a speed that still makes me shake my head. If you want to talk about bush-busting, that's the girl you want to hire. Hell, if she'd charged the hippo, I would have put even money on the outcome.

My next concern was to correct my weaponless condition with the greatest rapidity. I ran like hell for the Toyota, where my .375, crammed with solids, was leaning on the front seat. If that sonofabitch hippo was right behind me, I didn't pause to look. I saw that Fiona was clear and devil take the hindmost.

We have all the time in the world to discuss hippos, but bear in mind that they kill more people than any other vegetarian. No, not buffalo or rhino or whatever you will. Hippos.

I was later very sorry to have met dear old Karonda at the door of the hunting car because he was between me and that .375 H&H Mauser. In my haste, I grabbed the poor chap by the front of his jumper and, with a strength I never suspected I possessed, picked him up off the ground and threw him one-handed through the air. Happily, I didn't hurt Karonda, nor was the hippo directly on my heels. I had that .375 in hand in one big hurry, though, and was running as fast as I could back to the water, having tipped the scope mount off and leaving the open sights. Bulling through the bush, I passed Northcote, minus his gun, swaying in a treetop and caught up with Gordon, who was dunking solids into the Westley Richards .500. I hoped they worked better than the softs he had tried to use on the lion.

When it comes to hippos, *that* was a hippo. He was, without any doubt whatsoever, the biggest I have ever seen. I can't begin to imagine what the one that threw him out of the herd must have looked like! And Jesus, but did he put on a show! The first time he emerged, he came a whole body length out of the water not twenty yards away. That was for practice.

Presuming, quite correctly, that we were impressed, he carried on with the performance. He false-charged a dozen times, Paul being so unfortunately pie-eyed at never having seen something like this before that he neglected to photograph most of the dramatic moments. Ah, hell, that's safari. The bloody thing sure had *my* attention.

Karonda, or somebody else, had brought Gordon's side-by-side shotgun, and Old Hangfire decided to have some fun trying to drive the hippo out of the pool.

Now, you don't *do* that with injured hippo—not without provoking a charge. Gordon, as the photos that did come through show, did not actually shoot at the beastie, but merely laced the water to its bow and stern. It didn't like that very much.

At one point, with the thing about ten yards away, me with the .375 and Gordon with the .500, it looked as if it was *really* coming. No kidding coming. He was actually pushing a wake at least two feet high in front of himself and blowing a wave six feet around the periphery of the pan. I had thought our lion had been slightly out of sorts, but you should have seen that hippo! When he was within thirty feet, I asked Gordon out of the side of my mouth, "Shall I take him?" The scope was tipped off the Mauser and I had him dead to rights, in quite a literal sense.

"Oh, give him three or so more paces," said Cundill, the wash of the charge wetting his shoes.

To my surprise, he stopped. I covered him as he backed off just to be safe, there having been several fatal hippo incidents in the area in the past couple of years.

Cundill is one of the very cool ones. The distance would have been the absolute limit of proximity to that biting machine we would have wanted, as we would at that point have been well within his territory. The hippo might very easily have continued the charge. I'm not certain if Gordon was aware it was a rogue or if he was trying to provoke a charge, although he never shot directly at the animal, which most likely would have done the trick. He was most certainly a very bad one, and had he come a-charging while we were on the other side of the pool and unarmed, there's not much question somebody very probably would have been killed.

Cundill was having a wonderful time trying to drive the bull out of the pool,

Prelude to the "hippo incident," as described in text.

but the water was most obviously his security blanket and it would take a missle-armed destroyer to move him out of *there.*

I was finally able to convince Gordon that we were *hors de combat* and that if we wanted any sand grouse shooting at all, we had better get our butts in gear and find some other place. It was Karonda who advised that a second pan that offered excellent shooting lay not half a mile away.

That one, I am happy to report, lurked not with behemoth. If it did, he had a much better lung capacity than the previous bull. We had about forty-five minutes of excellent shooting, in which I did not particularly distinguish myself, but it was sure pretty as can be. Although we killed quite a few doves, ring-necks, and the usual potpourri of minor African pigeons, the sand grouse were a bit late.

The cloudless late afternoon sky was transfusion red, freckled with hurtling flocks of birds, mostly double-banded sand grouse. Now, if a man can hit sandies with any consistency, you can bet he's pretty fair. The difficult part is that they not only change direction at what seems to be right angles, but, when they find a wind they like—such as usually occurs at that time of day—they vary speed from feathered cannonballs to butterflies.

To my immediate left was Northcote (we'd gotten him out of the tree, although how an old bastard like that could have gotten up one in the first place without constant practice is beyond me). To his left was Mike Hissey, who had shot a couple of sand grouse in his time, you may be assured. Next was Gordon, who held down the left flank, while I held down the right. Behind me were Fiona and Paul, while scattered among us were the safari crew, ready to pick up those rare birds so unlucky as to arbitrarily collide with a charge of shot. They were not kept very busy on this particular afternoon.

I opened a few eyelids with a triple as the first bunch came in against the bleeding sunset, but it seemed to be all downhill from there. Still, we took a goodly enough number of birds (which are, interestingly enough, virtually never shot in most of central Africa, owing to the cost of shells. Francolin are mostly snared, along with the odd guinea fowl. Doves are killed with slingshots, or as they are known in British parlance, "catapults").

Monday morning. Gordon had clear symptoms of cerebral malaria, no small problem in the bush. This particular form of the disease involves parasites that die off in the bloodstream, impeding the flow of blood to the brain through the veins and arteries. Gordon has had it twice, the only man I know to have doubly survived it. I was worried as hell, even though I have always suspected some sort of brain problem with "Hangfire" Cundill.

Gordon does not take antimalarial pills or prophylaxis. According to him, it can mask the disease and blood tests will not show positive, even if you have it. In a cerebral malaria situation, hours are critical. As Gordon, who ought to know something of the matter, commented: "The problem with malaria is that the medication to treat and prevent it, readily available from drug stores or chemists in Africa, and on prescription in the U.S.A., recommends doses based on *average* body weights. Let's say the average man weighs a hundred and fifty pounds. Fine. The dosage is probably correct. If, however, he's the size of a Peter Capstick, he will probably need considerably more to either ward off or treat the disease. This is one of the major problems of these blood parasite diseases."

I am certainly no doctor, but when one lives for some years with the Big Three—malaria, sleeping sickness, and bilharziasis—one does pick up a few tips. It is my understanding, from those who have had it happen to them, that some of the drugs used to counter malaria can block or mask sleeping sickness—trypanosomiasis—and possibly, but don't quote me, bilharziasis as well. Whether this is in fact true, I don't know. I take malaria prophylaxis every week practically by my wristwatch and, despite the extraordinary places in which I have spent large periods of time and where one or another form of the disease proliferates, I have—touch wood—never had it. But then, I have a lead-lined constitution, never even having had amoebic dysentery.

(There is, I regret to advise you, a new form of malaria, especially in the Zambezi Valley of Zimbabwe, as well as in some pockets of the Luangwa Valley [so I am told] which is absolutely immune to the "chloro"-based drugs that form the phalanx of resistance in the fight against malaria. Gordon advised me to take a particular product as a precaution, but I caught sight of a special notice in the Safari Club International magazine that gave a strict warning against the drug's side effects.)

We watched Gordon very closely with the SSB radio on in case we would have to fly him out, but, a strong man, he passed the attack and was back in the field in a day. Fortunately it had been an exceptionally mild episode that he overcame.

To slip back as smoothly as possible from the minor problem of bloodsuckers to the major nonmeat-eating mankiller in Africa, the hippo. Just nine days before these lines were typed, the following

Author shooting sand grouse against a splendid African sunset.

headline appeared in the *Natal Mercury,* published in Durban, the continent's principal cargo-handling port, on the east coast of South Africa:

MISSIONARY FLOWN TO SA AFTER
MALAWI HIPPO ATTACK

I'll spare you a blow-by-blow account, but, if you live in rural Africa, such incidents are by no means rare. Sister Corrie le Gemate, a fifty-year-old Dutch missionary in Malawi, a country to the north, was mauled by a hippo on Christmas Day, 1985, while wading in a lake quite near her mission hospital. "The water," to quote the unfortunate woman, "was a bit muddy and warm, so I went in a bit deeper. Then I felt something heavy around my legs.

"I then felt something cut into my leg. I was surprised and fell back underwater. It must have bumped me then," said Sister le Gemate from her hospital bed, "because I was terribly sore."

She looked toward the children on the lake shore and saw they were all wearing expressions of horror. Turning in the water, she stared back smack into the face of a hippo, sex unknown, but most likely a bull. By lucky happenstance, some colleagues from the hospital at the CCAP mission came by and got her out.

"I was in terrible pain," reported Sister le Gemate. "I couldn't walk, so they put me into the back of a station wagon and took me to the clinic, but there were no painkillers."

Spare me rural Africa where there is rarely anything in the medical line. I carry my own kit and trust nobody else, despite some firms' claims to having full emergency medical facilities. In Africa, you look after yourself, me boy, if you are still able.

The missionary was indeed badly hurt. The ischial nerve in her upper leg, controlling all sensation and movement of the limb and foot, had been chomped through, her pelvis was fractured, and her foot lacerated by the saberlike edges of the hippo's teeth.

After the trip to a nearby hospital, where a doctor was eventually available, a preliminary operation was performed to stabilize her condition, after which she waited in great discomfort for four days before an aircraft was available to fly her to the Tygerberg Hospital in Cape Town, South Africa, and more sophisticated surgery was performed during a five-hour operation. She is now in a plaster cast up to her waist and is recovering. She came very close to dying in that lake.

Should you think that the hippo data I have been spouting for the past ten years and more is a bunch of crud, have a look at recent newspaper clippings, which are just the tip of the iceberg, so to speak, since hippo attacks tend to leave few victims alive. Of course, the hippos themselves don't eat them, but for bloody damned sure the crocs do.

I have already written in *Safari: The Last Adventure* of the American safari client who had the horrid misfortune of emasculation in October 1982 near my old camp on the Luangwa in Zambia. Hippo. It was an unprovoked night attack right in camp, which makes me think of the uninvited little bunch that dropped by ours at Saile. You may not, however, have heard about some of the other horribles that don't make the "SAVE BAMBI" U.S. press. Let me throw you a few.

From the *Pretoria News* of June 30, 1983: HIPPO ATTACK: MAN LOSES ARM. That happened in Zimbabwe. Or the item in the *Natal Mercury* of Durban: WAYWARD HIPPO SHOT DEAD AFTER MONTH OF KILLING. That happened in Zululand. There is also the report in the *Pretoria News* of August 8, 1984, telling of a man who had to have his leg amputated after a brush with hippo in Lake Amu, Kenya. A little closer to home there's the incident reported by the *Daily News* Africa Service on March 12, 1983: YOUTH DIES IN HIPPO ATTACK. That was in a river in Botswana. Just for the record, the youngster's skull had been penetrated by a tusk.

The foregoing is only a small slice of the melon because, considering the remoteness of most areas where hippos happen to exist, nobody is likely to pick up a telephone (a what?) and report that subchief whoever got his chips from a hippo under the following circumstances. Part of life in rural Africa.

End of thought.

It was the twenty-fifth of June, 1985, when Fiona, Paul, and I flew back with Gordon to Kasane and cleared Customs at the airstrip before flying on to Victoria Falls, Zimbabwe. Gordon, with his usual panache, pointed out the splendid sight of the confluence of the Chobe and Zambezi Rivers below, then gave our pilot explicit instructions to do a series of rather daring passes at various angles over the falls themselves. The thundering waters, ravines, and rainbows seemed to bear out Fiona's statement that they truly are the eighth wonder of the world. Paul thought he was back in combat as he rapidly changed lenses and position to get as much as he could of the roaring action.

At Vic Falls Airport, we were picked up by Keith Essen with his usual efficiency and taken to the renowned Victoria Falls Hotel to check in for the night. It was another homecoming for me, as I had picked up many clients there in the past. The doorman, a giant of a man named Ordwell Makamure who is probably emblazoned with more pins and badges than anybody on earth, was right on hand to greet us. He grinned in delight upon recognizing me and asked me why I had taken so long to come back. Every hotel of note should have a Makamure. It makes you feel good.

It was real *tagati*—magic—to be back at the Vic Falls and be reminded of days past. Paul had taken Keith up on his offer to go down to the falls for some spectacular shots up close and on foot. As mentioned earlier, I had bumped into Eric Wagner on our way through Vic Falls Airport when we were headed for Botswana, and he had invited our party down to the old Matetsi Unit #4 where I used to hunt. That was where we were going the next day.

Fiona and I were relaxing on the expansive terrace, under those fine, shady trees, to the sounds of the famous marimba band after a buffet lunch, when whose rather impressive outline should appear on the horizon but that of Stuart Campbell, one of my friends of longest standing. I cannot give you Stuart's story precisely, not having all the details, but I do know that he was for many years the chief game officer of Zambia's southern province and that he fought with distinction in Burma during "the Big One." Stuart is generally and specifically one of my favorite people.

Stuart bellowed a greeting from the upper terrace that would likely have put any resident members of the cloth into

Mr. Ordwell Makamure, the doorman for the ancient and revered Victoria Falls Hotel.

shock. The marimba band was playing but that never slowed down Campbell. You really had to hand it to the kids at the giant marimba. They never lost a beat. A few minutes later, Eric Wagner and his departing safari clients pitched up on the famous terrace and we all partook of some sustenance, if not exactly of the solid kind. (Well, olives *are* solid food, aren't they?)

A bit later, we packed off down the road to Matetsi Unit #4. I had been immensely impressed with the service and attitude of the Victoria Falls Hotel staff, where people fell all over themselves to be of excellent service. My personal congratulations to the Zimbabwe government for maintaining the very high standards of such a great landmark and its immediate environment. Everything was immaculate, the staff was courteous as well as efficient, and it was a real treat for an American—or anyone else, for that matter—to return after so many years. To go to southern Africa and not visit the Vic Falls would be similar to visiting Rome and not seeing St. Peter's.

We drove down the A-5, on our way to another of my African homes. I was truly touched at still being able to recognize individual trees along the way. We turned off at the familiar crossroad for Matetsi Siding and continued on the corrugated dirt until the left turn that led up to Geoff Broom's old place, which was on top of a hill named *Mongu* after the small stream that ran in the *vlei* below.

Well, it wasn't the same, but it wasn't that different, either. Although a touch more tattered for not having been lived in for several years, it was still a fine headquarters for a safari operation. When Eric Wagner had moved in, in March 1985, there were dead owls and all sorts of deceased *mammalia* strewn hither and yon. He had had the place cleaned out and disinfected, got the garden and sprawling lawns going in fine style, and was even building on extensions to an already rambling thatched home. I was delighted to be back, and to have the chance of not only getting to know Eric better but to spend some time with Stuart Campbell.

Speaking of Stuart, he was possibly the first man to operate safaris in Zambia, together with Lou Erasmus. By all appearances, this was some time before Norman Carr and Peter Hankin set up the outfit I eventually worked for, Luangwa Safaris.

There's a fascinating story of how Peter Hankin (tragically killed and partially eaten by a lioness on September 2, 1974) and Norman Carr (author of several books and a hunter and game warden) met. It was during World War II in Ethiopia at some remote place, as I remember the story from Peter over the years. They were seated next to each other at what might have passed for a bar drinking *arrack,* a local brew capable of peeling the paint off a tiger tank. As might be expected, both men being British officers, they got to talking.

It soon came to light that these two men had spent years of their lives avoiding each other. Hankin was reputedly the top ivory poacher in the Luangwa Valley of what was then Northern Rhodesia, and Carr its first game warden. It almost became a joke, with Norman working out elaborate ambushes while Peter thought up equally devious evasions. They would even leave notes for each other in obvious places in the bush—such notes having been delivered by the faithful locals—wedged in a cleft stick so that the perspiration of the runners did not soil the paper. Norman never caught Peter, but they did join forces after the war to create their safari firm.

At any rate, before Fiona, Paul, and I arrived at Matetsi, Stuart had told the household staff that "A prince is coming, a man you will know." Lord above, the whole of Zimbabwe was abuzz with such tidings! I don't know if they were expecting Bernhard, Andrew, or Charles and Diana. They could have been most heartily disappointed at the arrival of the old *bwana* of eleven years back. Still, they had had it firmly graven on their brains that I had somehow achieved princehood.

I discovered the extent of these proceedings upon the arrival of the first evening's dinner, when a really magnificent impala pie was carried in. Across the top of the crust, in finely whipped mashed potato, was emblazoned WELCOME PRINCE. Oh, well, my own ideas of princehood are rather vague, so I reckoned it would do no good to ruin any-body's party, especially considering the trouble the chefs and staff had gone to. We toasted Prince Peter I and his princess. As the real item would undoubtedly have observed, a jolly good time was had by all.

On asking the name of the elderly chef so that I could express our appreciation, I was rather amazed to be told that his name was Nick Campbell—not a typically African name. It was simply too much for Fiona's curiosity, and she wormed the story out of Stuart. Apparently, the chef had been in Stuart's employ for some twenty years, and such was the rapport between the men that the African had gone to considerable legal trouble to change his surname to that of his employer. It didn't stop there. The chef's eldest daughter had been named after Stuart's late wife, Joy, and the man's youngest son was named Stuart. Needless to say, this anecdote reveals a great deal about my old pal from the Luangwa days.

Before going any further, however, I must tell you of an amazing change that had occurred at Matetsi #4.

The Victoria Falls, the "smoke that thunders," displaying its magnificent cascades of water at the point where the Zambezi River falls into the gorge discovered by Dr. Livingston.

When I was there as a professional hunter, years before, I never saw even the spoor of an elephant. Now, however, the place is crawling with them. Matetsi adjoins the Hwange (previously Wankie) National Park, which had scads of the critters, and upon which large helicopter cropping programs had been implemented. You would have thought some elephant would have strayed over into Matetsi. No. Although we had no elephant quota whatsoever, it certainly was not a matter of hunting pressure or of poaching. They just stayed out.

I am not absolutely sure, but, in speaking with the chief game biologist of Botswana during a later safari, I may have gotten a hint as to why elephants appear and disappear in an area the way they do. But more of that further on.

While on the subject of elephant, I have a tale I must be extremely careful in relating. I acquired the court documents and medical reports through Eric Wagner, who served as an expert witness on the case. I choose not to use names for obvious reasons.

In 1982, an American woman was horribly mauled in Zimbabwe by a bull elephant that hadn't read the rules and that came in a full-out charge from a hundred and ten meters (or seventy-eight meters, depending on whom you want to believe); there was no shortage of witnesses. Now that's a hell of a long way for a jumbo, possibly explained by the fact that he had foot-long parasites up his trunk and was not very pleased with things in general. There are many versions of the incident but here is what happened, as best as I can determine.

The elephant, a very good one whose tusks weighed sixty-one and seventy-seven pounds respectively, was being photographed from what I personally consider a prudent distance. But when it winded the party, it spun and charged. All the people present agreed that the charge from that distance took no more than eight seconds. To give you an idea of how fast an elephant on a mission can move, the humans were able to cover a mere five yards before it was on them. The major problem was that nobody immediately handy was armed—not the professional hunter, the assisting "learner-hunter" doing his apprenticeship, or the client. A game guard in the car was armed with a 7.62mm assault rifle.

It chose the woman.

She got behind a *mopane* tree that was later measured and found to be eighteen inches at the base. The bull broke it as easily as I can break a matchstick and neatly dropped the tree on top of the woman, breaking her leg severely. The bull then proceeded to pick her up with his trunk and tried to tusk her, but he couldn't seem to get his act completely together. The game scout, who had no moss growing on him, got into action and shot the thing twenty times, including nine metal-jacketed bullets in the head. The elephant dropped the lady and fell back on its haunches, very badly wounded.

At this point, the professional's tracker came up with the express rifle, according to most accounts a .458 Winchester Magnum, and he fired two rounds at the animal as he approached the unarmed party. The pro finished the jumbo.

In shock and terrific pain, the woman was put onto a contrived stretcher—shortly you will see why. I have in front of me seven medical reports detailing her injuries. How she is still alive boggles the medical imagination. Her injuries, as ascertained by this gaggle of physicians, were as follows:

1. After a trip of some six and a half hours by car over some of the worst roads this side of Afghanistan, shock had reached the point where her blood pressure was 80/60. She never lost consciousness, which, of course, made matters all the worse for her. She then endured a traumatic flight crammed into a light aircraft that finally landed near a hospital.

2. X-rays showed a transverse fracture of her right femur as well as a displaced fracture of her pelvis. Both

breaks, although multiple, were set the same day, after which she was given intravenous fluids as well as five pints of blood, not exactly the replacement for a shaving nick.

3. At that point, they almost lost her. She went into pulmonary edema that evening and required days of intubation and ventilation. Worse was to come.

4. Two days after the attack, the woman also had a cardiac arrest. Complete heart stoppage, one of three in all, although she did live. For a time, she was a triplegic, owing to crushed vertibrae, which were not even discovered until a considerable time after her admittance to the hospital.

5. The woman had several broken ribs, which were further broken and driven into her lungs when efforts were made to resuscitate her from her multiple cardiac arrests. Add to this profound depression and you have some idea of the horror.

Now, I could go on with the woman's injuries for quite some time but I don't want this book to sound like a train wreck. I do not have the transcript of the actual trial, but the foregoing is, to the best of my knowledge, accurate. While I was not party in any way to the legal

Elephant bull.

proceedings, it's sometimes curious how one gets involved in what seem to be unrelated matters when one writes books.

Eric Wagner told me, while we were out wing shooting at Matetsi, that a reference to *Death in the Long Grass* appeared in her husband's deposition, I believe. The woman had instituted suit against, as I understand it, both the husband and his or their insurance company for an astronomical sum of money. The basis of the suit was that the husband was responsible for her safety and did not perform the implied function. According to Eric, the gentleman's deposition before a considerable number of witnesses included the fact that he had read the elephant chapter of *Death in the Long Grass* and was aware that elephants were both dangerous as well as unpredictable. From what I gather, it convinced the jury and the woman was awarded the money.

Shortly thereafter, if my information is correct, the couple entered the bonds of legal disenchantment. Bad luck all round. . . .

I also have before me a copy of a letter from the provincial warden, Matabeleland North, rather severely chastising the professional hunter in charge of the show. I have had nightmares of being in the same situation, and it is so simple and safe to second-guess a seasoned bush professional after a tragedy has happened. I shall not do so here. He had his professional license canceled for two years but was at least granted a "learner's permit" for the same period of time. It must have broken his heart, and I sympathize; but, goddamnit, you have to *always* be in a position to protect the client, no matter how unlikely the situation may appear at first appraisal. He failed to do this. Thus, he was up to his neck in boiling oil. The assistant professional as well as the gun bearer were completely exonerated.

The entire point of the story is the fact that the *dramatis personae* were entirely unarmed, and therein lay the infraction that led to the woman's hammering. And that is precisely the way the game department saw things.

No, the elephant should not have charged from that distance. But it did, and people got hurt. *Sic semper Africanus.*

• • •

Now, I really hadn't come to Eric's to shoot anything except game birds bent on attacking us with intent to inflict grievous bodily harm. As it turned out, we were attacked quite consistently.

The following morning, Thursday, June 27, 1985, Eric, Fiona, Paul, and I, as well as two gun bearers/trackers, went out looking for feathered trouble. Francolin and partridge of half a dozen varieties were absolutely all over the joint. We would drive along until we spotted a good covey, park the car, and walk in a couple of hundred yards, flanking each other. There were Swainson's, red-necked, and heaven knows what else, as well as some fine bunches of guinea fowl. I was shooting pretty well, but you have my guarantee that no flies were alighting on Eric Wagner's gun, either. He really shot magnificently on both days we went out and is clearly a pro, at least behind any kind of a long gun. I have never seen him shoot pistol or revolver, so I can't comment on that aspect, but I have no reticence in saying I'm not such a hot *pistolero* myself.

We were really just driving along the original track to my old home, Vlackfontein, referred to in the last book. It literally means "Spring on the Plain." After a couple of miles and a goodly number of birds, I noticed a figure in the path ahead. Sure enough, it was Rota, the assistant gun bearer under Amos, my num-

A previous residence of the author's.

ber one when I had hunted there. We
went through the formal as well as the
emotional greetings, and he told me that
Amos himself had gotten word that I was
coming and was walking some phenomenal distance to see me.

Rota was always rather an odd kid by
my lights, but he was an extremely tal-
ented sculptor. You could stop for an
hour or so at a particular pan that had a
type of clay he liked and he would always make the client an elephant that was
an awfully long way from being a "primitive." Unfortunately, he knew even less
than I did about glazing clay figurines, so
I doubt any still exist.

Rota was anxious to join us, so he
piled on the back with the other two

senior men, Alfred and Champion. Both were fine-looking chaps, tall and distinguished. I would guess they were Matabeles, a northern offshoot of the Zulus. Rota was a black/bushman mixture called Masarwa in Botswana. His old boss, Amos, was a Karanga (or, as Amos and his people always pronounced it, "Kalanga").

We covered the remaining three or so miles to Vlackfontein, with wonderful bird shooting the whole way. This was rather strange, since it was now mid-morning; one would not expect to see many game birds at that time of day. Usually, these creatures are early morning and late afternoon feeders who spend the rest of their time hiding in thickets from smaller cats and baboons.

There is, however, a story behind this game bird explosion. I once did a two-part article for the National Rifle Association's publication, *The American Hunter,* in which I described in detail the reduction of baboons on the Matetsi Unit #4 through a personal war with a large troop of them that were resting in the Prince of Wales feather trees that grew in such verdant magnificence around the Vlackfontein house. The stench and carryings-on were unbelievable, and I was determined to sort things out after a big male had killed a child and mauled a woman rather badly. This was during the bush war, and I had acquired a 9mm MAC-10 minima-

chine pistol along with nineteen clips and quite a bit of ammo as insurance. At last, I decided to "rev" this bunch and move them out of the area. It was never represented as a sporting situation, as I hate killing baboons; they're too bloody human. Whatever the case, it was the only article I ever wrote that brought cries of disbelief.

Before giving you a précis of the article, as many of you will have read it, let me point out that baboons have gone mad in the past years in various parts of Africa, Kenya in particular, due to chronic drought. They have been tremendously hard on the migratory herds of calving wildebeest in the Serengeti and elsewhere; they have more than decimated the game bird population of Botswana; and they have even taken to eating goats and smaller stock in East Africa, as well as the occasional child.

As I mentioned, this large bunch at Vlackfontein was roosting in the huge grove of Prince of Wales feather trees. Naughty fellow that I was, I contrived to have a shallow trench dug around the grove of trees, with only one escape route . . . right past the point where my submachine gun and backup spearmen would be stationed. (One contrived such an excavation, at least in those days, simply by saying, "Do it.")

We waited until after dark, by which time the *mabobojoan* were pretty well settled in. I then sent a couple of men laden with cans of mixed crankcase oil and gasoline to thoroughly slosh the hard ground in the trench. At my signal, they took torches from three positions and ignited the works.

Well, results were *not* the problem. I had a flare fired so we could see beyond the fire, it being essentially a matter of slaughtering a man-killing colony. All the details of the ensuing battle, which entailed one hell of a lot of machine pistol fire, some spearing with assegais, and a large part of my ammo, are recorded in the article mentioned above. In any case, the result was one hell of a lot of dead baboons, as well as a tremendous increase in the game bird population over the next few years.

I really don't know if that's playing God or the opposite, depending on whether one happens to be a baboon or a francolin chick. I never let myself think on the matter too deeply. But when I returned with Eric Wagner to the outskirts of Vlackfontein, I carefully checked the same grove of trees. Still no sign of a baboon, and this about eleven years later! Compared with Botswana, where baboons are protected and the bird population is not, the difference was obvious. Needless to say, the wing shooting was phenomenal at Matetsi, and I am personally certain that the moving of that huge troop at Vlackfontein had everything to do with it.

It's funny how the different kinds of African stimuli hit one, even after years. For me, smells seem to be special. Whether it be the magnificence of fresh bread baking in a hole or the waft of fresh elephant or buffalo dung, the odors bring back memories—and warnings—all of which are part of being a professional hunter, and upon which your life may often depend. A pleasant aspect of this phenomenon occurred on our entrance into what used to be the Vlackfontein complex. Gone was the gagging wave of baboon excreta, but the reddish dirt still smelled the same. You could have put me in a bank vault in New York City and I would have identified it. Perhaps Africa *is* eternal after all.

Textures also greatly affect me, as do colors and tastes. One *vlei* is never quite the same as the next, whether hundreds of yards or thousands of miles apart. No two rivers are even remotely the same; no, not even portions thereof. Yet they fit, and as they have done so in my own experience, I have grown to recognize the vastness and—much more importantly—the complexity and frangibility of the entire ecosystem. Africa is huge, violent, benevolent, savage, stupid, and, perhaps unknowingly, wise. It is mere chest-thumping to try to figure her out. But there she is, and she am what she am.

I'm one of those rare foreigners who happens to like such African foods as fried *mopane* worms; I'd kill for a good biltong in its "wet" stage and could eat —and have eaten—not one helluva lot more than the corn mush called *mealie-meal* for months, through my own preference. Although born elsewhere, I suppose that—when it comes down to it— I *am* an African.

There *is* no Africa per se. There are hundreds of thousands of them.

I had a curious sinking feeling as we came into sight of my old home. I knew it would have been damaged during the fighting in the area, but I really wasn't expecting the complete devastation our party encountered. I suppose you can look at the before-and-after pictures and make your own judgments. The roof was gone; the story, true or not, was that it had taken a couple of direct hits from insurgent 60mm mortar shells. From my own inspection of the house, I could see that it had been heavily scarred with automatic fire.

Okay, I guess war's war, but I hope nobody was home. I'm especially glad I wasn't.

In any case, it was a weird feeling that perhaps only survivors or refugees of re-

cent wars would appreciate. Vlackfontein *had* been my home, replete with lions on the lawn, buff in the *vlei* next door, leopards up the garden trees; a whole fantastic menagerie that made living in such a remote area even under wartime conditions worth it. Yeah . . . to a point. (Kindly be advised, any who are officially or unofficially interested, that I was not involved in the war. I was a professional hunter. Period.)

The lot of us took our time rooting through the ruins of Vlackfontein.

Eerie.

The ruins of Vlackfontein, the author's old home, after the bush war. Note the pockmarks from automatic AK-47 fire.

About all that was left was the bastion of a fireplace I had had built in the corner of the living room, which I guess hadn't been worth anybody's explosives to destroy. It had been one hell of a fireplace. . . .

But it was late afternoon, and we were quite far from Mongu. Knowing how cold the *vleis* got that time of year, we elected to head for home. Eric horrified me by putting on a rock tape as loud as it would go, but I shortly made it clear that we couldn't enjoy conversation and the magic of twilight in the bush with acid rock blasting away at the same time.

The temperature was noticeably warmer as we climbed Mongu hill. The first person I saw, even before considering my initial cold beer and, perhaps, a wee touch of wine, was a crimson-jacketed Amos, waiting for me with a broad grin. We spoke of his children, cattle, wives, and fortunes, all of which appeared to be in pretty good shape. I gave him some money for old time's sake, which pleased him no end, and we chatted for some time about the old crew: Gladstone, and Jazz-Eye, the one-eyed Masarwa whose real name was Julius and who, despite being in charge of such matters, always managed to forget the water, the lunch box, the ammo box, the beer, or anything else physically possible to forget. (It was actually Gladstone, one of my favorites, who, when mending the chimney on a hot water "donkey boiler," breaking down and dropping bricks as he tore them loose, could think of no more appropriate warning to those below than that of the railway crossing at Matetsi siding: "Beware of train!" And believe me, those below *did* beware of train!)

Though by no means my best gun bearer, Amos was truly loyal, brave, and reliable. An incident in particular cemented the relationship between the two of us.

Knowing his skill at tracking, I used to lend Amos my Collins machete, telling him to hie off and find some bloody leopard spoor or sign. After three of these trips had ended in the eternal African shrug, I became suspicious and decided to remedy things. Obviously, Amos wasn't doing what I'd told him to do, as I had twice found leopard tracks myself in the same area I was sending him. Thus, one afternoon I sent him out again, only this time I tracked him to where he was lying asleep at the base of a tree.

Now, you may agree or disagree with what I did next, but my life depended on this man virtually on a continuous basis. So, I stuck what must have been the relatively cold muzzle of my .375 H&H in his ear and advised him that he mend his ways. He agreed most heartily and, in the guileless way of rural Africans, expressed admiration at my tracking, since he had taken some care to cover his spoor. Apparently, it raised the value of my stock not inconsiderably, as there were later comments about my being the man who could always find Amos.

There was a fascinating incident that involved a pair of BSAP (British South Africa Police) leather leggings. Now, the BSAP were neither British nor South African but when Rhodesia chose to declare independence, the members voted to retain the ancient and honorable name.

And, so it was.

What I could not figure our was why, on one given day, one of my men would be wearing the leggings, which protected the shins from thorns and bush, and somebody else would have them on the next.

It turned out that the leggings were either stolen or won from a policeman. Whatever, they would daily change possession from one of my men to another —unless one got lucky two nights in a row—and he would have the privilege of wearing them for that day or until he lost them at gambling.

Owing to failing light, we did not go past Vlackfontein after the next day's wing shooting and general exploration, but instead headed straight back to Mongu, where we enjoyed something more substantial in the line of liquid refreshment before the dinner gong sounded. It had been a grand day, capped by some of the finest wing shooting I had ever seen (and that includes one hell of a lot of territory, from northern Scotland to Patagonia).

The following day, I was determined to find the site of my old camp on the Dumba (mentioned in *Safari: The Last Adventure*). After more than ten years, I wondered what the place looked like. I hoped it bore no comparison to Vlackfontein.

It didn't.

It was as cool, gurgling, and graceful as ever, a poet's dream of paradise. The fig tree was still there, bigger than ever, and the mark of man was not upon the land. All signs of my previous tenancy had vanished. But the same green pigeons of which I have spoken elsewhere were still there, and though the banded cobra I had killed at the tiny pool upstream had left no apparent progeny, I nevertheless watched my step.

There was nothing left to see, except for the giant fig tree. Everything else had been burned years ago or taken for the thatch, wire, and seasoned poles. Well, at least nobody could have made snares out of the wire; it was too short and twisted. I saw to that. . . .

(In those days, during the bush war, I carried a Ruger .38/.375/9mm revolver for self-defense, just to keep international relations reasonable. It was with that revolver that I shot the cobra.)

We had shot a few guinea fowl on the way down to the Dumba, and one of these was duly roasted on a sharpened stick under the great fig tree, which

The floor of the shower built by the author in 1975, finally rediscovered by Rota . . . archaeology strikes again! Reads: "PHC JULY 1975".

formed the canopy that protected the campsite. I was astonished at how tender and thoroughly cooked it was, as guineas are traditionally rather of an anvil-like consistency, but this one was not only tender as butter—through what black magic I don't know—but it proved the centerpiece of one of the best lunches I have ever had, including chilled white wine preceded by beer and the entire *schmaltz*. Alfred and Champion should be awarded the gold medal of the Paris Cordon Bleu school.

After lunch, I started showing Fiona and Eric where things had stood. Not a mark remained. But then, suddenly, I thought of something that might in fact still be there.

I had gone to immense trouble, back in 1975, to build a really nice shower for my clients, which included a thirty mile trip to the nearest stand of giant bamboo. Apart from being beautiful in its own right, the bamboo stand was near an abandoned and totally ruined farmhouse near the Bembe River, which was said to have a mated pair of especially aggressive black mambas in residence. With some trepidation, I led the way with the shotgun as my men cut behind me. We collected enough staves to make a lovely shower floor that would permit the water to flow through into the catchment area

Linyanti River reeds.

and carry on down into the river. When I finally stepped back to examine my creation, the thing was truly a delight. But in order to be completely finished, it needed a concrete or cement slab for clients to stand on while drying off. This I duly laid, and through some whim, I inscribed my initials and the date by means of a stick in the wet cement. (Getting cement during the bush war years was like collecting gold dust, but I had managed to get enough.)

Right. I had been heavily into anthropology and paleontology at the University of Virginia at what seemed a couple of centuries ago, and I couldn't resist the challenge of trying to find the shower slab. After half an hour, Rota (who had been there when I built it and who had helped pour the slab) came up with something hard under the layer of leaves and eleven years of accumulated detritus. *Aha!* Fiona was as delighted as I was at the rather short-term "dig," and Eric even took an extended video of it. (You'll see pictures in this book.) To come across a piece of your own past like that was like finding your personal skeleton; at least, that is how I felt. Dumba Camp has always held a special spot in my soul.

The Dumba, a small stream with a relatively large pool in proportion to its width, looked much the same. Paul, a fanatical fisherman, had spotted some spinning rods at Eric's and insisted on dragging them along.

"Hayikona, Nkosi," said Champion and Rota almost in unison, as Alfred nodded in agreement. No fish in the Dumba. Paul took a small cut of raw guinea fowl meat, baited up, and, before their words had died on the breeze, had a magnificent carplike fish flapping on the bank, followed by many others. There were also barbel and an assortment of stuff I couldn't identify (I had spent all my time in that area hunting with clients and never had the chance to get to know the fishlife as I should like to have). My best guess was that it was one of the *Cyprinidae* that, logically, should be there.

With a bellyful of white wine, guinea fowl fresh off the fire, and ensconced under my favorite tree on earth, I decided not to waste the moment snoozing. Even Eric grabbed a rod. To the astonishment of Champion, Alfred, and Rota, we caught fish as fast as we could bait a hook. Okay, it wasn't the Miramichi, or Malangsfossen Pool, or Iceland's Hitara, or even the Owenmoore or Ballynahinch in Connemara, but we took a *lot* of fish, which was a welcome change in diet for the blacks. Even Eric got so excited he practically wet himself as we caught the first fish just as the black staff were saying that there were no fish there.

Hell, I knew there were fish there as I had secretly lived there! There was also a croc about four feet long but, after ten years, I had no idea as to his size now. I didn't see him this trip and, in an odd way, I missed him.

Eventually, darkness started to fall and we regretfully decided we had better push off back to Mongu.

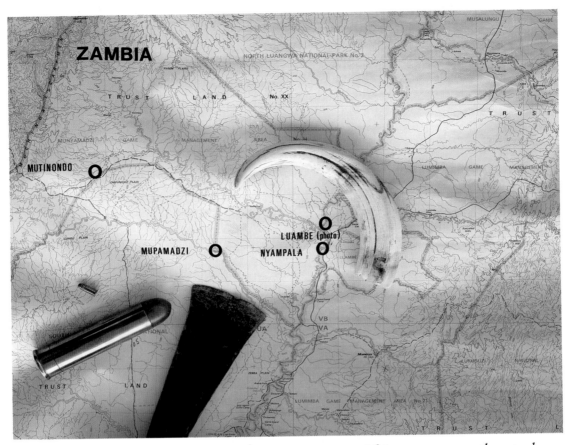

Luangwa Valley area of Zambia, showing Hunters Africa camps, warthog tusk, antique 4-bore and .22 short cartridges, and the head of an Awiza ax.

PART TWO

Mupamadzi

I was hardly back in South Africa before hearing of the terrible mauling suffered by Soren (pronounced *Sern*) Lindstrom in Botswana as a result of a severe misunderstanding with a lion.

Fiona and I took the first opportunity to drive over to the Johannesburg General Hospital, where Soren was being treated for the complete loss of his right bicep as well as for other injuries. Although he was still in obvious pain, we were fortunate enough to be able to talk to him. Fiona sweet-talked the nurses into allowing her to take a few photographs, while I managed to record the story. It turned out to be one helluva tale.

I asked Soren when he was attacked, but he couldn't

come up with anything better than the seventh or ninth of July, 1985. He had been on the Selinda Spillway, which connects the Okavango with some of its major feeders, and had as clients a woman, her son, a friend of the son, and one of the woman's younger daughters. They had been out for nearly a month when the incident that almost killed him occurred. To quote him directly from his hospital bed:

"We weren't even looking for lion. We were going up the Selinda to find a kudu and came across this very big, good-looking male lion. So, we drove over to have a look at it, as it was in some fairly high grass, and it just came for the car. It was actually trotting off when we first saw it. Then it lay down. We couldn't see where it had actually lain down, but the next thing that happened was that it simply came for the car.

"It didn't appear wounded or crippled from the way it moved, but it did give me the idea that it may have been because of the determination of the charge.

"Um, well, I wanted to get a close look at it from the first, as I wasn't sure, but it settled matters with its charge. One of the young chaps in back was convinced that it was going to get in the rear of the hunting car and he fired a shot at it with a three-seventy-five H and H.

"The lion ran off into the long grass across an open valley and quite a dense thicket on the other side. We followed it with the car, and the lion nearly got into the back again."

I was starting to worry that I was taxing Soren too much by asking for the details of the incident. He looked like last week's reheated pot roast, groggy and in obvious pain. Suggesting that we take a break, I asked him to relax and collect his thoughts before we got together again, barring the nurses, in about ten minutes' time, and then wandered off somewhere safe to have a smoke. Tough and strong as he was, I didn't want to be the cause of any kind of relapse. When I tell you this guy was hurting, it's only a suggestion of the agony he must have been in.

I came back after the agreed upon time and had to pass the head matron of the ward (or senior ward nurse), I got a look that would have turned a vulture into biltong at three hundred yards. Smiling with my usual charm, I edged past her with the implied threat of a karate chop. Soren seemed to have recovered a bit, however; perhaps they had given him a wee something.

"So, what did you reckon on being the best tactic next?" I asked him.

"Well, I figured I had better get rid of the clients before somebody got hurt. So I went and found a suitable anthill with trees they could climb up a long, long way from where we had last seen the wounded lion, and then I came back with the two trackers to have a look around.

"We cruised around with the vehicle, the grass and stone-hard ground making tracking impossible. We saw nothing of the lion, so we went back to the place where we had last seen him. We left the car, and I took off with the two trackers; I left the son (who had insisted on going with me) sitting in the vehicle.

"We found a bit of blood and some faint tracks, and I satisfied myself as to where it had gone—or at least in which direction. We started heading back for the Toyota—we'd only gotten fifteen, maybe twenty yards—and there was a growl and a snarl and the thing leaped out of the cover.

"He charged us from behind a fallen *mopane* that still had a lot of grass around it. The charge certainly wasn't more than five or six yards. I had turned my back, and he wasn't a yard away before I could get off one barrel of my double Ferlach four-fifty-eight Magnum." (Being left-handed, Soren found it an easier action to use than a bolt, usually made for righties. As it turned out, considering the damage he was about to sustain on his starboard side, he's fortunate to be a southpaw.) "Anyway, it was on me and grabbed me by the right upper arm and just shook me like a rag doll.

"He shook me until my thoughts were that the lion had broken my arm, but I later found out it was, technically, a com-pound dislocation. I didn't even think I *had* an arm at that stage. My last memories were of it coming up my body to grab me by the head or throat, and my ultimate thoughts were of it grabbing me on the left arm."

I examined the wounds on Soren's left arm. Savage and deep though they were, they had seemed to have healed nicely thus far.

"At that point, one of my trackers took fright—I guess I had started to yell and scream a bit. The lion got up and went for him. So, I got up and walked to the car, holding on to what I thought was a stump of an arm. I was convinced it was gone. Then I felt something thumping me in the back, which turned out to *be* my arm, still dangling despite the bites and tearing of my meat.

"Somehow, I was still conscious and managed to get into the Toyota, but I'll never ever forget walking past the lion, which was just standing there, growling; standing there with the tracker. I was able to get the young client to drive straight at the lion to scare him off the tracker. The other tracker wasn't much use as he was up a tree, a position he had achieved very quickly some time ago.

"Anyway, one guy came down out of the tree and into the back of the car as the lion ran off for a little while and we put the other tracker, who had been mauled, into the back of the car. The tracker had been bitten but rather lightly in comparison to me; he had bites in both arms and on his thigh. He was released from the hospital within two weeks and is just fine.

"Well, my whole bicep was torn off and all the cartilage around the elbow as well. And then, a lot of infection in both arms. Fortunately, I retained consciousness the whole time and directed the young client to drive back to where I had left the others up the trees. Then we drove around until we found a place where a plane could land. The arteries were severed in both arms and I was losing a lot of blood. I realized that I could never survive the drive back for help.

"Like most professionals, I had quite a comprehensive medical kit in the back of the rig and I put on a couple of tourniquets to slow the bleeding. I then put up the radio antenna and got through to Safari South."

Soren works for Safari South on a more or less equal basis with Hunters Africa, the two companies being friendly competitors in the same area and often making deals with freelance hunters. Although he was attached to Safari South at the time of his mauling, any safari company in the area would have responded in a similar situation. It's rather a close club in Botswana, despite personal rivalries.

"As I advised this young chap, once we had found a place where an aircraft could land, we got in touch, and Tim Liver-

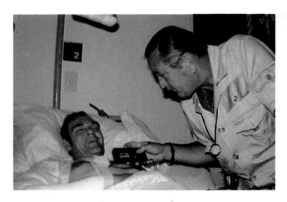

The author and Soren Lindstrom.

sedge [whose family you will hear more of in this story] flew in and talked another plane with a doctor on board in.

"Anyway, the doctor gave me quite a lot of sedation and they flew me down to Maun, where they took me to Maun Hospital, put me on a drip, gave me a transfusion, and—ten hours after the whole thing happened—I found myself in the Johannesburg General Hospital. The backup and support were absolutely fantastic."

I asked Soren what had happened to the lion, the major factor in the entire drama.

"The next day, Harry Selby, Duggie Wright, and several other professionals went down to this area, but hyenas had fairly well obliterated the spoor. They were able to pick up my rifle, which I had obviously dropped, as well as the rifle of one of the clients. Unfortunately, on top of the hyena spoor, a gang of elephant had been through, completely eradicating any sign of the lion.

"Well, they looked around for two days for that lion and there was no sign of it at all. To this day, I have no idea if the lion was wounded by a hunter or a poacher; certainly, we collect enough with bullets of one type or another in their bodies."

I thought back on the lion I had shot at Saile, not so far away, which also contained a considerable amount of buckshot.

"Actually," continued Soren, "they have an amazing ability to get over even major wounds. If he had one at all, it was superficial."

As it turned out, Soren was to remain in the Johannesburg General Hospital for over two months, and underwent major surgery there involving the grafting of part of his leg muscles to his arm where the lion had torn off the bicep.

"Point is," said Soren, obviously still in pain, before we left, "I'll only get fifteen to twenty percent movement out of the arm. I'll keep hunting, though. All they have to do is wedge the fingers into a vee so I can support the rifle.

"Reminds me," he said of my being there, "of having been on safari with Harry Selby; we were in a place filled with sticks and stumps and long grass, and I saw a really terrific kudu there. So, I

called Harry on the SSB radio and took him back the next day to show him where the place was.

"I spoke with him about lunchtime and said, 'Hey, how're you doing?' 'Fine,' he replied, 'but I know now what Capstick meant when he wrote *Death in the Long Grass.*' "

Perhaps you believe that half the fun is getting there. I would take exception to such an observation. This is not meant as a reflection on South African Airways, which delivered us with their usual efficiency to Lusaka, the capital of Zambia, from Johannesburg on July 24, 1985. But we spent the rest of the afternoon in that lousy airport because the visas for Paul and Fiona were not properly endorsed. Of course, as might well be expected, the only person who could endorse them was at a funeral—one of the greatest excuses

The author and wife, Fiona.

for an African beer bust. Cecil Evans of Hunters Africa, bless his soul forever, finally got in touch with the senior official involved, who made his appropriate scrawl, accompanied by enough stamps to keep a philatelist busy for a year. (African airport officials absolutely love the concept of stamping something, usually in red ink, presumably to reinforce their authority.) In any case, it was five hours before the deed was consummated.

Cecil then got us out of the half-lit airport terminal and whisked us off to the Pamodzi Hotel, the local Ritz. Although we checked in with no problems, plenty were to follow. . . .

I've learned from personal experience that most so-called "emerging" countries are absolutely paranoid about their currency: it must not leave the country. Consequently, one must fill in a complete declaration of all moneys carried or they will be confiscated on leaving. And this quite apart from the host of other forms one has to plow through!

Right. I note that because my wife and photographer were from South Africa, their visas cost 100 *kwachas* each whereas mine was free. Interesting, but clearly not racio-political.

Oh, no.

I had brought about 500 South African rands with me as well as a couple of hundred U.S. dollars, which I always carry when traveling. Armed with a number of credit cards, I wasn't expecting problems.

The Pamodzi Hotel, Gem of Lusaka, takes only the American Express card and Diners Club, which I did not carry at the time. That meant cash and I just managed to cover the hotel bill for the three of us with 20 *ngwee* left. It's a charming feeling to be broke and mighty far from home.

Finally squared away, we at last sat back and enjoyed cocktails. The firearms and cameras were in the hotel safe and we were at last able to unwind. In the meantime, the white bush telegraph was at work, and I was to learn just how efficiently when old friends soon began pouring in.

The first to arrive was Jolyon Irwin, whom I had had out on safari in Botswana when he was a child. Jolyon eventually held a professional hunter's license. He and Chris Beardmore introduced a safari client from California who was on his way to the bush the next day. We cracked a few beers together, and I noted that, in Zambia, there are no brands of beer as such. Beer is beer, often served in unlabeled bottles. We found the place very expensive but the service excellent, the rooms fine, and the food extremely good.

No sooner had we said good-bye to Jolyon, Chris, and the client than a great pal and hunting companion from the old Luangwa days, Joe Joubert, arrived. I was delighted to see Joe after so many years, and couldn't help being astonished at how little he seemed to have aged. The same thick head of hair with not a sign of gray, the same jovial face and slim physique. All those years in the bush had not seemed to have affected him.

Joubert at last sat down smack in front of me, and I got my tape recorder primed and ready to get a story I have been after ever since I first met him. A few Pamodzi beers later and soft-spoken Joe was ready to roll with the extraordinary tale of how he landed up with two wounded lions and a wounded leopard all at the same time, never mind the same day! Joe reactivated his memory banks as we laughed and reminisced about the old days and about old friends, many of them now dead, married, or worse, here's his story:

"I remember giving the two clients nicknames. One I called Hemingway because of his beard, and the other I called Selassie because he was dark and slight in build. They were from the States and were out on a twenty-one-day safari on a two-on-one basis. We all got on very well through the first week and we bagged a lion and a leopard.

"Peter, do you remember Chief Chitangulu?" Joe asked me.

I answered in the affirmative; the chief had controlled the area named after him where Peter Hankin had had his camp.

"Well, the chief came to me during the Hemingway/Selassie safari and asked me to please do something about the lions which were running around his area. I agreed. The lions were apparently coming into the village at night and were wandering freely, chasing people on bicycles, and generally scaring the bloody hell out of everybody. I only had one lion permit left but I told the chief we'd kill a buffalo, hang the whole bloody thing, and leave it near a water hole where these lions were active.

"We went to the water hole every morning, and it was after the third or fourth morning that things began to happen. I drove up to within a couple of hundred yards and could hear that the lions were there.

"I decided to walk into the blind we had built. It had a little shooting hole, and there, in the golden early sunlight, I saw four male lions! Two were feeding, one was lying about ten yards in front of the blind, and the other was a little way off, lazing in the tawny grass.

"So, I figured on taking the lion closest to the blind, as he was a good one. Hemingway was up on the toss of the coin and Selassie already had his. After some time spent in pointing out the lion to Hemingway—the shadows of early dawn were still heavy—he shot from about thirty feet. It gave a hell of a roar, jumped ten feet into the air, and took off. . . ."

Sound familiar?

"We obviously had to follow the blood trail. I didn't like the look of it. Guts. The thing had crossed the road right where the Land Rover was standing and, after a couple of hundred yards, entered a very thick patch of grass.

"I said to the clients, 'Look, we're not going to go through that stuff because somebody's going to get hurt. We'll take the Land Rover and skirt it and come in on the other side.' They understood. You see, one of the major reasons for this was that I had seen his silhouette in the grass.

"Understandably, we thought it was the wounded one, so I had both clients shoot at him. As soon as they shot, this lion jumped up and we all realized that it wasn't the wounded one at all. It was a new lion. Actually, all three of us shot at the lion, but it didn't go down."

Joe, as was his habit—and this may get him chopped one day—was shooting a 7 × 57mm cartridge, which many authorities feel to be too light for even nondangerous game. Well, Joe is an expert, too, and has a hell of a lot more field experience than most who write magazine articles and books. In any case, it's his tail, not mine.

"Okay," continued Joe, "we knew the first lion was still in the grass, but we decided to follow the second. We followed the blood spoor for a couple of

hundred yards when, all of a sudden, my tracker tapped me on the shoulder and said, 'Bwana, look up in the tree.'

"Hell, there, with all the artillery, was this leopard, a big male, fast asleep! The other guy, who hadn't yet shot a leopard, took a whack at him, and he boiled out of the tree, making that wounded noise they always make."

If you hear it once, you won't forget it, I promise you.

"So, what do we do now?" asked Joe. "I thought things over—very carefully —considering we now had two wounded lions *and* a wounded leopard in high grass. I decided to go in on my own with one man. I picked a tracker and stuck him behind me, since I had seen the movement of the grass and knew more or less where the leopard was lying in wait. I figured I could nail him without too much trouble.

"As it turned out, he was lying behind a log in the really thick stuff. We were throwing sticks and clods of dirt as we followed the spoor, but he never gave the slightest sign of being there until I was literally two yards away from him.

"He came for me like a shot—and believe me, a leopard can cover six feet like a flash. I had no time to fire, so I stuck the barrel of the rifle down his throat, pulled the trigger, and managed to hold him off as he was dying. I don't want to do it again. You simply cannot believe the speed of these predatory animals from very close range."

Joe didn't have to tell me that one twice.

"We hauled the leopard out and then, after a council of war, decided we would follow the trail of this second lion, as our problems were only one-third over and lions are a hell of a lot bigger than leopards. Besides, there were two of them.

"We'd only gone about fifty yards when this lion came for us from behind a bush and everybody ran away; the gun bearers, the trackers, all the local staff, and the clients as well.

"I was standing perfectly still to receive the charge with the 7 × 57mm when I immediately realized that the lion had not noticed me but had gone for the rest of the party. I also clearly saw that the bloody thing would run right past me, which it did. So I made a deposit of a bullet in its brain.

"At this point, having had to stick my rifle barrel down the throat of a leopard and shoot a lion a couple of feet away, I knew I was now overdoing it. So I called for the Land Rover. You don't push your luck with lions and leopards or sure as can be you'll get caught. That hurts. I therefore figured that the best way to approach the third wounded cat was by vehicle. Three times lucky, as we say.

"I sent the driver and the armed tracker a very long way around, and when they arrived, we loaded the lion and the leopard. We then returned to the point where we had left the first wounded lion.

"At this point, I decided I wasn't going to drive but that I would stand up in the back. One client would be topside and the other inside the cab, which had those half-doors with which one can equip a Land Rover. I carefully explained to the driver that, okay, as he went in, he was to keep on the left edge of the grass and work his way into the center so that I always had the grass on my side. But it didn't work that way. This lion came from the *client's* side.

"It happened so fast that I couldn't shoot because he was in the way; he got such a fright *he* couldn't shoot, and, the next moment, the lion jumped clean into the front of the Land Rover! The only part of the bloody thing sticking out were its hips, and you can imagine the noise going on in there with the lion, the client, and the driver! My only thought was that for sure I had somebody dead in front.

"At this point, all I could do was lean over and shoot the lion through the hips; the only part visible. The lion sort of slipped back on getting the bullet—a hundred-seventy-five-grain pill—, and on doing so, he saw me and reared up, slashing at me with his forepaw. Well, it just missed my face but shattered the rear window of the Land Rover."

Now, I should mention that I have personally tried to break a Land Rover window with a rock when I had locked myself out—without success. More proof of the power of that swipe by the lion.

Joe shot the lion through the head as he finished his swipe. His results were better than those I got on the lion hunt at Saile with Cundill. His dropped. Dead. Still, Joe was terrified to inspect the cab of the vehicle, as he was certain it contained dead people.

"I will absolutely never forget how one of the clients was sitting on the driver's lap," Joe told me. "He had a three hundred Weatherby Magnum rifle, which he had stuck sideways into the lion's mouth, certainly the only reason he was still alive. Somehow, the client was able to keep the lion off that way. Having just had the barrel of my own rifle down a leopard's throat for an emergency tonsillectomy, I knew how he felt.

"The rifle itself was a grand trophy; the teeth marks were an inch and a half deep, the scope all bent and twisted. Probably a better conversation piece than the lion skin!"

Joe doubted if the two clients ever went on safari again.

• • •

Not long after the lion episode, Joe traveled to the Central African Republic, formerly the Central African Empire under Emperor Bokassa I, and had some very interesting observations on *that* state of affairs. Amazing what you can gather from old pals around a cocktail table.

Not speaking a word of French—the lingua franca of the CAR—Joe had an obvious problem, one he solved in a most unlikely manner. I asked Kenyan-born Joe to tell the story of how he had overcome the communication problem and, at the same time, hired a gentleman of the cloth.

"Well, you know there's a little town up in the northeastern corner called Ejjale, where we had our base camp. I was in town one day and saw this priest, obviously a Roman Catholic, since the people are almost entirely Muslim up that way. One of the guys on the truck just happened to mention 'Eengleesh, Eengleesh.'

"I stopped the vehicle and started speaking to him. I ended up offering the priest a job as a tracker! He accepted, saying he needed the money. He threw away his Bible and his robes and has been my head tracker for the last five years now!"

Joe, Fiona, Paul, and I talked for hours, and we eventually got to know something about Joe's knowledge of the cannibal emperor of the Central African Empire, Bokassa I.

"I have actually been to his 'palace,' where he would sit and pass sentence over anybody who was accused of doing anything wrong. According to those who lived there at the time, and I know them well, he gave the guilty an option: lion cage or crocodile pit."

Joe had actually seen and been into the freezer where Bokassa the First—and, let's hope, the last—kept his human cadavers before throwing cannabalistic orgies. He confirmed that this was in Bangui, the capital city. Obviously demented, Bokassa returned in 1986 and was promptly jailed. He thought he would be met with open arms.

"I didn't personally see what came out of it—I was too late—but I can certainly describe the freezer and its contents. It was a built-in, walk-in freezer, rather like those you find in a butcher's shop or any other commercial freezer. The carcasses of human beings were just hanging there on meat hooks.

"In fact, if you ever come to the CAR, I can introduce you to someone whose body should have been hanging among the lot I saw. He was an English teacher at the local university. It was Bokassa's policy to have all 'clever' people or intellectuals killed and used for meat. This chap, however, saw the palace guards come up the walkway of his building, so he bailed out of a rear window and made it to the bush. He was one of the very few who survived.

"That was 1978, and if you figure in the cannibalism of Idi Amin Dada of Uganda, it's still unbelievable how many people are eaten by other people in Africa."

The next morning, we took one of Lusaka's ramshackle cabs into town to call on the Hunters Africa office, situated in Cairo Road. Super-efficient Ivy Mhinde attended to some business for us while we chatted to Pauline Finaughty whose husband is the great nephew of the famous elephant hunter, William Finaughty. (The first edition of his book, of which only two hundred and fifty were printed, is the pride of my Africana library. It certainly gave me a kick to meet one of his descendants and enjoy a chat.)

That night we were once again to discover that Africa is full of surprises.

As we would be checking out early the following morning to catch our charter flight up to the Luangwa Valley, Paul and I thought it best to remove the cameras and guns from the hotel safe so as to speed our departure in the morning. We duly did this with no trouble, and everything was stored in the bedroom Fiona and I had.

At about ten o'clock that night, Fiona

was busy doing whatever women do at such hours—probably smearing her face with some incredibly expensive gunge—which did not require my presence. So, I pushed off to Paul's room, around the corner, for a nightcap.

Half an hour later, the telephone rang, scaring us both nearly to death. It was Fiona.

"You'd better get back here immediately. The hotel security staff are looking for you!"

"What the hell's going on?" asked I in not a slight state of panic.

"There's trouble with your firearms. Get back here!"

"Why?"

"Because you removed your guns from the safe and put them in our room. The security men have demanded that I hand them back to them. I have refused and won't budge. Get back here!"

Oh, brother.

The front desk had reckoned we were checking out immediately, but such was not the case. Apparently, somebody had reported to them that firearms were being taken into one of the bedrooms, and this is taboo at the Pamodzi. A crowd of security men then banged on the bedroom door, demanding that Fiona open up. She did, in good time, and, on being told that she was to hand back the weapons immediately, she made it exceedingly plain to the security people that she would do no such thing.

"These are my husband's possessions, duly licensed and here for our early departure tomorrow. Your front desk had no complaints about releasing them to us, so what are you doing here, thumping on the door like the bloody gestapo? We are guests in your country, not criminals. Now get me your night manager!"

They did. And a more charming, quiet-mannered, and efficient gentleman you would be hard-pressed to meet anywhere. I am merely sorry I never recorded his name so I could thank him here for sorting out what could have developed into a vicious confrontation—Fiona's Irish heritage would have seen to it that they would *never* have gained possession of those guns.

The night manager explained most apologetically that the problem was one of chronic theft from hotel bedrooms, and that firearms and expensive camera equipment were prime targets. So I was escorted upstairs with four of the original gorillas (all of whom towered over me, and I'm a six-footer) to retrieve the guns and cameras and redeposit them in the hotel safe, together with the ammo.

I didn't tip the men for helping tote the equipment. Now don't get the idea that Zambia is negative toward foreigners. It most certainly is *not,* and, further, it realizes the huge importance of foreign exchange to its ailing economy. But the authorities *are* paranoid about anyone attempting to take any of their currency out of the country, so make doubly sure you have all the correct forms concerning any currency deals, duly stamped since there is also a crackdown on what I have been told is a flourishing black market in foreign currency. And be prepared to be pocket-searched, as we were upon our departure. Even though I used to be a Wall Street stockbroker, I cannot for the life of me figure out what the various customs officials had in mind to so thoroughly search an American carrying guns and so obviously on safari. What in hell would any foreigner want to usurp their currency for? To have a razzle on Fifth Avenue? Well, guys, it's your joint so do it any way you want.

I did notice in my short time in Lusaka that there was no diesel fuel at all and that there were lines for gasoline, or "petrol," as it is locally called at some service stations that stretched forever. Rumor had it that the country had run dry and that it was experiencing problems in paying for its fuel needs. (Thank heavens we had aviation fuel to charter out when we did! But we very nearly didn't at the end of our safari. But first things first.)

I am no political analyst. I can just say that Zambia strikes me as a single-issue socialist state that exhibits the shortages and problems I have come to associate with such political arrangements. For starters, if you are not a citizen, you may only pay for hotel accommodation in foreign currency, as I was to discover the next bleary dawn when we were checking out. I tried to pay in kwacha, the local shekel, and was asked in stiff terms where I had gotten it. Happily, I had already paid most of the tab in South African rands and American dollars, so we weren't talking about a great deal of money and the police were not called, although they might have been. The incident sure got our attention, though.

I was eventually able to convince the powers that at least were that I had borrowed the money from Hunters Africa, since the hotel had taken bloody nearly every cent I had and would not accept any of the credit cards I held, numerous though they were. This was true and, happily, the hotel believed me. But kwachas from a foreigner were still out, so Cecil Evans, because he was a citizen of the country, had to pay the remainder of our bill.

I was highly pleased to be the hell out of Lusaka, taking my currency problems with me. I don't wish to sound negative, but one must know the rules before playing the game, so check what credit cards are kosher and watch your arse when it

Lew Games.

comes to any currency deals and firearms arrangements.

We took off—guns and cameras collected—under the rather hairy wing of genial Cecil Evans, who deposited us at the Lusaka Airport, where we struggled on to the charter aircraft, pushing the one rickety baggage cart available. Our pilot a delightful young Hindu by the name of Suresh Verma, was on hand to greet us, and flew us beautifully over wild, magnificent country that seemed as familiar as my equally lost brother. *"Home!"* it screamed at me from the barren koppies and dull green-and-gold *vleis*. "Home, Peter. You've made it back. You've actually done it!"

Well, it took two and a half hours to do it, but we arrived eventually at Waka-Waka airstrip, near the Luangwa River.

(I spell it that way because nobody has yet had any better idea, and it is at least very close to the way it is pronounced.)

Lew Games was waiting for us at Waka-Waka. With him were Mabhena, his driver and general foreman; Banda, his gun bearer; and Blackson, the other gun bearer. Also present was Fighting, who is not only a gun bearer and tracker but also a skinner of high repute.

Rural blacks are usually astonished to find a white person who speaks Fanagalo or any other black language, especially if they discover that the whites are not *maBunu,* or Afrikaners. That an American would be able to speak to them in Fanagalo really cracked the ice. (Nobody, of course, was quite sure what an "American" was. I have had bush blacks ask where they could get the train for America. But then, I think of fellow foreigners and their often breath-stopping ignorance of anything African, despite all the advantages of education, travel, and a media-saturated existence.) In any case, there were broad smiles all round, and we were soon on our way through the bush to the Luangwa River and an area of Africa that had been the site for a true turning point in my life. Lew Games and his wife, Dale, were our hosts for the next ten days, and I'd like at this point to at least partially describe a man who has become a good friend, and who shared the odd event or two with me.

Lew Sturdee Games is one of the finest professional hunters in the business. I know. I was there. Now in his early fifties, he is the general manager of the entire Zambian operation of Hunters Africa, and a more fascinating man you will never meet. Dale Games runs a safari camp and sets a table that can vie with the best. Supremely capable, the pair of them.

Lew's great-great grandfather was hanged by the Union Army for infringements unspecified. Lew's father fared none too well either, after he stole the horse of the commanding officer of the United States Second Cavalry. He seemed to like the way people spelled *Australia,* when most of that outfit was on his tail, and he set sail in the nick of time. To be perfectly accurate, he lit out through San Francisco for Hawaii and Tahiti, running cattle successfully in both places, before arriving in Australia. He must have been one tough dude to have produced Lew, who is himself no wilting lily.

The geographic fortunes of the Games family absolutely fascinate me. As a fourth generation American, I have done some moving around, but it is mere child's play in comparison to the Gameses'. For one reason or another, Lew's father and mother took passage to Durban, South Africa's great port, and then asked the station master for a ticket to "Grahamstown, Southern Rhodesia."

Dale Games on the SSB radio.

"Sorry, but we don't got one," answered the bored man.

"Watcha got?" asked Lew's father.

"How's about Salisbury, Southern Rhodesia?" asked the ticket master, not mentioning that Grahamstown was in South Africa and not Southern Rhodesia.

"Fine," said Lew's dad. "Do it."

They did.

He must have been a fine old mustang, Lew's dad. Born in 1887, he ran away from home at the age of thirteen and hit Laramie, Wyoming, on New Year's Day, 1900. To his dying day he said he'd never forget it: everybody was boozed to the earholes—Indians, cavalry, cowpunchers—as he put it, "all good stuff."

As I was shortly to find out, he'd passed along a hell of a lot of the "good stuff."

Lew is also fractionally American Indian, and you can see it in his dark eyes and high cheekbones. Hell, he might as well be a full-blooded Indian, as well as he tracks in the bush. Lew ran cattle for years where I used to hunt in the Matetsi region of northwestern Zimbabwe. He was also on game control, specializing in buffalo. As a cattle rancher, Lew frequently had to do battle with lions to protect his stock. One night, in fact, he killed ten lions. As he puts it—even if it is something of an anachronistic approach by today's standards: "When it comes to killing lions, which eat cattle, all means, fair or foul, are valid. . . ."

One has to look at Lew's side of things, too.

This particular incident took place in the southern African winter of '65–'66. Lew was not chest-thumping when he said, "Hell, there's nothing to shooting a bunch of lions in the open at night. I even shot them *among* the cattle with an old Parker-Hale, but ammo was deadly expensive, especially as this was a three-seventy-five Mag."

But back to business. The vehicle loaded and the locals aboard, we set out for Mupamadzi Camp, about an hour's drive by safari vehicle, waving good-bye as we left to the hordes of small children who had flocked to the aircraft at Waka-Waka. We were astonished by these children. What in hell they ate was beyond me, since there was no corn or maize—the staff of African life—anywhere nearby. And I just can't believe they got much protein from the poaching activities of their fathers. The die-off must be something like Ethiopia, but then, what does one do?

The problem, obviously, is a mushrooming birthrate. Nobody bothers to think about who will feed a child a few years after it is born, and if you doubt me, check the official figures: Kenya has the highest birthrate in the bloody world! Who's going to feed these people? Who will doctor them?

It was back in this same area, the Luangwa Valley, at a time when the tendency was to regard every white person as a medical doctor, the 1960s, that I made the mistake of trying to help the locals medically. I was a professional hunter, not a doctor, although I had a sound knowledge of first aid and knew how to deal with simpler injuries. I also carried a comprehensive medical kit. In the end, perhaps inevitably, I was forced to make the decision to let people die. It was not easy, and it still haunts me, and the scores of children brought all the memories crowding back.

The most common cases brought to my attention were those involving toddlers who had fallen into campfires and often been badly burned. I honestly cannot tell you how many of these little mites were brought to me for help when

I first arrived in the Luangwa Valley, but they must have numbered in the dozens. I was out of medicine in no time.

The problem was further complicated by internal diseases, which I was about as well qualified to treat as I am to command a flight of the space shuttle.

White man's *muti* is big *tagati,* and if one of your pals is ailing from heaven knows what and is helped by the medication given him by whites, then often the rest of the rural folk gathered are eager for a dose, too. I suppose that, socially, it's like sharing a bowl of traditionally brewed beer. That is the way things often *are* in the African bush, not the shiny, international agency concept of how they *should* be. In the end, the children *had* to be ignored, and this upset me for a very long time. I couldn't conduct safari clients around the bush *and* play Florence Nightingale. I couldn't be a one-man, self-financed clinic. The medicines gave out, and I had to give up. It's a hell of a thing to turn away a badly burned child and then look at yourself in the shaving mirror, knowing that the child would die, covered as it was by flies. I went back to being a professional hunter, with a few more calluses on my soul. You would have had them, too.

Such were my thoughts as we pulled away from Waka-Waka and followed the tracks to the banks of the Luangwa River.

For all that, though, I did do *some* good in the medical line. It was in Ethiopia, in Borana on the Dawa River, just across the border of the Northern Frontier District of Kenya, a couple of years before those early Zambian experiences. (I was with Chris Pollet, the circumstances of whose death are still a total mystery to me. If there is anybody out there who can tell me what happened to him, maybe they can write to me care of my publishers.) One day, a Galla or Gherri tribesman walked into camp with a hole in his right calf we could actually *see through.* He had, as was the local custom, stuffed the infected insect bite or thorn wound with camel dung. The wound, not surprisingly, had become a horrid, smelly mass of meat, and I wondered (and not for the first time) if this standard remedy had something to do with the absence of an overpopulation problem among the Galla and Gherri. I was young and tender, with all my illusions still intact. So I gave this gentleman, as I recall, a 100cc shot of penicillin in his butt. He loved it. Rural Africans often regard medicine as being more powerful the worse it tastes—or the more it hurts, in the case of injections.

It chanced, after a couple of ambushes and shoot-outs with *Shifta* bandits, that we ran into this same guy roughly a month later. I purely couldn't believe what I saw. The hole in his leg had completely healed over with new meat, and he was as fit as the Resurrection. I guess his mint condition was due to the fact he had almost definitely not had any kind of drug before, and thus his system had not built up any kind of resistance to penicillin. He was fine, and I felt heroic.

Well, this digression has dragged me a long way from Lew Games in Zambia, who was meanwhile dutifully putting the Toyota into gear and driving us off through the Luangwa Valley bush to my old haunts.

We stopped first at a camp under construction on the banks of the Luangwa. Called Luambe, after the Luambe National Park, it was a photographic safari camp and enjoyed a splendid location. I felt a huge surge of emotion on seeing that wide and muddy river again after some sixteen years. I have no idea how often my thoughts have returned to that part of Africa, how often I have escaped in spirit to the Luangwa.

I felt as if I had had a damn good bottle of Moët & Chandon all to myself as we drove onto the ferry and negotiated the croc-infested waters to the wide sandy bank on the other side. Once there, Lew drove us a very short distance to a fine camp at what actually was more or less the site of Nyampala, my old camp. On hand to meet us with drinks and a fine lunch was professional hunter Andre de Kock, who was in charge of the place. (It

was Andre, you may recall, who had gone to such trouble to find out the fate of Silent.) He was between safaris, and had some free time to entertain us with his genial company.

We settled back in the cool, immaculate surroundings of a first-rate hunting camp and began to relax after the Lusaka adventures, a long flight, and a dusty ride to that little piece of personal paradise. Once seated, I quickly recalled that it was at Nyampala the "Gin Nyampala"—a drink calling for large lacings of gin, orange squash, and Indian Tonic—was invented once upon a time by Ian Manning and yours truly during a lull in the hunting activities.

It was delightful meeting Andre in person, since I had heard much of him through old and mutual clients as well as through the trade itself. And I found it a pleasure that a man of his talents and outgoing manner was holding down Nyampala. It will always be my favorite spot in the Luangwa Valley.

Andre promised to drop by Mupamadzi Camp a few days later to tell me his "leopard story." All too soon, however, we had to leave; we still had quite a way to go and the light was beginning to fail. I was glad we had crossed the Luangwa in plenty of light, because I recalled how many times I had been across that great body, very often in dreadful fear of losing my Land Rover to

Mupamadzi Camp.

the primitive, rickety apology of a ferry we had to use, never mind the risk of losing my life to the crocs. It sounds dramatic now but, by sweet Jesus, it wasn't then, as anybody who was there will tell you. We had to make our own pontoons out of empty forty-four-liter gasoline drums and lash on a framework with space for a vehicle's wheels on top.

The Luangwa, if you're not familiar with it, is very deep in places.

The crocs are huge.

You can give me all the antibravado stuff in the book, but to drive a loaded vehicle onto one of those matchboxes and be held in place and pulled along by a cable (laid by a brave man who was rather ineffectually covered against crocs) from the far bank was something to experience. Try it sometime. You can be my gun bearer.

Lew steered us through the bush and the late afternoon shadows to the Mupamadzi safari camp, situated on the banks of the Mupamadzi River. The reed-and-thatch camp was perched on

Interior of a client's kaia *at Mupamadzi, showing camp beds.*

—although running a safari camp can sometimes be anything but tranquil. Godfrey, the head waiter, beautifully turned out in green and crimson, looked after us as we enjoyed the twilight. Away to our right, against the setting sun, was the great dark smudge of the Muchinga Mountains, so robustly described by the late Owen Letcher in *The Bonds of Africa* as "a great towering wall of blue."

Both the Mupamadzi and the Munyamadzi rivers are *Bemba* terms, the former meaning "water bringer" and the latter "dark water." I had spent a great deal of time near the confluence of the Munyamadzi and the Luangwa, but I had never hunted the Mupamadzi area. From what I could tell, the country was identical to the areas further south where I had previously been headquartered: slathers of long grass, *conbretum* interspersed with *mopane* and sausage trees, the latter famous for their heavy salami-like fruit.

The smells were also essentially the same, the nasal twang one got from the mixture of dust and distant bush fires saturating my soul in seconds and wiping away years long gone. Hell, it might have been yesterday. And, the strange light late in the afternoon, that golden, liquid glow of sunset in a usually cloudless sky that pours over all the bush, as if sprayed there; this Central African light is a tangible thing, almost the sort of phenomenon you can pick off a bush and rub through

high banks overlooking a fine stretch of wide, shallow river, punctuated by tongues of sand and grassy islets. On the other side lay the South Luangwa National Park.

Fiona, Paul, and I instantly hit it off with the Games. It was a lot more than the standard client stuff. Dale is a highly competent and pleasant person who was on hand to welcome us and help us settle in and put our gear in proper shape. This meant unpacking, cleaning lenses after the dusty journey, checking ammo, stowing rifles, and freshening up for cocktails around the campfire and a fine dinner later on.

Lew and I got on like pigs in the same trough. He and Dale had been trapped in Lusaka most of the time with paperwork, and both were delighted to get away to the bush and a touch of instant tranquility your fingers. It should have a smell of its own.

But then, perhaps it does.

It has the smell of freshly crushed grass, new and clean, mixed with the acrid, musky odor of the sweating gun bearers and trackers to whom the white man undoubtedly smells as foreign. It smells of the twilight beer on the way home to the leaping flames of the campfire and supper coming out of a hole in the ground. It smells of elephant and buffalo dung, sweet and fresh and exclusively African, as well as the smell of your own sweat-encrusted bush jacket. It smells of the shotgun powder of the short stop for a brace or two of sand grouse, the empty shotshells never left behind but carefully picked up. It is not just light. It is Africa, and you won't find it anywhere else.

I talked earlier about the smells of Africa. Africa has its sounds, too. The cooling coo of ring-neck doves, blending with those of the emerald wood dove and half a dozen other species; the slow, quiet, but incessant swirl of the river; the clink of ice in your glass or the pop of a chilled beer being opened; the gurgle of your hot shower water being poured into shower drums by Jim or Fountain, the men looking after such matters at Mupamadzi Camp; the adenoidal honk of the hippos, and the splash of giant *vundu* catfish in the river a few yards away.

And now that evening is approaching, the lions and hyenas will soon be tuning up, as the gold of the sky fades into the richest of burnished amber. Their calls—especially those of the big male lions—will carry for miles, as they warn one another out of their personal hunting grounds. The hyenas will echo them, sometimes in their weird *whoop* and chittering, sometimes in such perfect imitation of a lion's roar that it takes an experienced professional hunter to tell them apart. It is fire time. Somehow, at least for me, a fire in a fireplace just isn't the same as the similar item on safari.

And then, as I was getting good and comfortable, the leopard called. He was a couple of miles away, but Lew said, "I rather suspect that's our boy. Direction's right. So's the distance. Yup. That's him."

We hadn't gotten around to the fact that, having escaped the horrors of Lusaka, Lew and Dale had been up on the Mupamadzi setting things in order, and that Lew had already hung a couple of baits with which he had promptly attracted customers. One was a lady leopard with a half-grown cub, but the other looked like something of a whopper—seven feet, easy, judging from the spoor.

The object of my trip to Zambia—besides seeing old pals and getting to know Lew and Dale Games—was to take a leopard of my own. Sitting there at the campfire, I hoped very much it would not be under circumstances similar to those of the lion charge. In a couple of ways, it turned out even worse. But I'm getting ahead of myself.

Listening to that leopard calling on the first night, he became *my* leopard. As with lions, big buff, and elephants, I had successfully hunted a lot of leopards but had never had one actually *belong* to me. The animals taken were always either client or government property.

The bait we were interested in was a couple of miles from Mupamadzi Camp but within easy reach. The next morning, after my by now habitual soul-cleansing hours of stargazing, we went off to look at what might or might not be going on.

There was *plenty* going on.

The bait, a *puku* ewe, had been hung in a fine-looking tree and been laced with wire so that the leopard would not be able to gnaw through it and carry it off. A great deal had been eaten, and I suggested to Lew that the big tom would only show up after dark, since he could have a full feed any time he felt like it. In fact, he had managed to loosen the wires with his tearing at the thing, and what was left might not be enough to hold him. We therefore decided to smack another *puku* (an animal that rather resembles a stocky version of an impala but with shorter lyrate horns), the idea being to wire it to the underside of the branch in such a manner that a leopard could get a good taste but could not

Hanging a female puku *as fresh leopard bait.*

gorge himself. Then, frustrated and still quite hungry, he would return while there was still shooting light, whereupon I would ventilate him with the .375.

Well, it *almost* worked out that way. Only it didn't.

It being the heat of day, and since the leopard was probably lying up at some distance due to the disturbance caused by the vehicle, we decided to build a blind. Considering that we had a photographer in tow with equipment (courtesy of Contax) worth about the same figure as the American space program, the blind had to be a rather special setup.

I don't know why, but I've always had a great deal of luck in second-guessing leopards, and ran an extremely high percentage of success with them for my clients. In fact, I never lost one or had a client on safari for a reasonable length of time who didn't have at least a sky-lighted shot in the clear. My success was probably due in part to the fact that leopards fascinate me, and so I've really studied them—which isn't easy, considering how secretive they are.

Perhaps a small digression here would not be out of order. My reason for this aside is to explain that your life is always on the line with dangerous game, and that even though you may be carrying the finest equipment in the world, nothing is guaranteed—neither rifles and their cartridges nor bullet performance. Your reputation as a consistently fine shot does not stop the hemorrhaging.

The incident I am referring to took place in roughly the same area we were now in. My client at the time, a Texan, and I just couldn't get a particular record-book tom to come in while there was still shooting light. (I do *not* shoot at night with lamps or torches.) We had had him feeding for five nights, and I was becoming damned frustrated. So, the thought occurred to me: Why not checkmate him with a preemptive strike?

I sent Silent and Invisible, covered by me, to see if we could find where the big bugger was lying up during the day, and where he undoubtedly paused to survey the scene before proceeding to the bait after dark. Eventually, we found his lying-up spot, as well as the spot from where he watched us: the head of a tunnel of the eternal *conbretum* thickets, just where it emerged from a *karonga*. From there, he could see the whole area without exposing himself, and he could walk up, bold as a lion, and have his evening chow-down, courtesy of Luangwa Safaris and my rations license. So, I decided to throw him a spitball, a slider, and a corkscrew curve all at once.

My client, the Texan, was a hell of a good shot with a .300 Winchester Magnum, and he had on an excellent scope. I decided to build a much smaller blind with a view of *nyalube*'s favorite spot to lie and lick his chops until dark, and to stick three or four of my men into the old blind rather obviously.

Twenty minutes before daylight faded, they left with some noise and chatter. Sure enough, up popped the head and neck of the huge leopard . . . right into the crosshairs of my Texan, who gave

Building a blind. The postholes are dug with ax-heads lashed into mopane *sticks.*

him 220 grains of imported trouble up the nostril. Didn't do a hell of a lot cosmetically for the skull, but the leopard *did* tape out at seven feet four inches between the pegs. So, double-guessing is also part of leopard hunting.

Lew, Paul, Fiona, and I had something to drink and eat as the men cut grass and poles for the blind. It was directly downsun and the prevailing breeze seemed to be in our favor, depending of course on which way he came in. That is, *if* he came in.

I noticed a curious thing on returning from an inspection of the bait. As I walked back, I noticed that my rifle, which before had been leaning on one side of a large *mopane* tree, was now on the other. Since it was only a couple of steps from where the blind was being built, however, I thought little of it at the time. Somebody had found it was in their way as they carried bundles of grass and *mopane* poles to the spot about thirty-five yards away from the bait, and had moved it out of the way.

Wrong.

Big mistake.

I should have realized what had happened when we went off to shoot the new *puku* bait. From fifty yards offhand, I missed him cold.

What??? Impossible!

Actually, I had nicked him, as there was a blood spoor that we followed for about three hundred yards to where the sturdy antelope had lain down. Suddenly, he bounded out of the long brassy grass and I swung the sights well ahead of him, having tipped off the scope. He went down as if smacked with a howitzer, the bullet placed perfectly through the shoulders at a three-quarters away angle. Well, I figured, I guess nobody is perfect, although it *had* been years since I had missed a shot at game. I reckoned I had somehow just pulled this one. I should have known better and checked the scope there and then, but it was getting late and we had to get the bait into the tree before the leopard came back and found the larder bare. (If *that* had happened, we might have had to wait for days before it got ripe enough for him to rediscover it. The hunter must not break the feeding habits and patterns of a leopard or, thinking there's nothing there anymore, it might never return to the spot.)

It was almost four o'clock by the time we hung the bait, and on the off-chance that the leopard might show, we decided to stay. We had wired the *puku* tightly to the bottom of the branch in a very awkward feeding position for the cat and sent the vehicle a half-mile away with the usual instructions to the staff to come like hell if they heard a shot or to show up just at full dark, when it became illegal to shoot.

We had had the forethought to bring along the camp chairs. All that was left was for Paul to figure out how he wanted his cameras and flashes placed. He would hand hold one Contax with a 150mm lens while we had the other, a highly sophisticated remote-control radio-operated job, loaded with special Fuji 3200 ASA film, about ten yards from the bait and well camouflaged. We taped it to a convenient *mopane* sapling where it seemed quite unobtrusive. Then we cleared a port in the grass wall for him and got my rifle perfectly lined up above the bait, resting in a pair of forked sticks sunken into the hard gray ground and insulated with a couple of extra bush hats so the recoil would not throw the shot high. We were set. All we needed was the leopard.

He came all right, but some hours after we had to leave. I had not really expected him during shooting hours anyway, as he had fed so heavily the night before. It turned out I was right.

This new bait, however, baffled him. It was wired snugly to the underside of the branch and he had been able to eat only about three or four pounds of the carcass, compared to the fifteen or so pounds he had been taking nightly on previous occasions.

We had waited patiently and quietly but it was no go. At least, not that night. . . .

When ideas filter through the moss of my brain, it seems a good thing to record them, since, the next moment, they're usually gone.

That same morning, before the rifle had been moved from one side of the tree to the other, I had had occasion to go out for a small warthog. Dale (for whose cooking abilities Maxime's would kill) has a speciality—roast crackling warthog. Now, a warthog is not exactly the same as a nice, fattened, domestic suckling piglet, but it's mighty fine fare. I had been told the night before that the lady required a baby warthog so that she could do her thing, and I was more than willing to do my share.

Now, it was a bit late in the season for a really young *ngulube* to be wandering around, but Lew and I had noticed a rather large bunch across a *vlei,* and we decided that the runt of the litter would do nicely for Dale's nefarious purposes. I bailed out of the car, followed by a cou-

Leopard bait with much of brisket eaten away by big male leopard.

ple of stalwarts, and stalked the little chap as Lew backed off three hundred yards or so. I got within about one hundred yards (as you can see from Paul's pictures), stood up, and placed the bullet exactly through the skull at the ear—a solid, as Dale had instructed. You can clearly see the shot, and that it went through the porker's brain at a slight angle. Fine. It wasn't a bad shot. Now, I shot that hog through the skull—on purpose, as I have explained. A mighty small skull it was, too. I walked up to it with two of the men, who were probably fearful of my being mauled, glanced at the bullet hole made by the .375 solid, and walked away. I don't shoot young animals for fun, but

Dale had put in a very specific request for a young warthog and I complied. (It was rather like having a close friend and neighbor request that you pick her up a pack of lamb chops at the supermarket, since you were going anyway. Let's not inject any sporting concept into this; it's not why I fired the shot.)

At dinner that night, after we had returned from the leopard blind, and just before the pork was served, I asked Dale if she was pleased with the piglet for her larder.

"Yes," she replied, "but I asked you to shoot the thing through the head, not the shoulder!"

"What on earth are you talking about?" I asked in complete bewilderment. "I shot it with a Remington solid through the brain."

Author looking for tracks with gun bearer.

"Nope," said Dale in her best Las Vegian. "There was a fresh hole in the center of the shoulder, apparently from a three-seventy-five." She even brought out the skin to show me when I expressed my extreme skepticism. Sure as rain. But how?

Obviously *tagati,* black magic. We all of us had seen the hole in the skull that collapsed it quicker than a stroke with a poleax. Maybe we hadn't seen the shoulder hole, however, since it wasn't bleeding, the heart having stopped when the brain was destroyed. Still, consider the following:

1. There was a single shot fired. We all agreed on this.

2. There was a hole through the skull, obviously freshly made by a .375 solid, the same having exited on the far side of the head and all of it having been recorded on 35mm motor-driven film.

3. The pig was standing, facing away from my right to my left when I shot him.

4. The other bullet hole, also obviously fresh, was in his *left* shoulder, which was facing me when I fired at his head.

Conclusion: there was no logical explanation. There was no entrance wound on the pig's right side, proving that there hadn't been a ricochet. There was only a clean and neat exit hole in the skull. Stranger things have happened in Africa, but I haven't seen many that have been more inexplicable than that one.

Lew agreed with me that very odd things come up in the cartridge field. My first so-called "high-powered" rifle was a 1936-vintage .219 Improved Zipper, which was a fire-formed case created by letting off ordinary Winchester .219 ammo in the expanded chamber of the rifle. This blew out the malleable brass into a different shape, permitting the creation of hotter and faster handloads. (The cartridge was actually .224 caliber, although it was known as the .219 for some reason.)

I got the Mauser-action, Douglass-barreled rifle with an old Bushnell on it for being my late brother's best man in 1957. At the time, I was a student at the University of Virginia, in Charlottesville, prime woodchuck pastureland. (The use of the term *student* is perhaps not entirely accurate. As I recall, I went to a class or two for four years running, but unless there was snow on the ground, I was shooting woodchucks and crows.) I had a reloading outfit in my room and shot most days, always experimenting with different handloads. My usual partner was Tom Goode, a fellow rifleman, who, as I recall, shot a Winchester Model 70 rechambered for .270 Weatherby Magnum. We did quite a bit of damage over the years.

The point is that I normally shot the 53-grain match hollowpoint by a major component maker, and with excellent results. Then one day I happened into a gunshop (in New Jersey, if I remember correctly) and saw a box of 60-grain .224 slugs that intrigued me mightily. Of course, I loaded up a batch and went out to the range to see how they would perform. The weight was extremely heavy for that caliber, and I was fascinated to see what would happen.

Damndest thing I ever saw! The rifle threw those bullets into fantastically accurate groups at two hundred yards. The only thing was that it was doing it in a rather odd fashion.

Sideways.

If you don't happen to be a hunter or a rifleman, remember that the concept of a rifle is in the rifling itself, those lands and grooves that swirl up the interior of the barrel and are meant to impart the same stabilizing spin to a bullet that a quarterback imparts to a perfect spiral in American football.

The bullets, having lost their stability, should have been all over the place; but for some reason, they weren't. Center-to-center, they were the best group that rifle ever produced. I'm supposed to be a ballistics expert, but the answer to that one has always evaded me. I swear to you that the group was clustered three-quarters of an inch at two hundred yards and looked like a daisy.

In *Death in the Long Grass,* I described what happened when a .458 Magnum became compressed and nearly cost me my life, so I'll spare you a repetition of *that* show. Another incident, however, was almost equally odd. I was hunting and had a leopard bait up that had shown handsome activity. In tow were two American clients and my usual field crew. Through a corridor in the bush, I could see that there was a hell of a lot more meat missing, and decided we should probably sit in the hide that afternoon.

I left the car a full half-mile away and took my .470 Evans double rifle and a couple of spare rounds between my fingers: 500-grain soft-points with their big blue/gray lead noses and cupronickle jackets. Figuring that the fewer the people, the safer and quieter it would be, I

A sample of the incredible elephant damage in the area, much of it fresh.

went in alone, through what wasn't really terrifically dense bush. I slithered, snaked, and slimed my way toward the bait, taking about forty minutes to do so.

Trouble was, I did it too well.

I don't know what drew my eyes up —perhaps it was just instinct—but suddenly I was looking full into the face of a huge male leopard crouched on a thick limb about thirty yards from the bait. Our eyes locked, and, just as with Andre de Kock's terrifying experience, I knew he was coming. Right then.

I'm fairly fast with a shotgun, and although this was a double express rifle, I forgot the difference and pasted him in the chest, literally in midair. I threw him completely off balance, as one would think five hundred grains of lead would do from eight feet, and he fell about three feet from me on his back. I remember thinking that if he landed on his back, he was badly hurt; how this sort of thing races through your brain in the microseconds involved is extraordinary to me.

The sonofabitch then got up!

I socked him straight on with the second barrel, and that pretty well seemed to be *it*. I reloaded in a blink and had him covered with the fresh rounds under the ivory night sight like a wet horse blanket. He gave a last sigh, and then there was nobody home.

I explained things as carefully as possible to the clients, who were not especially entranced with the concept of their professional killing the leopard they had come so far to hunt. But when I walked them through the exercise and they saw the claw marks, as well as how close it had been, they eased off and reckoned they were lucky to still have a pro. I shared their sentiment.

Now, you'll recall that Gordon and I had nearly been sorted out by using an especially popular British brand of express ammo from an old batch—the newest having been made in 1956—and, although I had no hangfires or duds on this frightening occasion, the soft-point bullet performance was atrocious. The first round had completely broken up, and this on a leopard of no more than a hundred and forty pounds, fairly hit and still able to do damage. The second did the same, but, luckily for me, one thousand grains in total was enough to cancel his life memberships.

I have a little leather sack in my safe with the chunks of those two .470 softs, and I never cease to marvel at how they failed to hang together. It could very well have been my life.

Lew and Dale joined Paul, Fiona, and me around the fire, and, crammed as we were with warthog, Lew and I got to talking. One of the stories that came out was one I personally consider the most extraordinary, unbelievable lion episode I have heard in my seventeen years in Africa. Lew, Paul, and I cracked cold Lion Lagers —appropriate—as he told us about his mauling.

Before becoming a professional hunter, Lew had run cattle in the Matetsi area, where I used to hunt after they swapped cows for game. Adjoining the Hwange (formerly Wankie) National Park in what was then Rhodesia, the place practically crawled with lions, which, naturally, caused heavy cow depredation.

It was November 11, 1965, which had become known as UDI Day, standing for Rhodesia's Unilateral Declaration of Independence from Great Britain. As Lew put it—and he can tell the story much better than I can—"It was a matter of carelessness, stupidity, bad luck, bum ammunition, and that's about it.

"I was running cattle at the time and was hunting one hell of a lot of lions. I was in the Dende area of Matetsi with a friend who was along for the ride.

"Everybody else was celebrating UDI and I landed up celebrating pussy bites. These lions were heading some distance away but they were going straight for my cattle kraals and I knew what they would do when they got there.

"Well, I jumped out of the car and shot one of them, a youngish male. I *think* it was a young male, but we were only

Paul Kimble, our photographer. (Photograph: Peter Capstick)

interested in protecting our cattle. Didn't matter what it was; if it was a lion, it ate cattle. And we shot one hell of lot of lions any way we could.

"I walked into the long grass to see that it was dead and I noticed that there were lions scattered all over the place. In fact, I counted eleven at one point, but I think there were more. In any case, I started walking towards them and they started down the road like a bunch of bloody cattle ahead of me. I, however, ran into another one and it immediately charged me."

I asked Lew if it was a male or female, and he said he was sure at the time that it was a male. "Had a helluva lot of hair," he added.

"I was carrying a Browning bolt-action four-fifty-eight Magnum and I knew I had only three shells in the fool thing, and there were a lot more lions than that about. What I do remember was that in those days, the ammo was a well-known American brand with a thing like an ice-cream cone stuck on the end of the bullet. It was not, in any case, the Winchester bullet, like a Silvertip, which I don't recall they ever made for the four-fifty-eight caliber.

"This bullet used to flatten out on just about anything, a fact of which I was unaware at the time, although I had had some very bad results with the bullet.

"This thing charged, and I got down on one knee to wait for it to get good and close if I was going to have to nail it for certain. I didn't want to have to shoot it, as by now the others had turned around and were looking upon the scene with a good deal of interest.

"It backed off a few yards and then came again, throwing dirt and little rocks —you know that basalt shield, Peter— and this stuff was actually hitting me, so

close was it. It stood growling just a couple of yards away and then backed off again.

"It was only ten feet off, but the others were now showing a definite interest and were starting to gather around. I knew the lion would go for me for real if I retreated, so I shouted to a friend who was in the Land Rover, a chap named Willy May, to bring the truck around and shoo the buggers off me. Unfortunately, he couldn't hear me."

Most unfortunately.

"But, anyway, this thing made another charge and, on the fourth charge, I was convinced it would do its stuff. As it came, I shot it, hopefully between the eyes, but I hit it just below the left eye, which should have taken the back of its head out, given any decent bullet, had I been using anything from the three-oh-three British service round upwards.

"It rolled the thing over, the lion flashing sideways to me behind a log. I was able to get another shot into its neck before it vanished behind the dead tree.

"It was onto me before I could do anything. I pushed the rifle barrel down its throat, but I was in the process of loading, and, as the lion hit me and the rifle, it tore it out of my hands and I went down on my back. The lion let go of the rifle and grabbed me by the leg and started shaking me in the grass like a terrier shakes a rat.

The hot springs near the Mupamadzi River.

"Actually, through what I thought to be the oddest luck, we happened to go back over the rifle, which I figured was pretty good news. I grabbed it, closed the open bolt, which I was reloading at the time I was hit, and carefully thought out how to handle the matter of killing the lion without blowing my leg off.

"I closed the bolt and put it up against the lion's ear, but the lion had my leg in its mouth, so I shifted the angle so that I wouldn't take the leg along with the lion's brain. I pulled the trigger.

"Nothing happened.

"At this point, I realized I had a problem, so I pulled the bolt back, worked it again, placed it on the lion's temple, and pulled the trigger.

"Again, it clicked.

"What had happened, I later realized, was that when the lion had taken the rifle away from me with the bolt-action open, a clump of dirt had gotten into the action. When I worked the bolt, I was just pushing the nose of the bullet back down into the magazine and not into the chamber.

"I was starting to realize that this might not be exactly the best approach to solving my problems, an observation reinforced by the fact that the lion had now decided that my more interesting end might be the other one. It let go of my leg and made a dive for my head. I was just able to jam the recovered rifle crossways in its mouth. Then we did a bit of a circus act for a while, ending with his jerking the rifle free again and slinging it away with a toss of his head.

"He immediately went for my head and, by reflex, I stuck both hands down his throat and grabbed his tongue as hard as I could. I nailed him as far back as I could reach and just got a death grip on his tongue. My right arm was well in and he was chewing me very badly, I could tell, but the left wasn't so deeply inserted down his throat, so there wasn't quite so much damage. Previous to this, the lion had managed to swipe me across the face, and I was unable to see at all out of my right eye. (I thought I'd lost it but it came right.) The problem, among other rather more obvious ones, was that it had a grip with one of the big teeth—what do you call them, canines?—and had sliced the main artery in my right arm. I was pumping out an awful lot of blood and I knew I couldn't hang on too much longer.

"In any case, I couldn't get rid of the lion, holding him by the tongue with both hands, and he couldn't get rid of me. So, we lay like a courting couple and rolled around and around and cleared three acres of bush ready for planting.

"The lion seemed to get exhausted, too, since it was losing a lot of blood from the neck wound. Then the guy, Willy May, came up in the vehicle, drove right up to us, and asked, 'What can I do?'

" 'Nothing,' I answered, 'but get the hell back in the car!'

"There was a spare three-seventy-five

behind the seat, but after a few seconds thought, I decided that Mr. May was far more likely, in his excitement, to shoot me instead of the lion. I therefore decided to take my chances with the lion, which I thought was getting weaker. Unfortunately, it was thinking the same thing about me, so it was a Mexican standoff.

"Mr. May, meanwhile, actually had a thirty-five millimeter camera on the seat next to him, and I was in fact speaking with him as he was pulled up alongside the lion and me. Nobody, of course, thought of taking a picture of me being eaten.

"Every time the lion lay down on me, it did so full length, its claws deep in my back, just holding me tight, and there was nothing anybody could do about it. I did have leverage, though, and was pulling the tongue as hard as I could. Neither of us could let go of the other.

"I was actually talking to this chap, May, and we were discussing with some urgency what in hell we were going to do. Well, I told him we'd resolve it somehow. This went on for what was really quite a while, and finally he said to me, 'Look, I can't take any more of this. I'm going back to get help.'

" 'Listen,' I told him, 'by the time you go off and get help I won't be around. I won't need it. Just hang on. Something's going to happen.'

"Now, you can appreciate his position.

He'd never seen a lion before, I don't think. Now was his first one, rolling around eyeball-to-eyeball with his pal, or what was left of him.

"It kept picking me up and carrying me around, so I told him again to bring the truck up and try to scare the bloody thing off me. Bump it if necessary, but let's try to get it off me! Well, every time he would do this, we'd get no results, and it was partially my fault. You see, I would tense and the lion would sense this and hold me all the tighter. I knew if I let go, the way it was looking at me and grunting and growling and making one hell of a noise, I was dead.

"One thing that oddly comes back and is of interest is that, well, his breath didn't smell too bad, so I had a Pepsi or Colgate-type lion—fairly hygenic.

"I was scared it would go for my head if I let go of the tongue. In any matter, it then literally picked me up and carried me across a little stream about ten yards away. Then it took me down through the water and put me down on the other bank.

"May said, 'What the hell do I do?' I told him, 'Look, go down about a hundred yards and you'll find a fairly shallow crossing and we'll meet up again. . . . I hope.' "

I asked Lew if he was still holding it by the tongue at that point and he confirmed my guess in the strongest terms: "If that bastard had lived, it would have had a tongue a half-mile long, guarantee you.

"Anyway, May managed to get around while the lion and I just sort of lay around gazing into each other's eyes in a very romantic manner. May began to ease up inch by inch, and I could see that the lion was turning its eyes and trying to turn its head a little bit. In any case, it was no longer lying on me, so I told May to get the truck up to one side, as the lion was now at a forty-five degree angle to me, and told him, 'Now, when I tell you, you rush up and smack it with the bumper while I let go at the same instant.'

"That's exactly how we played it. He hit the lion as I let go of the tongue. The lion immediately charged the vehicle, reared right up and actually got on the hood, scratching down the windscreen, before going over the bonnet or hood. It fell on the ground—between us. There was only one thing to do, so I stepped on the lion and jumped into the truck.

"I had long forgotten about the three-seventy-five behind the seat or I would have obviously plugged the bugger. I was, however, more interested in my not bleeding to death than killing the lion. Hell, I'd lost so much blood then, what with the severed artery as well as the chewed foot, I wasn't thinking too much about anything except staying alive. So,

we drove away, leaving the lion the victor for the moment, and May took me back to the house, which was only a couple of miles away.

"I had a major slug of brandy and a lot of cold water was poured over me as I was patched up and bandaged sufficiently well to enable me to undertake the long drive to the nearest hospital that could cope with a severe mauling. That was in Bulawayo, where I was treated by a good doctor friend who had mended a lot of my pals over the years. He never charged me a single cent. Even the medications were samples. He knows who he was but let me once again express my appreciation. He had to give me a hundred and forty-seven stitches.

"The game department went down the next morning, found the lion, and shot it. When it was skinned out, it was found to be a maned female. As far as I know, this was only the second true hermaphrodite among lions ever recorded. Of course, I had a lot of comments from my friends, who said that only I would be caught playing around with something like that."

Lew does not know how he survived that mauling, and his scars are a daily reminder of how lucky he actually was. But ironically, he was in for a *second* attack within a couple of miles of where the first mauling had taken place.

"It was almost a year later to the day

that I was attacked again, this time completely unprovoked. I had a hunting client from San Diego; it was only his first day and we were sort of wandering around, taking a look at animals. In fact, it was not really even a hunting day, just one spending time to give him some idea of what goes on during a safari. So, I drove up across an open plain and could see on a ridge ahead of me a whole bunch of lions. Ten, twelve, maybe, and I drove up to the far edge of this plain over a little hill. There was a little river there.

"As these lions were going over the hill, the male turned around and came running back in a sort of charge, and it came right at us from what must have been, at that stage, a good two to three hundred yards; a helluva way off. He watched us from the top of the ridge and, as we cleared it, he came straight at us.

"I don't know if, at that moment, you could have called it a real charge: more of a reconnaissance, since we were on one side of the river and he was on the other. It was pretty deep but easy enough for him to swim—only twenty-five to thirty yards wide. He got to the edge of the river and just stood there swishing his tail around, appearing most upset about the whole scene. The way he was acting, I said to the client, 'This may be your lion.' But then, I had a good look at him and said, 'No, no. This might be your last-day lion. He's not good enough to take on the first day.'

"Eventually, this thing started to walk away from the other side of the river, growling to beat hell. He was obviously a little uptight, but he went over the ridge and out of sight. So we started up again and continued east along the river —I don't remember its name. Anyway, we just followed it for half to three-quarters of a mile, with this high ridge in front of us, but just couldn't get across until I found a place to ford.

"We went across and carried on for about a hundred yards until one of the men tapped the roof and said in dialect, 'Hey! There's some kudu.'

"I glassed them and there were three kudu bulls. We stopped, but they really weren't worth shooting, it being the guy's first day and certainly not worth the stalk. This would have been around 1966 and I remember him particularly, since I had asked somebody else to check him out with his firearm and his scope so he was zeroed, as I was running late for some or another reason.

"When I got there, he said he had a pain in his chest, and I thought, Oh, brother! What now? However, it turned out that he had been zeroing his rifle from the middle of his breastbone and not his shoulder, which had obviously hurt him with the recoil. Well, frankly, it indicated to me that he hadn't done a hell of lot of shooting, and it made me wary of him as a client on his first trip out.

"In fact, he made it immediately clear that he was there on a 'fun trip,' and the interesting thing about the whole exercise was that he had no money! He'd just done his legal exams to try to qualify for the bar but was able to raise enough to come out to Rhodesia. One of the first things he said to me was, 'Listen, if I don't qualify and pass these exams, you'll have to give me a job.' I asked why and he said, 'If I don't pass these legal exams, there's no way I can go back to the United States. I borrowed all the money I could lay my hands on to do this trip on the strength of my being admitted to the bar. If I don't make it, I'm history. There's no way I can go back to my hometown. I've got to stay somewhere else.'

"Well, I shrugged it off as part of the crazier side of the safari business, and we went on looking at those kudu bulls. All of a sudden, somebody shouted out, *'Look out! Here he comes!'*

"I shouted to the back of the vehicle, 'Who comes?'

"The answer, in a bass chorus, was, *'The lion!'*

"Then I saw this thing burning right at us. We had the windshield dropped down flat and I told the client, 'Well, this may be your lion after all. You've got to take him or he's going to take somebody else.'

" 'Lew,' he said, 'my gun's jammed!'

"At this point, the lion was about to come over the bonnet of the car and join us in the front seat. As this furry head appeared on the hood, I stuck a four-fifty-eight into what looked like the biggest part and it just disappeared. The car and the front were then enveloped by a dense cloud of red basalt dust, caused by my sudden stop. It happened that the sun was directly in front of this dust cloud and it was very low on the horizon, just about to set. With that kind of light, vision was impossible. Unable to see, I just reloaded and waited for the whiskers to appear again.

"It took what seemed an age for the dust to settle. We couldn't see through it, and I was looking to every side, but we didn't even hear a noise. Slowly, it settled and I saw the lion limping away, quite a long way off from us. I used the vehicle to get as close as I could, but we had to contend with another river. I told the client to stay where he was and got out with the trackers to cover them. We followed as far as we could until it was completely dark and took up the spoor the next morning at first light. It led into what was then Wankie Park, where it is considered very bad manners to shoot lions."

Lew and his men spent the day looking for vultures or any other sign of a dead or disabled lion but came away without a clue. As Lew put it: "That's all she wrote."

I really can't recall Lew's mentioning whether the young man passed the bar exam or not. Presumably he did, since, to my indirect knowledge, he never went to work for Lew or his firm.

Dawn on the Mupamadzi is well worth the trip. It was on the twenty-seventh of July, 1985, that it blossomed into what had it been noise rather than color, could only have been thunder.

Several leopard baits were out, and we stalked them all in the hopes of catching a big tom with a full stomach and a lacka-daisical attitude. No luck. Nothing had been touched, so we decided to collect some camp meat and just wait to see what would happen.

Dale, most unfortunately, was down with a bout of malaria, so, except for her gallant attempts to join the campfire at night, we didn't see her for a while. In about two days, however, she was back to her old self. And there was other good news: we had the big leopard feeding on the *puku.* Having wired it up tight to the branch, the leopard was having quite a time getting at it and, the nature of the beast being what it is, it would not make a natural kill as long as it knew that free chow was available.

That afternoon, I shot a Cookson's wildebeest—found only in the Luangwa

Lew Games and author conferring over whether bait shouldn't be pulled closer to branch to prevent leopard from eating too much of it.

Valley—basically for meat for the men. Oh, sure, I could see he was a very good bull and well up in the book, but I was not prepared to share my boudoir with a wildebeest head of any description, so I only took the skin. (The Cookson's is a highly localized species that enjoys a "minimum measurement" in at least *Rowland Ward's* record book—which, by the way, is far too small. I don't think I ever had a client shoot one that did not "make the book." The skin of the Cookson's is, however, lovely: a collection of striations against a gray-beige background that makes a beautiful throw rug.)

It had been a perfect setup. Lew had dropped me off about four hundred yards from the animal, and I stalked through heavy bush—paying particular attention to very fresh buffalo dung and tracks—and made my way parallel to the road until I was opposite a fallen tangle of elephant-ravaged bush, to the side of which was a very low anthill that provided a perfect prone rifle rest. Paul was spooking behind me with his Contax, and the wildebeest was standing at the edge of the bush, about a hundred and eighty yards off. I cushioned my forestock on my folded fist, lined up just below the base of his horns, and squeezed off. The Silvertip took him exactly in the left nostril and pushed up into his brain, at which point he dropped, thoroughly dead. I was relieved, as head shots on things such as wildebeest are always tricky and, once wounded, it's not unusual to follow the bloody things for a couple of days. They have a habit, like zebra, of developing bulletproof propensities.

We loaded the bull and, with the sun slipping down as if on a greased rail, made for camp, not quite around the corner by some twenty miles.

What bothered me was not the fact I'd missed the exact spot I wanted to hit, but that as I was crossing the plain toward the dead wildebeest, there was a helluva wind blowing, which, having been in the thick bush, I had not realized.

I should have missed him to my left by a good foot with that gale!

Again, I should have rezeroed. For the life of me, I can't figure out why I didn't. It was to prove an expensive error.

As we pulled into camp, with everything making whatever kind of noise it does for a living, Dale was up and about, and had prepared the most pleasant of surprises for us . . . this time not culinary.

It was Wally Johnson, Sr.

For me, it was like returning to your campfire to find Karamojo Bell, Jim

Wally Johnson, Sr.

The author with Cookson's wildebeest (well in record book) in heavily damaged elephant territory. Brain shot at 180 yards, on the way back to the leopard.

Sutherland, and all the greats of the ivory days waiting for you. Wally and I were well acquainted with each other through mutual friends but had not had the opportunity of meeting until that evening, on the Mupamadzi. The atmosphere and setting could not have been more appropriate.

We all hit it off instantly, and in fact enjoyed just over a week with him, during which time he was coaxed to share some of his intensely interesting and often terrifying experiences as a big game hunter in Africa for over half a century. He had spent most of his hunting days in Mozambique, where he had eventually lost everything he owned when the commies took over. Then followed several years in Botswana, including hunting trips to the then Central African Empire. Then approaching seventy-three years of age, he had conducted his last safari as a professional hunter only four years earlier, which gives you some idea of his vitality and skill. He had taken some of the biggest ivory of any living white man, and is one of only two people known to have survived a full bite from a Gaboon viper. The clients he had had out on safari read like a *Who's Who,* especially when one considers that the late Robert Ruark engaged him as his pro on no less than five occasions after he himself had become *persona non grata* with the East Africans. (Apparently, they took exception to such works as *Something of Value, Uhuru, The Honey Badger,* and others, obliging Ruark to seek fresh hunting grounds. Ironically, the only place I have ever seen a complete collection of Ruark's Africana for sale was at the Nairobi Airport, Kenya!)

Adam, the head chef, and his sidekick, Donald, excelled themselves that first night, as Wally regaled us with his stories and sense of humor. He had with him historic and valuable photographs, as well as a scrapbook containing letters from clients, including letters from Ruark. Those documents were all the more valuable because they were the only things he was able to salvage after a lifetime in Mozambique.

I now have those documents and photographs in safekeeping, together with a whole series of taped interviews with him, conducted on safari and in my home. They will form the basis of my next book, which will be devoted to Wally and his amazing life. It was just as well that he entrusted his things to me when he did, because later that season he was robbed of his briefcase containing all his important papers—and in which he had been carrying that original material —when he visited Lake Tanganyika, on the Zambian side of the lake. The briefcase has never been recovered. The grand —and often depressing—years of Wally's life story are now under lock and key with me, together with our signed agreement.

Maybe it was the wine or the Mupamadazi cuisine, but old Wally composed an introduction to the forthcoming book by the end of that week in which he stated that, with the exception of the gin, nobody had reminded him so much of his late pal, Ruark, as yours truly, especially after he had hunted with me. I guess that's a weenie bit self-serving, but Wally is not the kind of person to say something like *that* every day. He said there was an amazing similarity in our voices and laughter and that the physical resemblance was strong. "Absolutely uncanny," said Wally to Fiona and the Gameses.

There was, however, no comparison made of our prose.

So, since nothing ate me in April–May 1986, when I contracted to do a series of videos in Botswana on hunting dangerous game, Wally is my next project—and what a grand one to work on.

The next day passed without incident, and suddenly it was the twenty-ninth of July, a Monday, and we were in business with a very good leopard, which ate as much as he could reach of the *puku*—which, to our delight, hadn't been much. He would be damned hungry, and would probably show up early. But who ever knows with leopards. Not even other leopards, I strongly suspect.

We were all worn out, though, and it wasn't just because of all the late, late campfire talk. At some unsanctified hour the night before, a gang of hyenas had broken into the kitchen enclosure by simply eating a large hole in the grass-and-wire fence. As hyenas are wont to do, they raised hell, chewing up pots and generally making the place look like ground-zero. Lew chased them around for a while, and I said to myself, "Screw it," something that applies to home carpentry and, checking the Winchester shotgun *sans* plug, I rolled over and went back to sleep.

Well, there was a lot to be done and a lot of guesswork on Paul's part. Nobody knew, presuming the leopard would show up, *when* he'd arrive or what the proper light reading would be. Now, I had a lot of money in this venture, and

Hunters Africa, bless them to eternity, had a hell of a lot more in the pot, both in cash and in time. What would happen if we flashed from the hide with the hand-held Contax? Would it blind me, freeze the leopard in place, or cause a direct charge? And what of the radio-operated rig, which we spent half our time trying to keep the hyenas from eating (although we never got a single exposure of them because of incorrect processing by the lab—may they be forever damned. The lab that is.) Nobody knew what would happen, but nobody ever does when hunting leopard.

I don't know what shutter speed or exposure Paul's hand-held Contax was on, but, as was previously the case, we had the radio rig loaded with 3200 ASA, which, correctly processed, should have made the inside of your appendix look like high noon on Midsummer's Day in Cairo.

We got into the blind early, about 3:40 P.M., and got everything into what we thought was Bristol fashion. The cameras were ready, the rifle was set, and there was little else to do but pray and watch the *drongos* and Little bee-eaters attracted by the flies swarming over the dead *puku*. Yeah. There was positively no question it was dead.

One can describe—or attempt to describe—waiting for a leopard a hundred times. No two experiences are the same.

Actually, he must have been lying up some distance away and well out of earshot, as how he eventually showed is still one of the minor miracles in my hunting experience. Nevertheless, just as it was starting to darken, the blind an anonymous blob against the tawny, yellow grass, I decided there was time to share a last cigarette with Paul. I closely cupped my hands and thumbed the little butane hoojigger, whose control wheel had somehow been turned to full on in my breast pocket. That being the case, it promptly relieved me of most of my right eyebrow and lash. Paul, sitting on my left and seeing me aflame, a long wisp of smoke rising from my face, instantly broke up, sounding like a gagged donkey being hamstrung. And that seems to prove that the leopard was not very close, at least at that moment. I was finally able to shake him into at least some semblance of control, though every few minutes he continued to threaten to break up again.

I was, however, to shortly get my revenge. Ten minutes later, as it was getting to be deep twilight, with even the bee-eaters huddling together for warmth, a presumably large beetle flew directly up one of Paul's nostrils.

Now, *there* was a show.

You would have thought somebody had dumped a pailful of scorpions in his underwear. Great God! Such carryings-on! All this just for one little beetle no bigger than your fist up your nose!

By the time we got the lot of sneezing, coughing, wheezing, scratching, clawing, and what-you-will sorted out, I didn't think there was the chance of a full bottle in an Irish pub of that bloody leopard ever showing up.

Waddya know.

Not five minutes later, I was astonished (as I am sure was Lew, who was next to me) to see the ethereal form of a whacking big male appear on the tree branch a couple of feet from the bait. There hadn't even been the hard whisper of claws on bark; perhaps he just jumped up. One second the tree was empty; the next, it was most definitely inhabited.

Actually, I'm a bit deaf—what?—because Paul later told me that Lew gave him a nudge and a slight nod. But in any case, I happened to be looking through the scope when it was suddenly filled with leopard.

Hell! At last! My own. And what a perfect setup.

My rifle was double-rested and insulated from recoil barrel bounce. I was smack spot one hundred percent *on* the exact portion of the precise shoulder rosette I had chosen to put the bullet through. I took a very quiet shooting breath and started to squeeze the trigger. As I did so, Paul hit the radio-controlled camera, afraid that the flash unit he was holding would frighten the big cat. But even I could hear it!

Now, what the hell is this? the leopard was obviously wondering as I watched through the 8X scope at about thirty-two paces. I could see every hair, even a split in his left ear, as he turned, standing like something peeled off a Norman shield, absolutely still and in perfect profile. I wasn't about to hang on any longer as he listened to the five frames Paul got off with the motor-drive. He was as still as he would ever be, and his profile would be lower when it got darker and he crouched to feed.

I eased the trigger back, knowing I hadn't jerked at the surprise of the recoil.

Following leopard at night through high grass under extremely *dangerous conditions.*
Author with shotgun, two gun bearers behind.

There was one hell of a roar, snarl, hiss, and gargle as he half fell, half jumped from the limb. (I couldn't see, since the kick of the .375 had put him out of the scope, but that's what Lew and Paul said later when I asked them what had happened. Although my ears were ringing, I heard him thud onto the ground and thunder away to our right at an angle, then the tearing of bush and grass and the same thumping on that hard earth that we had heard from the lions in Botswana. At forty yards, it stopped dead.

Uh-huh. Main pipes into the heart. A mad rush and then an advanced attack of death. Typical leopard chest shot. Or so I thought at the time.

We waited ten minutes, hearing nothing; no growling or any kind of movement whatsoever. At last I figured he was dead, dropped in his tracks. Still, better to wait for him to stiffen in case that ninth life had not quite run out. It was by then mighty goddamn dark anyway, and we only had two flashlights.

I can best describe the area into which the cat had run by saying that the designer was obviously a graduate of one of the finest landscape gardening schools in the world. The bush was such as to make leopards feel completely at home, even with holes in their chests. When I wrote *Long Grass,* I did not have that kind of terrain in mind. The stuff was a tunnel of horrors: sixteen-foot grass thicker than overfertilized redwoods, neatly embanked with a mixture of *conbretum* and assorted crud that would have stalled a herd of buffalo. Even with my big five-cell torch—carried by, I think, Banda, who most carefully searched the area around us at each step—it was nigh on hopeless. The thing could be wounded and a foot away and you'd have never seen him until twenty minutes too late, when they carried the shreds of your body back to the car, taking care not to drop any especially large chunks.

Lew was off on the right flank, covering the men as they tracked. He was also carrying a 12-bore with American Magnum Single-O buckshot, ammo I had given him. Blackson, one of the trackers, was carrying his light. One finds it difficult to imagine the nerve of these field staff members under conditions like that, unarmed, relying entirely on the hunters to save their bacon. Let me say here that I have never seen a more consistent level of bravery than that shown by those men entering such stuff armed only with lights. *We* had our naked bums well enough exposed, but at least we were armed. Had it been wartime, they would have all gotten the Victoria Cross or the Medal of Honor, as far as I was concerned.

We carried on about forty yards, having left Paul back in the car, as we did not

Pushing into a conbretum *thicket, expecting a charge at any moment.*

want the responsibility for his receiving a dose of impulsive plastic surgery. (Besides, how could he focus and get a photo of a charging, wounded leopard when you literally could not see more than five feet ahead of you? He was keen to come along, but we had to forbid it.)

Of course, to anybody not overwhelmed by general and specific stupidity, either genetically or acquired, this whole exercise was complete lunacy. Somebody should have gotten killed or at least badly mauled, even by this point. The leopard had stopped only forty or so yards from the blind and I presumed that he had cashed in his chips from a heart shot.

As it turned out, what happened was that the leopard had gotten into a sandy *karonga* that not only muffled its sound but concealed its movement. It went in a few yards and then cut back up the far side, where we couldn't hear it.

We had hell's own time finding blood, although all agreed that I had hit him with the .375 Silvertip. The problem, especially with a fresh wound like that one, is that when the animal runs, his skin slides back and forth over the rather small bullet hole and keeps a lot of the blood spoor inside, unless he has really big holes in the right place. That is what had happened with our leopard, because we later discovered that, though pretty well slugged, he had not thrown much of a blood spoor trail.

Council-of-war time. We went back to the vehicle, parked at the blind, and decided to go back to camp and recruit a few more anxious volunteers with better lights. We all knew it was a patently insane idea to follow up a wounded leopard with artificial light. But we decided to act that night. After all, the bloody thing might be lying dead a few yards away, and the hyenas would get his carcass.

Maybe they didn't realize what they might be walking into, but most of the staff at Mupamadzi were more than willing to come along carrying Cadac pressure lamps on their heads. Hell, yes. They'd purely *love* to prowl the deep thickets in the pitch dark for a wounded leopard the *bwana* had fouled up. Better

than a John Wayne movie. In any case, they came, and not a single man, from pot cleaner to wood fetcher, wavered the tiniest bit. They weren't stupid. They were brave, and they realized that their reputations, one to the next, depended a great deal on this sort of exercise.

Hell of a way to keep a reputation.

One man who certainly had *no* need to maintain a reputation was Wally Johnson. He borrowed my .375 with the scope tipped off and insisted on coming along. He, more than anybody, owing to his half a century in Africa, knew what might happen. But he was there.

I suppose we looked like some weird sect of light-bearing *djinn* as we formed a flanking line and made our way back into the grass to the point where we had left the spoor. Paul got some more photos from the top of the vehicle. After that it was foot by foot. The only thing was that suddenly, as I put a foot down, there was nothing but space beneath me. . . .

I seemed to fall forever through the dim light but I guess it wasn't really more than five or six feet. It was a hidden hole of some sort, completely covered with shrubbery and grass so as to be virtually invisible. I can remember it taking about four years to hit the bottom, a concrete-hard floor of dried mud. Pain shot through my legs, but I realized that if the bloody leopard were watching me, it would be the instant he would come.

Tracking leopard. Wally Johnson at left, the author at left-center, with safari staff.

Despite the pain, I immediately covered the lip of the hole with my shotgun as one of the men helped pull me out. Why there wasn't a herpetologist's paradise of mambas and puff adders at the bottom will always make we wonder, since that sort of hole, with its vertical walls, is exactly the sort of place where puff adders, in particular, get stuck. Once stuck, they seem to thrive, grabbing the mice, rats, elephant shrews, and demented professional hunters that drop in the middle of the night. And they kill more people than does any other snake in Africa.

That I still have a bruise bigger than my extended hand on the back of my left calf and lower thigh today—February 5, 1986, half a year later—may give you some indication of how hard I fell. When I had finally determined that there were no bones jutting through anything useful —like a shin—I decided to ignore the pain and go on with the men, after first completely inspecting as best I could the surrounding grass. The hours of unbelievable pressure wore on. We had been in that grass for four and a half hours and it seemed like as many ages. The possibility of the damned thing tearing out from behind the tiniest piece of cover was excellent. The only thing was that there were no tiny pieces of cover, just stuff that made the Amazon Delta look like a well-tended putting green. And then I saw Lew's lantern-jawed face headed toward me.

"Hey, chum," said he in that odd American–Australian–Rhodesian accent of his, "I think we're just buggering things up for when it gets light. We're obscuring spoor that we could follow much more quickly, easily, and safely in the daylight. Let's call it a night and come back at first light."

"Yeah, Lone Ranger," I agreed. "As Arthur Godfrey used to sing, 'Heap Big Smoke, No Fire.'" I suggested that we instantly repair to the campsite and the goodies therein, where we might toast in true devotion the ill health of yon *ingwe*.

We ate, I think, haunch of impala or *puku*, and somebody remarked on how positive I seemed to be, considering that it didn't look immensely likely that we were going to find the cat. I advised that

person that I did not let such things concern me, but tried to do the best I could, given whatever circumstances. Sounds like the *C'est moi* business from *Camelot*, but in fact I have developed a rather fatalistic philosophy on hunting and life in general, as well, I suppose, as on death. You do your best and that's the best you can do. If, through my own fault, I had cost that leopard pain, I genuinely regretted it. Although it would be difficult to justify in some quarters, I did put my life and the lives of our men up against the life of the cat; first on my terms, then on his, with the cloak of night and the shroud of blackness all on his side.

Nobody really won, except a third party.

Considering that we had to be life-saving sharp the next day, we sacked in relatively early and were back on the last bit of the spoor we could find from the night before. Wally was again with us and was carrying my .375, while Lew and I both toted shotguns that would have had us in U.S. federal prison on sight. We poked around on the old and rather thin spoor —as the hyenas had been eating the blood off the grass stalks—until our line was about a hundred yards wide.

Mightn't you know that it was Wally, rather than the kite-eyed trackers, who finally picked up the spoor on the hard ground and figured out what had happened. He had come across a matted-down area the size of a big dog's bed, sopped with blood that had partially dried. Obviously, the cat was very hard hit, since this was later paced off at two hundred and eighty yards from the blind. The slug probably caught a major vein, but I'll never know. Next to this lie-up were a pair of saplings, not as thick as your forearm, which were heavily scarred with leopard claw marks.

From a dry streamlet, Wally found what looked to me like fresh and nicely cubed goulash meat. This puzzled us: the leopard had not had a chance to get stuck into the *puku,* since I had shot him first. So, what the hell was this?

We backtracked and, in a couple of patches of softer earth, found the fresh pug marks of a big lion. He had apparently picked up the scent of the blood and had followed the spoor, found the leopard dying below the saplings, and charged it. The leopard had somehow gotten into the slender saplings and then, probably because the lion was trying to pull him out of them and had actually grabbed him, broken loose and made for a bigger tree a couple of yards away. Too late. The lion was on him before he could get out of reach (and don't get the idea that lions can't climb) and chewed him down to what resides today in a steel cigarette tin as "my leopard."

The scars on the big tree were fierce.

The claw marks where the leopard tried to hold on and was pulled from the tree by a lion.

For a leopard not to be able to escape a lion is a pretty fair indication that he was *badly* hurt.

I really believe we would have picked up the leopard's body the next morning, had it not been for the strange chance of that lion taking him first. But, as I had said the night before, that's hunting. A waste, and a damned expensive one, but that is what Africa is all about: the unexpected.

I gathered all I could of the scraps of the beast and put them in tissue paper to dry out. He was big; in my opinion, in "the book." But he was not to be mine. I didn't count the hours that Lew, Wally, Paul, the crew, and I spent on the late leopard's spoor, but it must have been from dawn to early afternoon before we conclusively decided—given that we had actual pieces of him as well as chunks of skin—that he was gone.

Strangely, particularly for an ex-professional, I was not disappointed. *C'est la guerre. C'est la chasse.* It was spilled milk in its most classic form, but at least nobody cut his finger on the bottle. And that counted most.

I had lost the leopard, the one remaining trophy I really wanted, through my own fault in not rezeroing. Had the lion not picked up his spoor, however, I am sure we would have found the cat curled up peacefully in the spot where he had made the bed beneath the twin saplings.

Well, he will have to share my den from his cigarette box, which offers not much in the way of a view. But I am far, far happier that the lion took him, rather than having had him escape, sick and hurt, as much as I would have cherished his memory. I can still do that. . . .

So goes Africa, true love, and my leopard.

Before we could wallow for too long in any sort of regret, Andre de Kock and Derek Evans, a well-known former pro, arrived in camp to enjoy the twilight and dinner. It turned out to be an evening of true tales and much hilarity. And, after hearing Andre's leopard story, we all realized that, in fact, we had gotten off lightly. Here's why:

"We were," Andre began, "in the area of the Luangwa, near Joe Joubert's place called Yacobe. It was a four-on-four safari which was split with Bo Illingworth and a chap by the name of Boetie Bothma. We were on our way with our clients up into the hills on the Kangwa River. You know, it's on the southern border of the Luambe National Park and is east of the Luangwa itself.

"Curiously, it was an area Joe used to hunt quite a lot, and I even happened to have Joe's ex-tracker with me, Shorty. We had a leopard feeding on the Kangwa. Our clients were Mexicans, mine being a gentleman with the first name of Enrique. The bait that had been taken was hanging in a sausage tree by the edge of a little *karonga*.

"Actually, although there was hell's

Andre de Kock.

own *conbretum,* there wasn't all that much grass. We'd been sitting up the first afternoon for the leopard when, at about six o'clock, I looked through the loophole in the blind, putting my rifle scope through. The leopard was there okay, but I made up my mind that we couldn't shoot. The sun had completely gone.

"I whispered to Enrique that we'd just have to try him again in the morning. I stood up, and as I was ready to leave and walk back to the vehicle, Enrique said to me, 'Do you mind if I just put my rifle through and look?'

"As I got ready to open the door of the hide, a shot went off!

"Now, when you wound a leopard, there is a very deep series of growls. And when that happens, there's no doubt in your mind what has taken place. The worst.

"What had happened was that when Enrique put his rifle through, he suddenly saw the leopard. As we unfortunately found out later, he'd opened up a great big vee on top of the leopard's shoulders, and off he went.

"We spent about an hour in the dark, looking for blood with a torch, but there just wasn't any. So we decided to call it a day and come back the following morning. I explained the situation to Boetie, that we had a wounded leopard on our hands, and he agreed to help me sort matters out first thing.

"We were back on the scene at first light, about six in the morning. We left the clients with the vehicle, and Boetie, his trackers, my trackers, and I all went in. We picked up the spoor of the leopard where he had come out of the tree and the very occasional spot of blood. In fact, we picked up the tracks of the leopard going through the *karonga* and, after about an hour, came up to a big, very thick *conbretum* bush, where we both decided, after walking completely around the cover, he was still inside. So we decided to put a couple of shots through that bush.

"I fired a couple of rounds of LG [a British designation for medium buckshot] and there was nothing. At all. We carried on around that patch of bush, putting in another couple of shots, and Boetie stuck a four-fifty-eight Winchester Magnum through the bush.

Nothing.

"Well, we cut up chunks of sausage tree fruit and also threw in anything else we could lay our hands on.

Still nothing.

"Pretty clearly, to our reasoning, the leopard had died there, or whatever."

It turned out to be "whatever."

Andre continued. "Boetie walked up the bottom of the *karonga* and actually looked into the bottom of the bush. I went up on top of the *karonga* and most cautiously peered in from the side. As I did that, the leopard was only a couple of yards away, looking straight at me.

"I've never seen a pair of eyes like that in my life. It still haunts me today. Bright yellow, glowing coals in that dark early bush. Funnily enough, when something like that happens, you know *immediately* what's going to happen . . . and I *knew*.

"It charged instantly and I got a shot off with my shotgun. It was from the shoulder, from about ten feet. I hit it in the shoulder, too, which did absolutely nothing! The leopard just took off through the air, coming down on top of me."

I asked Andre what happened next, and he said that he tried with his left hand to grab the leopard by the throat but must have miscalculated because, the next instant, his left hand was in the cat's mouth. His shotgun had fallen, but Andre is strongly built and was able to keep the leopard literally at arm's length.

"My shotgun had dropped to the ground and I decided that the only thing left, well, was that I would beat it. I punched this leopard with a number of blows to the body and the head and anywhere I could hit it with my right fist. I was, I realized, fighting for my life. And, every time the back legs came up to disembowel me, I would kick him as hard as I could right in the knackers. That's sportsmanship at its best!

"All this time, I was so charged up, I was holding him straight out in front of me. How my arm didn't buckle, I have no idea, but all that time I kept kicking him in the Rocky Mountain oysters.

"Later, Boetie told me he had never heard such language in his life. He reckons just the things I called it should have turned it belly up right there and then.

"Actually, it was quite incredible, since he later measured out, *Rowland Ward*-style between the pegs, at six feet ten inches, a hell of a lot taller than I am, and weighed about a hundred and twenty pounds. Okay, I outweighed him by a bit, but the strength of a leopard is legendary. I guess I was just scared. Anyway, I don't have any claws and, remember, my left hand was in the thing's mouth.

"Maybe I'm in the wrong business, but he's now on the wall of Enrique's adobe hacienda and I'm still here. . . .

"Anyway, as this was all going on—and it seemed like a lifetime to me, although the whole business probably only took a couple of seconds—I must have seen my opportunity, slid my right hand in under the belly, grabbed the leopard by the skin of its stomach, and, in the next instant, picked it up above my head and literally threw it away from me, letting go of the mouth and the belly. Where I got the strength, I have no idea.

"He hit the ground quite a few yards away, took a look at me—which I suppose is enough to scare anybody—and headed back for the thick bush. As it did so, it gave an opportunity to the professional hunter with me, Boetie Bothma, to put a four-fifty-eight slug right through his shoulders. He hadn't been able to fire previously for fear of hitting me, but this really put the leopard down."

I asked Andre to what extent the damage ran.

"Not nearly as bad as it might have been if he'd reached my guts with his rear claws. Still, I had claw marks across my face, and chest and across my throat. If they'd been a fraction deeper, that, I believe, would have been *that.* There were also deep lacerations from his claws on my back, so, at some point I don't recall, he got that close.

"I think the difference, really, was that my reach was just that bit longer than his was, and every time he brought his paws around, he just missed me. I think I was especially lucky with the throat scratches, as that could have truly been the end.

"When the rifle shot went off, my knees literally buckled; I heard the shot and actually didn't have the strength to pick myself off the ground. The crew and Boetie had to carry me to the Land Rover and put me in, I was so exhausted from nervous tension. I washed my face, noticing for the first time the severe bite marks on both my hands, which were enough to put me out of work for three months. My fingers were like cigars and

my hands swelled up like your American baseball catcher's mitts. Funnily enough, the scratches from the claws healed in ten days and didn't get infected, despite all the rotting meat lodged on the underside of a leopard's claws.

"The first thing we did was to finish a bottle of Scotch. We then went into Chibembe, way south. You know, the place where Sanchez Ariño used to have his camp, yeah?"

I remembered it well.

"On the way we killed a bottle of Old Brown sherry. Once at Chibembe, we met Norman Carr's daughter, who got my hands into a bowl of just about neat *dettol,* which is quite a strong local disinfectant in southern Africa. I don't know if it did any good but it must have. Luckily enough, again, Cotton Gordon's clients were just about to fly from Chibembe to Lusaka, and they kindly put me aboard.

"It was Sunday, September 14, 1980. By one o'clock that afternoon, my having been mauled at ten to eight that morning, I was at Lusaka Airport with a Dr. Bush on hand to meet me. He had been radioed ahead and was there to give me shots against tetanus, rabies, and every other thing he could think of.

"That's the size of it, but I couldn't work for months, and those first few days were grim, I want to tell you."

Donald, the headwaiter, summoned us

to the thatch-and-reed dining hut with its marvelous openess, where a table laid beautifully with starched linen and monogrammed crockery was soon groaning with such delights as hearts of palm, game soup, *puku en croûte* with all the trimmings, and splendid meringues. Man, but did we eat well on that safari!

Between the wines and cordials, Derek Evans regaled us with a story I think all of us interpreted as the proverbial red rag to any hunter.

In the early eighties, Derek had a client out on safari who was oddly enthusiastic when it came to hunting. The hunt got off to a bad start when this chap wanted Derek to shoot all his animals for him and said the only thing he was really interested in was a leopard. Derek, like any true pro, refused.

Well, the safari wore on and the men went through quite a few exercises to find a leopard worth taking. Everything seemed to be either female or too small to satisfy the client.

Finally, they got a good male feeding. It even obliged them by coming in the late afternoon when there was still bright light. The client fired and wounded the leopard, and it took off into a clump of thick brush. Derek got the vehicle and drove up a little way toward the point where the thing had disappeared and— telling the client to stay where he bloody well was—went in after it.

Lunch at Mupamadzi Camp.

He could hear it growling but couldn't see a thing. He got fairly near to it—it was in extremely thick stuff—and then got his tracker to throw a clump of wood just outside the bush at a right angle to the cat. The leopard, like a dappled flash, tore out of the bush, grabbed the wood, and then ran straight back into the cover before Derek could get off a telling shot.

When a leopard's in a hurry, he moves. My personal word on it. So, they tried it again, with exactly the same results: the leopard rushed out, attacked the wood, and was back into the dark and hairy before a shot could be fired.

Well, figured Evans, there's only one way to do this. And he did it. He threw a stick directly in line with him and the leopard. Again, it flashed to the attack. As it grabbed the stick, however, it saw Derek and the tracker and came straight for them. Derek was down on one knee, an elbow resting on his knee, as this thing came. He hit it, and . . . it didn't react at all! He fired a second shot as it was right on top of him, and he hit it again, this time killing it instantly. It was so close that it actually rolled right up against his knee, deader than yesterday's stock market reports.

At this point, the client swaggered up and said, "Hell, I enjoyed that! I've always wondered what you guys did to earn all that money you charge. That's the first time I've seen a professional hunter earn his salary, and it's paid for my whole trip."

I'm rather surprised there weren't two carcasses in the rear of the vehicle that afternoon. Having taken a .375 H&H slug through the collar—courtesy of a careless client—I can well imagine how Derek Evans must have felt that day.

We took it pretty easy after the leopard because, except for camp meat and the odd guinea fowl, I was pretty much out of business. But that didn't mean we stopped having wonderful days and nights in that very special part of Africa. While Wally, seated in his little thatched *kaia,* worked on filling in gaps concerning his life to supplement a whole series of tapes he let me have, I unwound.

One morning, while some of us were out, Fiona and Dale saw an extraordinary and fairly rare sight. Dale, now much recuperated from her bout with malaria, was enjoying coffee when she suddenly called my wife to bring her binoculars and come straight away to where she was sitting.

Across the Mupamadzi, on a sandy tongue jutting into the shallow water, was a pack of about fifteen Cape hunting dogs, *Lycaon pictus,* which had hit a herd of *puku* watering on the sandbar. The dogs pulled down a female and started eating her alive—Dale saw this actually happen—as is their fashion. A male *puku* most bravely got into the water to cut off any of the wild dogs from picking up another of the herd; the male standing in knee-deep water in a threatening attitude. Nobody of the *pictus* bunch tried him out. The male *puku* is strong and not to be fooled with, as I guess the wild dogs knew.

Dale and Fiona reckoned this entire process lasted better than an hour, during which time two huge hyenas, probably part of the bunch that had been breaking into the kitchen, waded from our side of the bank and stood watching the wild dogs with no little interest. But they were afraid to come too close. Hyenas, unless they are in a very big pack indeed, do not fool around with wild dogs on kills. Certainly, two of them would never take on a crowd that big. The hyenas hung around for some time and, when the wild

Camp waiters in full regalia.

dogs eventually pushed off, they loped onto the sandbar, sniffed what was left, and then melted back into the bush from which they had come.

Now you see it, now you don't. African ecology on its most basic level. . . .

One day, Lew treated us all to a meandering drive along the Mupamadzi, which I was anxious to see more of. It was low, very low, but when we turned a bend in the river where a huge slab of rock stretched well out into the water, we came upon an exhilarating sight: there, in the hundreds, was the largest herd of hippo I have ever seen, splashing, rolling and wallowing, bumping and grunting in the early morning sunlight, some of the animals yawning, their awesome tusks a reminder that the hippo is lethal.

We loved it. I wandered off to have a closer look as more and more hippo

The most incredible herd of hippos the author has ever seen; on the Mupamadzi River.

Author with hippo herd.

streamed out of the long grass on the far side to join their pals, until, in many places, they were piled up three deep. With the river so narrow at that point, they had no other place to go. I had my .375 over my shoulder, the magazine loaded with solids. Except for a few false charges, however, they just milled around. I knew I was safe, since there hasn't been a hippo born that can cover twenty yards of flat rock and grab me, fast as they are. The fact that the trackers were throwing rocks at a spot near the hippos probably didn't much help their collective temperament, but I was hardly worried—at least I could see.

We drove off with great reluctance after a couple of hours, while I wondered if I'd ever see such a sight again. That was an awful lot of protein in a meat-poor, people-packed Africa. . . .

But then, I thought of the elephants. *What* elephants? In the entire time we had been there, we had only seen the spoor of a single young female. And bones. Lots of them, lying bleached in the Zambian sun, including the skulls of baby elephants and the remains of half-grown brothers and sisters. The poachers have had a field day in the Luangwa Valley, where Bob Langeveld and I once worked flat-out to help thin the huge herds of elephant to prevent further damage to the countryside. Today, they are history. I lament their passing. A part of the Luangwa's soul has gone with the demise of its elephant herds. Wally had a very odd expression in his eyes, and none of us could talk as we rode passed a solitary skull on our way back to camp. The late Captain Chauncey Hugh Stigand said it all: "It is not compatible for elephant and civilisation and progress to live alongside each other."

Blue waxbills, Nyasa lovebirds, firefinches, the ubiquitous doves, and Grey loeries with their distinctive call brightened up the camp surroundings. I was feeling so well, so alive, and it seemed an odd time for Lew and I to start swapping stories about hunting superstitions and death, but he nevertheless told me of an incident that really makes one think.

A client who drops dead on safari is a

nightmare I have been spared. Not so Lew. But let me quote him as he tells this tale with the aplomb of an accomplished *raconteur*:

"This was in the early sixties, and we were hunting one morning in what was then Rhodesia when the guys up back said, 'Hey, there're some kudu over there!'

"The clients weren't very good shots and not exactly what you would call agile, so I hopped off myself and made a stalk. If there was anything there, I reasoned, I would then call whatever client's turn it was to shoot. I was halfway there when they shouted to me from the back of the vehicle, 'Hey, we can see them. They're standing over on the ridge.'

"There were between five and seven kudu, all standing rigid on the ridge, all bulls. I shouted to the clients that I just couldn't see the kudu from where I was. 'Glass them and pick out the biggest one and take him, if you think he's big enough,' I said.

"One of the guys did, and the thing went down, stone dead.

"Now, I used to have a nearly completely white kudu which I had watched for several years. It was a very strange animal as the stripes were reversed; the body was white and the stripes were, in fact, brown. Never saw one like it. It wasn't an albino, since it didn't have red eyes, just some sort of genetic sport.

"But I was as mad as hell that this man had killed it, since it wouldn't have reached real trophy size for another couple of years. Well, they were all full of apologies and such, but one of the guys, who was a general in the United Nations forces in the Congo at the time, was very concerned and said to me, 'This is an ill omen.'

"Now that's rather an odd turn of phrase, a bit medieval, if you ask me. I asked the general what he meant. He said, 'Well, surely you know that on the day that Frederick the Great was assassinated, he had killed a white stag?'

"I admitted I didn't know this. Just shows what hunting will do for you.

"But I was irritated as hell by this whole thing as we loaded the kudu onto the vehicle. It even had a white streak right up its horns and, because it was so recognizable, it enabled me to follow kudu bull movements all year long. Man, I was some kind of cross.

"The general kept mentioning that it was a 'terribly ill omen' to have killed this animal; in fact, he brought it up to me on several occasions, and this spooked me, although I'm not the spooky type."

The safari party finished their day and sacked in. The clients had a rather objectionable habit of calling Lew very, very early in the morning. But, when he went over to their area, they were never ready to leave.

One of the extremely curious aspects of this whole affair occurred that evening when the man who had shot the white kudu suddenly said, "Look, if anything happens to me, my wife must just go straight along to the bank."

"Well," continued Lew, "the next morning, they called me as usual, very early. I decided to hell with it. But I got up and drank some coffee, when suddenly the guy staying with me, an associate in the Vic Falls taxidermy business, said, after my men had called me several times, 'Lew, you'd better come over. We've got a definite problem here.'

"Well, one of the clients was dead. The one who had shot the kudu. Of course, the general said, 'I told you it was an ill omen!'

"I didn't have time for that routine, so we called the wife in Austria, after the devil's own time of complications. We advised her what had happened and that we would be back in touch in a few hours when we could make arrangements for the body.

"The major problem was that the late gentleman, who had died of a stroke, was Jewish, but nobody knew if he was orthodox or reform. This didn't help much solve matters concerning the funeral, as burial customs differ and we didn't want to offend anyone."

Right. There was Lew with a body in the bush on a very hot day. The corpse

Jawbone of a poached juvenile elephant.

was not local; there were no refrigeration facilities. What to do?

"The widow wanted us to ship the body back, but we were blocked right down the line because of 'health restrictions.' In the end, the diplomatic corps sorted out the mess; otherwise I just don't know what the hell we would have done. It was a terrible experience.

"Anyway, as a result of this incident, I missed a safari with a competing company for whom I occasionally worked. I'll always remember that general's words about an 'ill omen.' It sure was for me."

Nobody can spend any length of time in a place like the Luangwa Valley without talking about the croc activity. When Lew and I broached the subject, I asked Lew if he had had anything much in the way of croc incidents. "Hell, yes," was his reply.

"It's not that common to hear of a white person being chomped by crocs, but just last year a visitor to Chinzambo Lodge went to swim in the river, even though he had been warned not to. He got grabbed. And died.

"But it didn't end there. The game scouts went in and tried to recover the body for form's sake. Sure as hell, the croc grabbed one of the scouts. My information—secondhand—is that the croc was killed and, when it was opened up, remains of both the white visitor and the black game guard were found. I thought that was taking integration a bit too far!"

Crocs are extremely active and kill one mighty towering heap of people, if you take the time to do the adding up. My files bulge with incidents in various parts of Africa from the last three or four years *alone*. As I have written before, a successful man-eating croc, lion, or leopard rarely gets into the press because their deeds leave little evidence, and because the areas in which such things occur do not usually have an abundance of telephones and telex machines to let the world know what is going on at any given moment.

Think about it! For every attack you hear about, dozens or perhaps scores never hit the papers. This can give the false idea that croc activity is spasmodic or that they are not usually interested in people. Consider the following Reuters report of July 15, 1982, datelined Lusaka, Zambia:

Crocodiles eat an average of thirty people a month around a remote Zambian lake, the *Zambian Daily Mail* reported yesterday.

It quoted a village councillor as saying that the hungry reptiles had become so fierce that the Kapinda villagers had curtailed their fishing activities on the shore of Lake Mweru Wantipa, near Zambia's northern border with Zaire.

A shortage of fish in the lake had sent crocodiles ranging up to 500 meters (550 yards) from the water in search of human prey.

The following item gives you an idea of how severe things are—and these figures are direct from the Zambian Information Service as reported in the *Natal Mercury* on January 4, 1984, through Sapa–Reuter:

CROCS KILL 25 SCHOOLCHILDREN: LUSAKA—Crocodiles have killed 25 pupils in the past five years at one primary school in western Zambia, according to the Zambian Information Service (ZIS).

The figure was made public yesterday by the government-owned ZIS on the installation of a water pump at the school, in Senanga District, some 550 kilometers west of Lusaka. The pump is intended to discourage pupils from drinking from the nearby crocodile-infested Kalongola River.

Lord above, but you would think even children would figure out that drinking from the Kalongola wasn't especially conducive to growing up. Apparently not. "Never me," seems to be the credo, whether child or adult. Well, facts are that at least twenty-five people were wrong . . . and dead.

The article continues:

Crocodiles are common to most of Zambia's rivers and lakes, but there are no dependable estimates of how many lives they claim each year. Last year the hungry reptiles were reported to be taking an average of thirty people a month from the shores of Lake Mweru in northern Luapula Province. In another region, angry villagers beat up their traditional ruler and vandalized his palace after accusing him of not doing enough to combat the menace.

Obviously, crocs are still a major factor in Africa, despite the absolute trash you will hear on American and British television. They *do* eat people with a frequency that I imagine we hardly suspect. This doesn't mean they should be obliterated. They should simply be recognized and respected for what they are; carnivores of quite ubiquitous tastes —as Gordon Cundill would put it.

It was Mike Nicol, an authority on such matters, who said on March 3, 1983, in the *Pretoria News:* "Statistics show that crocodiles are as much a hazard in the lives of blacks living in the wilder, east-

ern regions of South Africa as they were 100 years ago." And *that* is a generally more developed area than the remote parts of Zambia we have been considering.

At this point, I must relate the Tale of the BSA. That's the Big Shot Author. Me.

Lew, who usually sacks fairly early and rises even earlier, was chuckling like mad the next morning when he greeted me as "the BSA."

"Well," I observed, "you're not mistaking me for the Birmingham Small Arms, so what's the story?"

Restraining a guffaw, he said, "I just got off the SSB [single side-band radio] and was talking with one of our younger hunters. He observed that I had the 'big-shot author' aboard. 'Yeah,' I said. 'He's right here. Want to speak with him?' "

Lew said you could hear his epiglottis bouncing as he gave that some thought. "No, no, just wanted to know if he was having a good safari."

Lew's like a bloody bulldog. "Sure you don't want to speak with him?"

"Nah, it's okay. Don't want to bother him."

"Oh, well," said Lew, "I would have called him back but he's just off on his ten-mile run and his calisthenics."

"Shame," quoth the other end of the wire. "I would have enjoyed a chat."

"Way it goes," said Lew. "Try about

four tomorrow morning and you just might catch him."

Not mighty likely.

Game at night can be very dangerous. Of course, this is true even in broad daylight. One must be damned careful about rounding a sharp turn in the bush for fear of instantly being whipped up in a bunch of, say, jumbo. At night, things are much more dangerous because animals, confused by lights, lose their sense of direction and will happily share your vehicle with you. In fact, in April of 1985, a Johannesburg man was killed outright in Zimbabwe by a large kudu bull that literally leapt from an embankment on the side of the road onto the car in which he and another three people were traveling.

Joe Joubert clearly demonstrated what can go wrong on a lion hunt, and I had a frightening experience with a bull buffalo in Botswana who had collected a hole from my client and decided he didn't like the color of the vehicle, which was really quite a distance from where he had shot him. We had decided to go back for some water when the buff boiled out of the bush and charged the hunting car, giving it a hell of a thump before taking the passenger seat. I exited, stage right, frolicking. It had been close.

Cundill told me a great story of a wounded lion that preferred to ride rather than walk, and a venerable gun

bearer who went some hundreds of yards hanging onto the springs under the vehicle before matters could be resolved.

But it was Lew who told us of a highly tragic incident involving a kudu that had become disoriented by car lights, resulting in a terrible situation in which a man was accused of murder. Lew preferred not to be specific about names or places, but it is an authentic story.

"A friend of mine had some people visiting him. Just prior to this, he had lost his wife. They had been driving along and, all of a sudden, she stopped talking to him. She was dead. Heart. Now, my pal was obviously going through quite a traumatic time, and these people called to see how he was and tried to cheer him up a bit. They all became a bit mellow after a few drinks, but his son and the son of his visitors were just out of the army and were becoming quite boisterous, using bad language and such."

So, Lew continued, one of the guests figured he'd cool things down by taking the youngsters for a night drive; not an armed "hunting" trip, but just a short trip as a sort of pressure valve to distract them.

"The guest and the two boys went for a drive and came out at the bottom end of the game farm where my friend lived. They were coming down the main road, which had a high fence on either side of it. As they were driving along, they saw a kudu that had somehow gotten through the fence and was coming towards the car. The guest realized that the kudu bull was a bit bewildered by the lights, so he cut to the dims, the parking lights, then said to the two young men, 'Hey, this thing is coming right for us. Better get your heads down!'

"It was an open vehicle with no top, doors, or windscreen. Well, they all ducked down, more or less laying their heads on the dash, and they waited for this kudu to go by in case it kicked or whatever."

Whatever. An eternal "whatever."

"Anyway, the kudu just jumped over and, as far as he knew, ran off. The driver saw that the thing had jumped the car . . . but the two youngsters were still lying down over the dashboard. He reached over and shook the nearest and said, 'Okay, he's gone. Let's get going.'"

Nothing. He was stone dead.

"So, the driver reached over and grabbed the other chap sitting on the far side. He was also dead. The kudu had somehow hit them both: broken their necks."

According to Lew, the driver then lost his cool, jumped out of the car, and ran screaming down the road to the gate of the property where the house was, only a few hundred yards away. When he got into the house, he broke down.

"We, of course, were all friends. The widower, on hearing the story, immediately accused the guest of having murdered the boys and was on the point of shooting the poor guy.

"Well, we saw to it that that didn't happen, but the situation was mighty dicey. We got on the phone and called the police over from the nearest town. As they were coming over to us, they noticed a truck which must have aroused some sort of suspicion. They stopped to have a look at it and found a dead kudu in the back! Thank God!

"The people in it said they had simply found the kudu lying in the road dead, 'just down there.' They took the police back to the spot and showed them exactly where they had found the animal. It was about a hundred yards from where the accident had happened.

"In the meantime, the widower had been taken back to where the driver more or less remembered the incident as having taken place. When no sign of a kudu could be found, my pal started up again and accused the guest of lying and murder. Just then the police showed up, with the other vehicle containing the dead kudu following close behind. Statements were taken and the poor guy was at last exonerated on the spot of murder."

As Lew so aptly put it: "People just don't realize how dangerous it is to hang around animals with vehicles and bright lights at night."

The tremendous versatility of a hunting vehicle.

• • •

It was August 2, 1985, two days to go before the end of our Luangwa safari, and a fine, clear day. We had a lot to do.

I was anxious to get some good hyena shots, since at the time the bloody things were practically in your mustache as you gave it a morning trim. They were everywhere, hovering around the loos, near or in the kitchen, practically standing in line to vote with you. So, I shot a waterbuck for bait while Lew organized the building of a superb blind quite near camp where we could sneak in and (hopefully) get some hyena action on the sizeable buck, which would be winched up into a sturdy *mopane* tree.

Paul positioned his cameras, and we indeed had a truly outstanding evening as we sat in utter silence in that blind, waiting and watching. There were lion about. We could hear them. Then the hyenas

came; first a bold one to case the joint and see what was on the menu, then the gang. They skulked out of the black shadows with that loping gait of theirs and began their tipsy chuckling and chattering as they attacked the waterbuck. They snatched and clawed, actually swinging on the carcass at times, before tearing off chunks of meat and some bone. One of the hyenas sat not five feet from the grass walls of the blind, noisily slavering over his dinner, his vicelike jaws crunching into bone, before he loped back to the bait and scrapped with the others to get more. It really was a thrilling experience, especially when some of the hyenas froze in their activities, turned, and stared for what seemed like an eternity at our blind. The bright moon picked out these animals and their malevolent stares. I couldn't help but think of the superstition so prevalent among black Africans that holds the hyena as the familiar of evil spirits, an omen of misfortune.

Curiously, for most of this unusual performance, Paul's flash hardly bothered the animals, so involved were they in eating and scrapping, like a litter of 150-pound puppies with teeth. But you will see no hyena shots in this book. *Aziko mapirri. Nikis.* No pictures, just a series of pitch-black, raven-winged, stygian shots that show what the African night looks like from the inside. Technical foul-up. Incorrect processing. A couple of thousand bucks of effort and licenses down the drain. Naturally, if we'd set up in the kitchen, we'd have won every wildlife photography award extant. Africa strikes again.

The sun was setting on this, our last day on the Mupamadzi. The river looked like molten lead from the dying sun and the night chill sent us for our jackets and then back to the fire and drinks. Lew came across and asked us to come along for a short drive.

Just east of the camp site, a sizeable area was being cleared for a new airstrip that would make communication with the outside world much easier for safari clients. All around us, smoldering fires were doing their work as the last of unwanted scrub and undergrowth was burned away. Like the sound of hyenas, the smell of grass fires means Africa for me. I inhaled the night. It was magic.

Now, the reason why this little excursion took on a new significance for me lies in something Lew and Dale told me months later when they came to my home for a visit before flying back to the States at the end of the safari season.

After we'd left for Lusaka, Wally Johnson had suggested to the Gameses that the new airstrip be given a fitting name. "Why not call it Capstick Airport?" he said.

They did.

. . .

It was time to leave, and Hunters Africa had gone to no little trouble to arrange transport by charter aircraft with Hilton Hudson, a pilot who also had a fishing industry on Lake Tanganyika to the northeast. Things were all arranged by SSB radio, and we duly set out quite early to make the Waka-Waka airstrip in time for our 11:00 A.M. departure.

As we pulled out of camp, having said good-bye to all the members of the staff and thanking them with well-earned tips for their first-rate service throughout, I knew that something of my calloused soul had been revived in the valley. And that I'd be back again.

On the way to the Luangwa River, we passed a strange little graveyard by the side of the bush track. Each grave had a stout stick-cum-pole that bore an old cooking utensil on top. Apparently, the pots were there to ward off evil spirits. I wondered who lay buried there, and the thought sent a strange mixture of chill and pathos through me. No grave had a name and the area was a mass of wild undergrowth. Was Silent there? It was his home area. I'll never know.

As we neared the confluence of the Munyamadzi, where I used to have my camp, I suddenly recognized a piece of bush that I had excellent reason to remember well. It was the same spot where I had killed a buffalo with a spear, a feat filmed by George Lenher of New York, and it was the same place where he, in turn, had killed his record-book leopard. Funny. The surroundings had hardly changed in all those years.

Naturally, I was all for piling off but for two items: first, we were starting to run a little late and still had a long way to go after crossing the Luangwa and, second, I couldn't get off the Toyota! There, directly where I would have jumped or climbed down, was a puff adder, sunning itself. I cursed the situation from the Muchingas to the Missouri, but there it was; Africa's most deadly snake, if statistics can be trusted.

Had we had the time, I would have taken off the windscreen of the Toyota and used it as a shield to get some really good shots of the snake striking the glass. But all we did was take a couple of desultory shots and leave him to develop his tan.

Actually, I had seen more snakes on this series of safaris than in entire years in the African bush. There was the mamba that had swum the Linyanti at King's Pool in Botswana when we were there; this chap; and, back at Mupamadzi Camp, another. Wally had ordered some tea one morning and, as Godfrey brought out the tray for him and Fiona, there was a sudden shriek and a clatter of falling crockery: *"Nyoka!"* shouted Godfrey, pointing under my chair. "Snake!"

There's always the chance . . . if a person had stepped out of the cab as we stopped to look at a thicket where I once speared a buffalo, he would have trodden precisely on this nicely proportioned puff adder.

Hell, I never even saw the fool thing, even though it must have gone right through my legs and under the seat as it streaked to the dense cover at the river's edge. Nobody had time to positively identify it, but at the time we felt that its speed and the marks it left in the dust suggested a mamba.

Now, Zambia is known for a most unusual and profoundly effective remedy for snakebite. Dale, in fact, showed it to us. The blacks in that part of Africa usually keep a piece of special black stone handy for snakebite, boils, stings, abscesses, and various other painful and sometimes fatal conditions. This stone is found at a place called Serenje, northeast of Lusaka, on the Great North Road.

Sunset over the Mupamadzi.

When placed over a bite, boil, or whatever, it has tremendously effective drawing properties. After use, the stone is washed, placed in milk overnight, washed again in the morning, and kept ready for further emergencies. Missionaries in Zambia use it, other white residents use it, and my old pal, Stuart Campbell —who is one of the last old northern Rhodesian/Zambian hands, with a lifetime of experience in remote African places—assures me this black stone the Zambians carry is no rural fairy story but cold fact, tried and tested.

We made the briefest of stops at Andre de Kock's camp at Nyampala and then went straight down to the pontoon to cross the Luangwa. It was now getting a bit late. An oil-and-petrol-drum affair, the pontoon was hauled by hand across the river by cable and the muscle power of the local staff. There was a slight problem, however, proving that Murphy was alive and well and living in the Luangwa. The pontoon would not budge because of a sandbar that had built up overnight. But Andre organized a team that eventually got us to the far side of the river, and once again we were driving as fast as conditions allowed in order to get to Waka-Waka to meet Hilton and our charter out. . . . No Hilton Hudson at the airport.

No sign of Hilton Hudson.

At last, the tiny whine of a single-engine aircraft pussyfooted over the horizon like the sound of a mosquito. It was, indeed, Hilton, with Hilton, Jr., in tow, on his way back to school in South Africa. Hilton, Sr., made a lovely landing, taxied up to the *mpahle,* neatly stacked with luggage ready for loading, and shut down the engine.

As we spent the next hour or two discussing, he shouldn't have done that.

Poor Hilton had battled that day to find aviation fuel in fuel-starved Zambia with its ravaged economy. There being hardly any foreign exchange—which was reflected in the price and availability

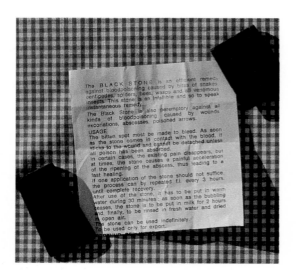

The "Black Stone." Believed by many to be a snake cure, it does have unusual drawing properties. Many professional hunters use it rather than a snakebite kit.

The pontoon at Nyampala, with our vehicle.

of gasoline, avgas, diesel, kerosene, and whatever—Hilton had had to traipse all the way up to Lake Tanganyika to try to fill the aircraft. That is not a trip to the local gas station, I can assure you.

We got the plane loaded, with Hilton at the wheel, Paul playing co-pilot, and Fiona and I in the middle back seats, together with Hilton, Jr. Everything was set; we had barely enough time to reach Lusaka for the connecting SAA flight to Johannesburg.

All went fine—except that the engine wouldn't start, and wouldn't start for nearly an hour. I then learned some facts concerning aircraft maintenance in Zambia I wish I had not dug up. They

were sufficient to send my stomach through my shoetops. . . .

We fooled around for a while, my anxiety increasing by the minute at the mere thought of spending another night in Lusaka at the Pamodzi with no foreign exchange on me. Finally, Lew hooked up a jumper cable from his Toyota to the aircraft and, after great reluctance, reticence, and what seemed internal chaos, the engine started. In a few minutes we were airborne without further incident.

We waved good-bye to Lew, Dale, Wally, and the crew, and banked neatly away from Waka-Waka.

After roughly thirty minutes, the engine quit. The single, sole engine quit.

I have, as the mossbacks say, "gone in" twice, once in Nicaragua and once in Africa. In neither case did we burn, although in the Nicaraguan incident at the edge of Lake Nicaragua, near San Carlos, both wings were torn off and everything drenched in aviation fuel. It was enough to make you quit smoking.

We had been whipping along toward Lusaka, everybody relaxed except Fiona (she loathes light aircraft), when the engine decided it had had enough and would go on an extended vacation over some of the most isolated, desolate-looking countryside you can imagine. At one point, Paul had even noticed a suspicious-looking gauge on the dashboard and brought it to Hilton's attention. He was told not to worry, since no matter what the gauge read, there was always some residual fuel. Hell, the artificial horizon didn't even work, Hilton added.

No. No. No.

It quit, essentially, because it had no avgas. It had no avgas because Hilton had forgotten to switch from the one wing tank to the other. The aircraft "windmilled," and all I could think was that we were all at the end of the long, long trail a-winding.

But then Hilton switched tanks and got the engine—the only one we had—running again. The problem was getting Fiona going again. She absolutely freaked out, and I had to make her take two

The "waiting lounge" at Waka-Waka Airport; author sitting with tracker, waiting for flight to arrive.

powerful tranquillizers. Just as well, for our problems were only beginning.

None of us was amused at Hilton's half-hearted remark: "Hope I didn't scare you folks too much. Just forgot to switch tanks." We are unamused to this day. Hell, we had battled forever to start the bloody thing on the *ground,* with a Toyota pumping current. So what were the odds of restarting it in the air? All I know is that it would have been the Burma March all over again if we'd survived a crash.

As we came into line with the runway at Lusaka, there, banking off to the right was SAA, on its way back to Johannesburg. Our aircraft going home. So what now?

Well, Hilton did us proud. He, on behalf of Hunters Africa, saw to the hotel bookings and sorted out any potential problems before they even arose. I, by now like a well-trained Pavlov canine, had learned to be a good boy, and all the guns and cameras were placed in the hotel strongroom. After a very satisfactory meal, we sacked. Exhausted.

In the meantime, Hunters Africa saw to our rebookings on an SAA flight the next day, as well as a transfer to the airport. In other words, they saved our bacon, as any jacked-up safari company will for its clients.

We checked out the next morning and were fetched spot on time by Des Caine, who held our collective hands until we boarded the flight south. But "Murphy" doesn't just lurk in the Luangwa. He lurks in Lusaka, too. Just before we cleared Customs, I decided to check on all my papers, especially my gun permits.

Surprise. No gun permits. Oh, dear Mother McCree. . . .

I stripped the black leather document folder in which I carry—or thought I did —all my important papers. I had everything from my dental records in 1948 to a couple of used marriage licenses. Gun permits for the Republic of Zambia? No.

We were in the upstairs bar—where else—when Fiona suggested I look in my wallet. Tough luck, Murphy, but nice try. They were there.

We went through Customs and Immigration without a hitch, although they insisted on body-searching me. That kwacha currency neurosis again; and all for a currency with no value at all outside Zambia and often not much good inside the country because of the chronic lack of consumer goods of all kinds—from soap powder to new vehicles. Hell, I was carrying an American passport and firearms receipts. But that impressed nobody.

We took leave of Des Caine and stepped into the departure lounge. A couple of hours later, we were home.

Shortly afterward, as we were later told, Hilton Hudson flew down again, this time with Dale and Wally aboard. He exhibited some rather remarkable cool when his compass went on the blink because of cast-iron fittings of some sort or another in the nose cargo hold. He eventually found the right airport and landed. The aircraft had been brought south for comprehensive servicing unavailable elsewhere. I bet the air mechanics had a ball. I'd like to know what the final bill was.

Safari is not all smooth, problem-free fun. You experience annoyance; get scared; know bouts of chronic fatigue; have days of pure frustration and disappointment; and sometimes ache for the right results right away. But there is no other experience I would rather have had than that jaunt back to the valley, where I could share such special memories with Fiona and the others in the very region from which they sprang.

The author in long grass, with Lew Games.

PART THREE

King's Pool and Etsatsa

By the end of the Zambian trip, the safaris had been plagued with everything but rains of blood and frogs.

To start off, I had been carefully coiffed to look like whatever somebody's idea of a professional hunter is supposed to look like. That was before Fiona and I accepted an invitation to go hot-air ballooning with some friends who live near Johannesburg and who actually own one of the flying machines. They thought a brief "balloon safari" would be fun.

In a fit of applied idiocy, we accepted, and heard the alarm go off at three on a Sunday morning, one week before the first safari to Botswana. We set out for the open country near the Magaliesberg hills.

"Right," said my pal, "just hold that gap open so I can pour in the fire"—propane, as I recall, in pressurized containers—"and we'll get this into the air."

Like a dope, I did.

My pal flicked one of these little spark-makers, and there was the goddamndest rush of dragon's breath you ever heard. The flash ignited the front of my hair as well as taking some of the same eyebrow and lash that broke up Paul in the incident at the leopard blind in Zambia. I looked like a badly shaven Hari Krishna type, but we finally got my head extinguished and, smelling like crackling pork, were off.

Way off, in my opinion. With all due respect to my friends, if there is a duller sport with more impossible hours, I have not yet been a participant in it. Perhaps full-body contact monopoly.

Well, after that experience, I wore my hat most of the time in Botswana and Zambia, except when called upon in suitably dull firelight to say something profound. I find this difficult enough *with* hair, but highly tricky after having been seared like a plucked chicken. (I don't have that much hair to work with anyway, and when they start deleting the bloody front, that becomes a bit too much.) Both my wife and I *greatly* appreciated the hospitality and considerable trouble gone to for that short-lived balloon safari, but it is the last time I'll ever get caught "holding the bag."

Gordon came by and spent a day or two with us on our return from Zambia and was most interested to hear how things had gone. I told him the leopard story, and, as a pro, he understood. Actually, had that cat fallen as flat as two-month-old soda water, where would the story have been? Although I lost the gallant beast to the lion, it *did* make the tale. Okay, nobody had to strangle him and he never got around to eating anybody, but we didn't know that at the time.

In any case, the story was "Cundillized" by Gordon, who stated that "in the fullness of time," we would put the whole show together. Just what did I need?

"Another crack at some hyenas and some fishing," said I, "to completely round the thing off."

"Just so," said Gordon; the wand was waved and I was booking air tickets through his office.

He called a couple of days later, advising us that we would start off back at King's Pool on the Linyanti River to try to fill in with hyenas and, if we got lucky, a leopard for the lens. Then, Gordon continued, down to the island of Etsatsa at the mouth of the Okavango Delta, where the main channel meets the

The chef cooking at King's Pool, on the Linyanti.

swamp of the Okavango. Spot on, thought I; should cover it completely.

Unfortunately, a serious incident occurred the night before we were to fly out for the final safari. It was a Saturday night, September 14, and there was an unusually cold snap. I complained to Fiona of icy feet, and she duly hied herself out of bed, heated a kettle of water to boiling point, and filled a rubberized hot-water bottle that had a fuzzy-wuzzy covering.

I am not the most gentle of sleepers and somehow, during my thrashing, I contrived to wedge my foot between the cloth cover and the hot container itself. At some unknown hour, I dreamed I was burning. Sure as hell, I was!

I honestly don't know what happened, but that bottle scalded me badly, and I've seen bad scalds before. Napalm it was not, but it burned every layer of my right foot, right down to bare meat, on the inside "corner" of my foot where the big toe meets the beginning of the first bone of the metatarsal arch. I promise you, bub, it hurt!

By noon the next day, the fifteenth—the day I was to go on safari—the bloody thing looked like a softball. Actually, it was as big around as two silver dollars and scared the hell out of me because I realized it was getting on in the season and the bacteria in the bush were starting to do whatever they do to make other bacteria. Tetanus wasn't really my worry, since I'd recently had thirty dollars' worth of booster in New York City. My problem was any number of septicemic surprises Africa has up its sleeve for open wounds like the virtual landing field for trouble on my foot. There is also a very popular local item called blood poisoning that is all the rage in rural Africa and which I dreaded.

But the safari had to be done and I did it, pain or no pain, risk or none. Perhaps you wouldn't mind pounding my chest a bit; I'm getting sore knuckles. I'm sure you understand: honor, duty, Queen, and, of course, royalties. No safari, no pay. Get thee hence. It doesn't matter if it hurts. Do it!

Well, I *did* my best.

I tried to do my best about the burn, which was bad enough to have one hospitalized at a glance by a physician. Right. What really mattered? I figured it in the following manner:

1. Keep it clean.

2. Use antiseptic until it leaked out of my ears.

3. Stay the hell off my feet or I'd aggravate the problem, which was already serious.

4. Keep it dry and the dressing fresh.

5. As a last resort, shoot myself before going to a rural African hospital. (That was my theory.) Oh, and always be sure to save a cartridge.

Paul Kimble was not available for the trip, but I was most fortunate to get my grubbies at short notice on Dick van Niekerk, a good pal who is a fine photographer and possibly an even better shot. Dick and I made a deal, and Paul could not have been more cooperative, which I shall eternally appreciate. It had been some time since Dick had photographed in the bush and his personal equipment was not really suited to the job. Paul supplied the Contax and the Yashica equipment without the slightest hesitation. (And I shall not let the great kindness of Fuji Film slide by the board. They were magnificent in their cooperation, which is hereby acknowledged.)

But had Dick, good friend though he is, had any idea of what he was about to go through, I rather doubt he would have accepted the assignment.

I sure as hell wouldn't have. . . .

Our problems started at Maun Airport, in Botswana, Maun being the headquarters of the safari industry in that country. It is a tiny place quite used to foreign hunters and heaven knows who coming through, and is composed mostly of main offices of the various safari firms (and, when I was there, the Ngamiland Trading Company. In my day, if you wanted to buy anything, either you bought it there or you went without). Today, I don't know.

There was also Riley's Hotel in which I actually spent a few honeymoon nights in the only bedroom that had a private bath. Ensconced behind what used to be a rusting Coca-Cola sign, announcing its presence to the discerning, visiting gourmet, Riley's was nearly the only accommodation in town. Ah, yes, then there was Crocodile Camp, owned by the Wilmots, a famous Botswana family. I cannot comment on Crocodile Camp as I have never been there but I did hear generally good reports on its facilities. My honeymoon at Riley's was highlighted by two inches of bat dung in the bathtub as well as less pleasant aspects. The marriage didn't work out, anyway. Maybe it was the bat guano.

Whatever the state of affairs used to be around 1970, it had not overly changed at the airport, at least. The officials were pleasant and, I am sure, helpful if called upon to be so. But I had fouled up and had to hand in my .375 and my 12-gauge shotgun to an airport official—let's call him Mr. Monare—who was highly courteous but well within his rights to confiscate my weapons. He handed me a receipt so that I could collect them when I passed through Maun again at the end of the safari.

You see, I had no valid license for them because my permits from the previous trip had expired. Now, Americans read dates differently from the way they are read in metric countries, and, as a result, I had let the damned things expire, despite all the work Hunters Africa had put into getting them for me in the first place. (For example, "9/12/85" is not September 12, 1985, but December 9, 1985.) Knowing the uselessness of argument from years of experience, I asked this Mr. Monare if he would kindly do me the favor of retaining the weapons for the ten or twelve days I would be in the bush and if he would place them in the airport safe under the good auspices of the Republic of Botswana. Of course, I knew he would do this anyway, and I figured that if I needed a rifle or shotgun, I could borrow one. I had no plans to shoot, but I don't like wandering around remote places unarmed. House rule, you understand.

The airport official was kind enough, and I realized that there was no chance of getting my guns into the country without the proper permits. I had to hand-count each round of ammo and was given a stamped customs receipt with the clear advice that when I left the country, I was to notify the officer on duty, show him the receipt, and the guns would be placed on the outgoing Air Botswana aircraft by the Botswana officials themselves. Well, it seemed reasonable to me and the man was very obliging.

Turned out, on my return, that Mr. Monare's replacement was not *quite* so accommodating. But I'm getting ahead of myself.

Fiona had not accompanied us on this last safari, as the single-engine-aircraft incident in Zambia had cured her of any lingering aeronautical curiousity.

We arrived after a couple of hours at the Linyanti airstrip, where a charming boyish-faced gentleman met us and announced that he was Steve Liversedge. Our destination was King's Pool, Gordon's personal camp, which we had briefly visited before. A most lovely spot, the camp lies on a fishhook of the Linyanti River and has its own resident pod of hippo and bream breaking the surface all over the place. (When the King of Sweden chooses it for his honeymoon, you can pretty well bet it's worth the trip.)

Although Steve looked young, he had held a full pro license for eighteen years,

so we knew we were not being shuffled off to the also-rans. (Liversedge is another of those very old Botswana names that are as much a part of the history of the country as the rivers are.) Steve, as we were also to find out, has a fairly sophisticated sawmill where he fills in his time when not hunting. I have a hunch he did this trip for Gordon as a personal favor, since his hunting talents are top-rate and the work he did for us couldn't have been better, especially considering that I could hardly walk. We arrived at King's Pool without incident and settled in nicely, Dick van Niekerk, Steve Liversedge, and myself. It was coming hard—or, better put, soft—on twilight. There was a slight ripple on the surface of the water like that of a well-aged but still young woman's cheek, the caress no less smooth.

The firelight had just taken over the sunset when, to my immense delight, ancient Karonda, Gordon's gun bearer, showed up at the campfire, squatted, and gave a respectful clap of his horny hands. Now that *was* pure magic as we suddenly had a chance to take fresh photographs of that classic face. And he was as delighted as a birthday party to see me. He, Gordon, Jehosephat, and Mack had all shared my lion with me. You don't just walk away from such an event, and old Karonda appreciated both this and my own delight at being with him again.

I carefully noted the time and saw that

Karonda, now over eighty.

This being September 1985, I was faintly alarmed. I had carried that bottle literally tens of thousands of miles, mainly as insurance against a leopard or lion mauling. It would now just have to do. And it damned well did!

The object of the exercise at King's Pool, as mentioned earlier, was to obtain, or at least try to obtain, some good hyena night shots. I asked Dick to obtain bait for me, since the pain in my foot precluded my stalking. He killed a fine zebra with one shot from a borrowed 7mm Remington Magnum, and we hung the bait low and quite near a road—which was later to prove a mistake—and sat back to wait.

Photographing hyenas *should* be the easiest thing in the world. Man, did we battle, and without results. The hang-up was a big leopard who came in and started feeding on the bait (baiting for shooting purposes being illegal in Botswana). Actually, *mapirri* were all over the place in addition to the leopard, and we had an excellent blind at the top of a termite heap. The hyenas could actually be seen ghosting between the *mopanes,* and the leopard was clearly heard, if not spotted (no double entendre intended). But could we get one critter into camera range over three nights? Not bloody likely. We did get some good bird and character shots, however.

So it sometimes goes.

at 6:40 P.M., one could comfortably skyline and take a leopard. The hippos were grumbling, grunting, and honking but showed no sign of launching an amphibious invasion, so I leaned the borrowed .375 against the chair.

I could hardly feel even my fingers for all the aspirin I had taken for my foot, which had been rebandaged with a layer of Neosporin powder. I cheerfully noticed that it had expired in May of 1982.

In any case, we did have the chance to chat over the fire with Steve, who, in reopening my huge blister with his hunting knife, came so close to taking my leg along with it that I eventually had to decline with thanks. He did, however, have one hell of an interesting story about a leopard down near his sawmill at Pandamatenga, one that bears retelling.

"One afternoon, a few months ago," he began, "my partner and I were sitting about and a couple of locals who worked for me came out of the bush, one of them obviously badly mauled and bleeding heavily. He had been a skinner for me during the safari season and was called Mfana. We had a safari camp about fourteen miles from the sawmill, and he said he'd been mauled while wandering around near the camp.

"Riland Wallace, my partner in the sawmill, and I had had a couple of drinks, the sun being well over the yardarm. Well, we both knew this old chap as a rogue and a poacher, and we were both sure that he'd had this thing trapped or snared and that he'd probably tried to kill the animal with an ax. So we took him to hospital at Kasane and thought little more of it until the next morning, as I was starting a safari there.

"I decided to take my safari gear into that camp just to be ready before the clients arrived. When I got there, all the men in camp said, 'Hey, come and see what this leopard has done!' They were all excited, so I wandered over to old Mfana's hut, you see, and it was pointed out to me where this leopard had gotten in. I don't think there was any doubt that this particular leopard was a man-eater, and that it was most obviously after this guy, Mfana. He had been mauled near a little pan near camp and had run back into camp, leaving a blood trail. The leopard had followed it, torn open the roof of the hut, and come in after Mfana. Now, if that's not man-eating, what is?

"Fortunately, he was in the hospital and not at home when the leopard followed up the blood spoor and tore open the hut, thinking the man was there."

I asked Steve how badly the skinner had been hurt. Although at first he'd thought the man's injuries minor, he recalled that he had been badly scratched, had lost a lot of blood, and had been badly bitten in the head, arms, and legs. "Actually," said Steve on reflection, "he had been badly mauled. He would have died without treatment.

"Now, Riland, my partner, got curious and, this being several hours after the event, went to Mfana's hut and tried the latch. One of my men, the waiter in the camp, in fact, took it upon himself to spread the reeds of the walls with his fingers and see what was going on inside.

" 'Eeeh, *Morena,* I can see something inside,' said the waiter.

"So, we all backed off to my Toyota, where I had a shotgun and a four-fifty-eight, and we drove right up next to the hut.

"If there had been a leopard, I would have expected it to come right out of the hole at the top. We waited for about ten minutes and there wasn't a sound, not a whisper. There was absolutely nothing.

" 'Okay, Riland,' said I, climbing off the back of the truck, 'I'm going to have a look.' I climbed off and peered between the reeds. Did I get a start! On this guy's bed there was a blanket piled up, one of those with imitation leopard spots—very popular among those people. Anyway, that's what I made it out to be and, in fact, it was. But the light was very dim inside and I wasn't about to open that door.

"I had a think about it and decided to go in and see what was going on. So, I took the shotgun with American ammo —00 buckshot—and went in.

"I got a helluva scare, as right beside the bed was a huge male leopard looking me right in the eye, his tail twitching like a bullwhip. I just raised the double-barreled shotgun and shot it straight in the face."

"Surely you killed it straight off with a shot like that at such close range," I observed.

"Nope. The bloody thing went round and round the hut, but eventually I said 'the hell with this' and shot it with the four-fifty-eight, which did kill it on the spot."

Steve told us about other close calls, as well. A great friend of Wally Johnsons Senior and Junior, he was present when they had a Cape buffalo bull pinned down by a tractor. All three men took turns sawing away at the buffalo's throat with a Swiss Army knife to kill it, since nobody had a gun at the time. But then, that's another story for another book.

The virtues of the Swiss Army knife don't end there, however. In a recent incident, a game rancher was charged by one of his wildebeest bulls and he was forced to kill it with the knife. I wonder if he had to use the magnifying glass.

It was Wednesday, all of a sudden, and a difficult day it was to be, especially for Dick. For starters, we needed a Cape buff for camp meat for ourselves and the staff. I was feeling such pain and discomfort that I had to stay back in camp—only the second such day in seventeen years. I offered Dick the buff, and he was delighted at the opportunity. As things turned out, however, he would have been a hell of a lot happier if he had been the one who stayed behind in camp that day.

On the basis that if I couldn't walk, I couldn't hunt, Dick did the deed. It was decided he would take the buff from a small gang of bulls—if they could find one—and he and Steve went happily on their way. Miles later, somebody got thirsty and they all decided to have a douse of water from the canvas sacks hanging from various protuberances of the Toyota. Dick drank and got back into the rear of the vehicle. Suddenly, there was a screech of agony, and he instantly developed his personal version of the Botswana St. Vitus's dance.

He'd been nailed. But good.

Somehow, as Dick was dismounting from the car into the shallow grass, he had accumulated a passenger. It was a spider which type will never be known; he crushed it accidentally between his bare foot and his desert boots, but only after it had given him three very poisonous lightning-quick bites.

I never saw the remains of the spider,

Part of a motor-driven camera sequence in which the author killed two warthogs.

although both Dick and Steve described it as being silver-haired and about the size of a U.S. dime. The white-edged mandible marks on his ankle were clearly visible, however, and made it look as if he had been branded.

Oddly, Dick at first suffered no reaction, apart from a terrific, burning sensation. He and Steve therefore decided to go on and get their buff, which they did, Dick killing it with one shot—fine shot that he is—a 500-grain .458 solid. Eight hours elapsed before the real trouble with his ankle started. Dick became sick; very sick. Since we had no idea what sort of spider it might have been, Steve and I rather arbitrarily decided it was the "jumping spider," as nothing else seemed quite to fit. To this day, none of us has any idea what species nearly ruined our safari.

After all those years in the bush, I still have never been bitten by a spider or stung by a scorpion, or had a client nailed in that manner. Even Steve knew of nobody else who had been bitten or stung on safari.

In any case, van Niekerk is a slender, wiry man and I personally suspect that had he had a bit more meat on him, things might have gone easier with him, but that's conjecture. He was in trouble.

I didn't know what we should do. Some sort of antihistamine seemed in order and I dug out a tube of cream, which I applied liberally, gave Dick pain killers and checked his pulse and heart as well as his respiration. Figuring there was nothing more we could do but make him as comfortable as possible, we stashed him away for the night.

Nice situation. Two cripples.

While Dick was letting most of Africa chew on him, I was in camp, as mentioned earlier. And I was up early—at least early for me, about 6:00 A.M. I hung around the fire from first light, surprising the hell out of the chef, who wasn't used to seeing me up and about at that hour of the day.

Now, let me explain that there is a system in Africa in which everybody knows what everybody else is doing and even with which hand they're doing it. It is the modern miracle of bush telegraphy —the SSB (single side-band) radio, which all camps use to keep in touch with one another and with headquarters. Word was out that, as Lew put it via the unknown caller back in Zambia, the BSA— Big Shot Author—would be in camp that day, his wounds preventing him from strangling leopards and other assorted sporting fare. (I might mention, at this juncture, that if you hear the professional hunter offer the SSB signal "I read you strength seven," it means he has a client standing at his elbow and cannot speak in any way openly. Back off. Give him his privacy.)

Right. The BSA was in residence. (I shall not offer alternative possibilities for these initials, since I believe they will come naturally enough.) Still, the weird thing was that people started showing up, for God's sake, with books under their collective arms. People poured in! It was incredible! I could hardly hobble but had to show the hospitality of King's Pool in the professional's absence. Of course, at that point in the afternoon, I had no idea of Dick's mishap with the man-eating spider.

One of the more interesting groups to come through on that Wednesday was that of George Calef and his lovely wife, Brodie, from Canada. They were there doing elephant research in the Chobe/Linyanti area. New in the country, they had a black game officer with them to show them the local ropes. Actually, George was the chief biologist for Botswana. I, having been a cropping officer in Zambia, soon got into a lengthy discussion with the Calefs concerning elephants and their weird movements.

I mentioned to him the situation I had found in the Matetsi region of Zimbabwe, and my surprise at seeing the place alive with elephants. But George astonished me with his report on elephant densities and populations in the Chobe National Park over the past several years.

For example, in 1978 the elephant count in the Chobe park showed less than 7,500 jumbo there during the dry season. A very similar count was conducted in 1984, and it showed a population of better than 40,000 elephants!

Where the hell are they all coming from? I wondered, and that's the question George and Brodie are there to try to answer—an answer I'd certainly like to know. It is the personal hunch of the Calefs that the jumbo are eating out their habitat because of their incredibly destructive table manners, moving on sooner or later to literally greener pastures. In this case, they may be coming over from Hwange, in Zimbabwe, or they may be crossing from the Caprivi Strip, or even from the Congo. Nobody has ever figured out where the great gray ghosts wander, or why.

As both George and Brodie so well point out, there has never been a thorough population density or quantity study done of the African elephant over an extended area. Nobody has ever known how many elephants were located in a given area, a point well borne out by the old ivory hunters. Here, one thinks of W.D.M. "Karamojo" Bell's weeks of searching a virgin place like Uganda's Karamojo region at the turn of the century and finding no elephant, only to arrive at Mr. Elgon and see the plains black with good bulls! Such experiences

Sunset over the Linyanti from King's Pool.

lead me, as someone whose life has largely been entwined with elephant, to conclude that much of the damfoolery we are fed about preservation is based on Walt Disney and his seven dwarfs, who knew about as much of the real side of elephants as I do of underwater basket weaving. Most is bull; my reference, of course, being to the male of the species.

Today, there is a great debate simmering and sometimes breaking into open flame concerning the three theories about elephant movement. The first theory (as I've just mentioned) is simply that jumbos destroy their habitat and then move on to better feeding grounds—a not illogical theory, I might add. The second holds that the "elephant problem" of habitat damage stems from the encroachment by man and his domestic stock, who force the elephants to over-forage. Hey, when an elephant goes a-foraging, he doesn't kid around. He smashes whole trees the way we pick asparagus. The last —and equally reasonable—theory is a sort of cousin to the first, but one that deals with the reasons for such destructive behavior. Unless I misquote, I believe it is the theory most favored, at least by the Calefs. It goes something like this:

The modern savannah or bush elephant, *Loxodonta africana,* had its origins in the rain forests of central and northern Africa, now the Congo Basin/Sahara region. These early elephants developed into the two major types of elephant in Africa today, *Loxodonta* and *Cyclotis,* the forest elephant. Because of the lushness of the vegetation, the bush was able to cope with their depredations. As the savannah jumbo spread south—the forest jumbo sticking with the real jungle—the behavior of the bigger and more populous critter became too much for his territory to support.

As I explained earlier, I did not take an elephant on this series of safaris, although (perhaps ironically) I had originally come to Africa in the late sixties as a cropping officer for the Zambian government. My job then had been to thin out the herds that were absolutely ruining the Luangwa Valley Southern Reserve.

The last of the visitors to King's Pool had left, and I could see and hear Steve's vehicle in the distance, coming towards camp along the river's edge. Before long, I had learned of Dick's experience and taken a look at his ankle, which was now swollen and pretty damned nasty. I gave him aspirin and then rubbed the antihistamine creme on his ankle, but it did little good. It was now dead dark and too late to safely call in an aircraft without running the chance of a crack-up. But I hobbled around and did what I could, considering that the nearest drugstore was a couple of hundred miles away. Dick is about the most uncomplaining man I know, but I knew him well enough to discern that he was really hurting.

That night, we poured a couple of conversation-makers into Steve and got him to tell us some of his adventures with lions.

He was driving along late one afternoon, he told us, when he and his client saw a marvelous lion just standing there by the side of the road, looking at them. They drove on, then doubled back on foot to try and bag the beast.

Sure enough, the lion was still there. The client slugged the beast, but it didn't fall over. It was getting monumentally dark, and the blood spoor led right into a dense thicket. It always does. So Steve called up the hunting vehicle on the basis that a lion not taken in the purest sense still had to be shot.

They drove into the thicket *very* slowly. At last, one of the gun bearers spotted the lion, just lying there, staring at them. Steve had a rifle lying between him and the door. Suddenly, he heard one of the gun bearers screaming to the client to shoot! As Steve tells it:

"The client *did* shoot, but I had no chance, as the lion piled into the door of the Toyota. He put his back feet on the running board and actually bent it with his weight. He tried, by his claw marks, to come through the window and do me, besides leaving a mighty impressive collection of claw marks on the door and window.

"Actually, when the lion came around the windscreen, which it realized was open, I shot it in the nose and was splattered with lion blood. I looked around at the client and saw that he was white with shock as he thought I'd, in fact, been bitten. I think he won't forget that night or that lion hunt as long as he breathes."

Actually, we were stupid as can be to have built the leopard and hyena set-up as close to the road as we did, but we never expected the influx of visitors that materialized. Even though we explained to all the pros and visitors about the blind, and they all assured us that they would, every man-jack of them, leave King's Pool by the back way so as not to disturb the area, human nature being what it will always be, hardly a soul paid any attention to the agreement. Frankly, it made me mad as hell. We'd spent a lot of time, money, and effort to put this together and it was all being wasted before our eyes. We sat helpless that evening as we watched bush car after bush car whizz by within fifty yards of the blind, which had been swarming with hyenas and at least one big leopard the day before. Goddamnit to bloody whatever. It angered me. And disappointed me. These were precious days, expensive days, but what could we do?

But there are always distractions and compensations! Steve, for example, runs a great kitchen. His headwaiter, Cumquat, serves some of the finest sable roast and soup in Africa, and the chef, whose name is Mkoma, asked especially to be remembered. Mkoma, you are well and truly remembered because food on safari assumes an importance you don't realize until you are there. (In fact, Mkoma was one of my personal chefs many years back, so there was no chance of his being forgotten.) Together with David, the head gun bearer/tracker; Blackie, the assistant chef; and *Morena* Pito, a marvelous old man of seventy-five who was the

Author shooting wildebeest.

chief skinner and who was always addressed by that august title; and not forgetting the more anglicized Mr. Bula, who looked after the tents, we were in excellent hands throughout. At 7:45 P.M., the lighting got buggered and we were down to the campfire and one very small Cadac pressure lamp with a net mantle. The wind was ferocious. I was wearing both my goose-down vest as well as a full jacket. At twenty-five to thirty knots, there was a hell of a chill factor. Three lions were roaring in the distance, and, after a monumental struggle, I managed to outwit Brewster's Patent and open a tin of mixed nuts.

It gets hot as bejeesus at midday, boy, but when nightfall comes, you'd better be prepared to play Baby-a-Bunting, since you'll freeze off some of your important

members if you don't. Tarzan's Africa? Forget it. He would have died of the cold before he was five years old. (Just for your information, Edgar Rice Burroughs had Tarzan born in Angola.)

With my permits fouled up and being armed with a strange rifle, I had a tendency to go to bed rather early (maybe because there was no reed fence and the camp perimeter was alive with lion, leopard, hippo, and jumbo, none of which inspire deep sleep in me).

I again noted that when the lions roared, the frogs stopped calling. As I was thinking why this should be, Cumquat came by, and I engaged him in conversation with a mixture of Tswana and Fanagalo.

I told him the KiSwahili tale of what the lion calls: "Whose land is this? Mine, mine, mine." He thought it very funny after a bit of consideration. I then told him the story came from East Africa, where KiSwahili is spoken. He had not heard of KiSwahili, Kenya, Uganda, or Tanzania. The rural African often has no idea of where he is in relation to the rest of the world. He relates only to the tribes around him, most of whom he fights. Unless living on or near a coast, the very concept of oceans separating things such as continents is inconceivable to such people. They cannot be expected to know what they have not been taught, any more than a white man, who has the advantage of extensive schooling but can still be ignorant about a great deal that goes on in this world.

I watched the moon fill like a tub of butter before wandering off to bed, trying to think of some appropriate Kipling /Cundillism. . . . I could not.

The next morning, September 19, 1985, found Dick much worse. In fact, I was considering having him flown out, but he insisted on sticking around. In any case, he wasn't about to miss the fishing at our next stop, Etsatsa. I had been bitten by a spider in, of all places, one of the movie theaters in Pretoria. It took more than four months to heal, although, for some odd reason, it never caused any pain. But the bite left a helluva crater for months. Who knows what *that* was. Perhaps the fact that I was bitten in the heavy flesh of the thigh permitted the poison to become less concentrated, rather than more so, as was the case with Dick's ankle where the meat lies so close to the bone. As things turned out, Dick was still having problems with the tendons in the back of his leg four months later.

Before we flew to the fishing camp later that day, Steve regaled us with more stories, maybe in an effort to distract his crippled clients from their woes. One of them was about a nightmarish encounter with a big croc that a client had shot with a .375. This was on the Savuti River,

which is is quite deep. Unfortunately, the client had whacked it in the neck, then kept firing until it disappeared. Steve, being young and enthusiastic, was determined not to lose the croc. Pretty sure it was dead after fifteen minutes, he decided to dive for it, but not before realizing that the place positively slithered with other crocs. (Not to mention the fact that the river was the color of toffee.) It was really a very brave thing to do. I have swum with crocs—big ones—and know the fear that lingers like lead in the pit of your stomach.

Steve took a deep breath and went under. Groping through the blackness, he finally located a scaly leg—a leg that retracted at his touch! Needless to say, he hit the surface in a hurry, clearing it by about ten feet.

The hell scared out of him, Steve "plucked up courage"—you can say that again—and forced himself to make another dive. Finally, he got hold of the tail and got a rope around it, dragging the croc to shore.

Interestingly, its stomach contained a baboon skull, the vertebrae of one or more buffalo, and some *lechwe* bones. There were none of the rocks or stones commonly found in crocs that are said to aid digestion. Steve was damned lucky no Liversedge bones wound up in there. . . .

Dick and Steve had been unable to get

hyenas as well as the feeding leopard on film. And there were also lions announcing their presence on all sides, slathers of them. In fact, in one day we had either seen or heard four of the "Big Five" at King's Pool—elephant, leopard, lion, and buffalo (which were watering just below camp). I had, in fact, spent the last afternoon with a bull elephant, although no money was lent. In chatting to Steve about the elephant, he told us of an incident at "Splash" camp—the one Daryll Dandridge and I had constructed in 1970 —where another professional hunter had killed a very good elephant, about an eighty-pounder, with his clients.

Later that night, according to Steve, two big lions started feeding on the elephant carcass. The clients were a family, mother and son. As they approached their trophy at early light, they found the two lions fast asleep, one with four paws in the air. The son took the shot and plugged him right between the eyes, which rather ended that side of the episode. As the other lion jumped up at the shot, the mother hit it in the front paw. Considering it was probably moving like mad, this may not have been as poor a shot as it sounds on paper years later.

Steve told them to wait with the dead lion while he took the trackers into heavy *mopane* scrub. But he just couldn't get a clear shot. Every time they got within range, the fool thing would rush off into heavier cover. And this continued for miles! Finally, they reached a patch of waist-high *mopane,* one of the trackers carrying the mother's .375 H&H.

Steve decided, quite rightly, I believe, that it would have been pure, undiluted suicide to enter that patch of bush, although they could actually hear the lion breathing. He then came up with a plan that called for getting into a clearing nearby and having one of the trackers fire at the breathing sound while he covered, in hopes of a charge.

Nothing. Silence. Had he by chance killed the lion with an odd shot? he wondered.

Steve was now out of soft-point ammo for the .458, so he took the .375 from one of the trackers and, with another tracker at his shoulder and one behind him, went in.

They hadn't covered five feet when a great roar erupted, followed by an even more impressive lion. Steve will certainly never forget those great dark eyes any more than I will forget the amber murder in the eyes of the Saile lion Gordon and I shot. He spun and shot from the hip with the .375 and hammered it in the center of the chest in mid-leap. As had Gordon and I, Steve shot this lion *eleven times* at point-blank range with a mixture of .375 and .458 solids—all he had left— before it died.

It did before he did.

Nyasa lovebirds (Agapornis Nigerensis).

According to Steve, as well as to local jurisprudence, the only method for hunting leopard in Botswana is tracking. Oh, how charming, especially when I am advised by Steve that the Kalahari leopard is much more aggressive than the lion, and that it has a penchant for charging vehicles—about ninety percent of the time, on the average.

Now, I have never tracked leopard in the Kalahari but I did pick up some "gen" on the process whilst in Zambia, Botswana, and Zimbabwe, midwifing this book. In fact, I must tell the brief story of some unnamed professional hunters who were one day summarily ordered to their HQ and advised that they must desist from using "rural dwellers" as leopard bait. One hunter looked at the other and asked what on earth "rural dwellers" were. They were advised that it was now the official Botswana term for Bushmen. The way it apparently works is this: !Kung Bushmen or other Bushmen tribes familiar with the Kalahari were run before the hunting car on the spoor as trackers. In doing so, they were often mauled.

Dick's foot was very bad and he had a great deal of trouble walking, as I did from my burn that was also turning nasty, although not septic as I kept it smothered in the outdated antiseptic powder. But Dick was determined to stick it out and go fishing in the Oka-vango with me. In an odd way, it was as well he did.

We both commented on a very strange phenomenon that I had noticed as we sat by the fire at King's Pool. You could almost set your watch by a weird noise. At eleven at night, a peculiar "BOING!!" would reverberate, then repeat a couple of times. We found out that the noise was caused by the contraction of the 44-gallon or 55-gallon fuel drums that expanded at dawn and then contracted in the evening as they chilled off.

Steve and his staff saw us off on September 19, the day we flew from Linyanti by Cherokee aircraft to Seronga at the northeastern corner of the Okavango Delta. We were both really hurting, and we felt worse when there was nobody at Seronga to meet us.

Seronga is a fenced in—or fenced out, depending on your viewpoint—airstrip in the middle of the proverbial nowhere. There was one official there who was most courteous but, beyond effusive greetings, he wasn't much help. Where was Etsatsa?

Fortunately, our pilot was a star. Although he had never flown to Seronga before, he hit it on the button. Then he took off again, not really knowing where Etsatsa might be lurking, went up quite a few thousand feet, and started a series of aerobatic maneuvers that would have

Author fishing in Mupamadzi.

made the Eagle Squadron flush with embarrassment. Hell, he was superb! The object of the exercise was to attract attention—and he did.

In the meantime, we had left our *mpahle* on the runway and had sought the shade of a large tree. Apparently, the aerobatics were effective because, half an hour later, we heard the drone of Bruce Riggs's boats, come to save us. In fact, we didn't need that much saving, since I had had the grand foresight to wrap four cold beers from Steve's stock in foam rubber. The beer eased our wounds considerably.

Bruce pitched up with a gargled roar. What had been a totally deserted compound now looked like a parade ground as people helped us load our stuff into the boats, Bruce having piloted one and his gillie, Frank, the other. A bunch of kids

appeared out of nowhere to help Dick and me with the luggage as we hobbled down to the boats. Then we sat back in luxury in what were truly first-rate craft and, within half an hour, were on the island of Etsatsa. By this time the Cessna 206 had gained altitude again, and the pilot waggled the wings in farewell. That man really had style.

Bruce had been expecting us later that morning, but it didn't matter; he was to prove a great host.

A Botswana citizen, as one must be to run a camp or hold a professional hunter's license, Bruce was waiting for his professional hunter's license, having completed roughly half of the three-year apprenticeship that even a citizen had to undergo. (There is, however, a proviso that allows a qualified person to hold a license for *half* the hunting season if he or she is not a citizen.) He also spoke a better Tswana than did most of the locals and his linguistic prowess was astonishing, which certainly is hugely important in such an off-the-map location as a fishing camp in the Okavango swamps.

"Swamp," as in Okavango, is really not an appropriate description of this unique, vast aquifer that essentially runs into the porous northern Kalahari. The delta is fed by the Okavango River, rising on the west side of the Angolan escarpment and flowing on to a watery labyrinth of rivers, islands, and trees, a maze where often only the primitive *makoro* dugouts, of wild ebony and other woods, can negotiate the channels and papyrus-flanked waterways.

Etsatsa, an island about three acres in size that looks mightily like some Melanesian atoll, is located just at the mouth of the Okavango Delta where the main channel joins the delta. The camp was built in October 1984, and is a pure example of what a good camp should be. Hunters Africa idea was to offer everything, including fishing, especially when it came to taking advantage of the tigerfish and bream in the area. It had magnificent palm foliage, excellent tentage and food, with cold, clear water and unimaginably lovely surroundings.

The water, in fact, was almost *too* cold, as they had had a freak cold snap that had left the main channel frigid. As a result, most of the large tigerfish (of the class *Characidae,* with the Latin designation of *Hydrocynus vittatus.* I thought that would make your day) had gone into the swamps where warmer and shallower water prevailed, along with the accompanying baitfish. There were still, however, any amount of smaller tigers to be caught, as well as various types of bream.

Bruce, with his impeccable Tswana, said that the name of the island is actually I'tsatsa, although it does not appear as so on the maps. I have chosen to go with the preferred spelling. It has always been a constant mystery to me as to who decides to change what place name and why in Africa.

We had had a huge breakfast at King's Pool before flying out, so we skipped lunch and looked forward to going out fishing that same afternoon as the sun dipped. There is a very definite correlation between the activity of fish and the time of day. This is true nearly everywhere, but especially in the Okavango. When I was on safari back in the seventies at "Splash" camp, at lunch times I was able to spear quite a few bream—mostly *Tilapia,* the so-called Egyptian mouthbreeder—with Bushmen fish spears made of slender wands tipped with barbed pieces of fencing wire. One would balance the butt against the middle finger and, to allow for the refraction of the water, aim low. The throw was accom-

Client's tents at Etsatsa.

plished with a flip of the wrist, or perhaps more accurately, a "snap." We were never short of fish.

Dick, Bruce, and I had a terrific afternoon, taking a lot of small tigers that would have been fantastic on a light fly rod, using a mylar or tinsel streamer. They seemed to like the Mepps, in any case.

I was originally a fishing writer before I started on my professional hunting career, my first pieces being about tarpon taken with a fly rod and harpooning freshwater sharks in Nicaragua. (The latter was then made into a TV piece for ABC's "The American Sportsman" back in the mid-sixties. It featured Jack Nicklaus, the man who swats the white dimpled pill so well). In any case, I was no stranger to a fishing rod, raised as I was on Lake Valhalla in northern New Jersey, and I've fished from Scotland and Iceland to the western Caribbean and Patagonia from the Amazon tributaries to the Indian Ocean. I learned to tie flies with, if I dare say so, some proficiency, and I had sadly missed the fishing side of things on African safaris. (One cannot run a safari and drag a fly or spinning rod around the bush.) Thus, until this trip, I had not had a chance to wet a line, except for a couple of recent aquatic safaris with the great Cal Cochran, out of Marathon, Florida, for giant tarpon on the fly. (A kind of fishing that, as Cal put it, resembled

Nice bream of about 2½ pounds.

"shooting an elephant with a BB gun.") So it felt great to get a casting rod back in my hands again.

Seems to me that the majority of hunters are also fishermen. In fact, it's really the same sport, depending on the species, and requiring a stalk, a shot (or cast), and the skill unique to outdoorsmen. The one aspect of fishing I like is that you can let 'em go. . . .

I am told there are two major kinds of tigerfish, maybe three. There is the common tiger I mentioned above as well as a dwarf variety. Then there is a huge lake species that can reach over a hundred pounds. Hell, I'd as soon take on a croc as one of those. I shan't bore you with Linnaean Latin concerning the large varieties of bream, but they are indeed numerous. The fish are shaped like a white perch or American sunfish, being flattened rather than rounded (as opposed to a bass). I believe they are the finest fighting freshwater fish in the world. None compares even remotely.

In camp, I noticed that the good quality spinning rods and reels were all what an American would call "left-handed." In other words, the African system calls for the rod to have the reel handle mounted on the right, instead of the left. I simply cannot figure this out. Most people are right-handed, so they cast with the right hand. But, with the cranking handle on the right, there is no way to control the cast and the reel at the same time. If, on the other hand, the handle were on the left, it would give perfect control, since one could either slow up the speed of the cast lure in the air, or completely stop it by turning the handle a bit and flipping the bail closed. Without this technique, you stand to spend most of your collective time hung up in the papyrus, which

A yellow-throated bream. Bream are renowned as excellent fighters.

lined both sides of our channel like a solid green wall.

Everybody was astonished when I started casting, and I'm hardly chest-thumping here. But bream lie under the overhanging papyrus and, unless you put the lure on their nose, the odds of a strike are greatly reduced. I was able to drop that little #4 Mepps spinner within a couple of inches of the edge of the reeds through simple reel control every time—well, nearly every time. As a consequence, and I don't think Dick or Bruce would disagree, I was getting somewhere between six and ten times as many strikes as they were.

Never having fished either tigers or bream before, I reckoned, since they were predators feeding on smallish minnows, that I could do no worse than to treat them the same way I would bass. And it sure as hell worked. Bruce had advised a fast, smooth retrieve of the cast and lure, but I figured that the mentality of fish doesn't vary, even from one continent to the next. A crippled, weird-acting "minnow" would attract more attention than a healthy, quick-swimming one. And so it proved. I was using a stop-start retrieve of the spinner, while they were reeling in smoothly with no "action." The results proved beyond a doubt that the fish were more interested in my offerings than in those of my companions.

Before I decided on my bass tactics and really got the hang of things, I did okay, but Bruce took a very nice bream of about two and a half pounds, which provided dinner for Dick and me. (What a shame to be running a fishing camp, yet to be allergic to fish as Bruce is.) Now, even though Bruce was the professional, I was able to prevail on both him and Dick to slow down their retrieves, so much so that almost immediately, they got more strikes. Bruce, for example, hadn't had a hit in over an hour, but as soon he started playing "crippled minnow," his percentage picked up.

The difference was astonishing. Perhaps it was the very cold water, I don't know. But both men started to take more fish when they began fishing more slowly and erratically. I believe we were "Jezebelling" the fish into attacking the lure, since not a single caught fish had anything at all in its stomach. Hell of an interesting exercise, especially for somebody who had never caught a tiger or bream before.

Though I love to fish, I hate for the most part to *eat* the resulting catch. The exceptions are American snook, swordfish, South African kingklip, and—provided *I* do them—whitebait and kippers. I do like crustaceans, especially lobster, clams (steamed!), oysters, and scallops, particularly those I found in Iceland. But, of all the seafood in the world, give me Okavango bream. Normally, I have only one meal a day, but at Etsatsa, I tripled my consumption, eating nothing but bream, the finest of all fishes.

While at Etsatsa, we had the chance to speak with a couple who were the only other people in camp besides Bruce and his staff. This couple, who will remain anonymous, spoke of a very odd and disturbing experience they had had recently.

They were leasing a home in a large city in one of the countries bordering Botswana when they began noticing an odor and a great increase in flies. Looking through the picket fence of their property, they literally saw piles of baby and adult ivory, as well as heaps of horns and tons of meat. Being responsible people, this couple contacted every authority they could, as well as prominent newspaper writers, including one of international repute.

Nothing. Nothing even from conservation officers who witnessed and smelled the products next door.

Nothing.

They reported that, along with another neighbor who was not stupid, this was an obvious poaching operation.

Not one official reply.

Makes you think . . . and it makes you sick.

One of the grandest aspects of the Okavango main channel is the fact that it is populated by roughly a dozen fish eagles, *Haliaeetus vocifer,* which are tame enough to take small tigers with a piece of papyrus jammed down their gullets to keep them afloat. Seeing this spectacle is really worth the trip, as the eagles soar and swoop, yellow talons extended before their bodies. Of course, like anybody else, they occasionally foul up, sometimes missing the fish altogether in the five- to seven-knot current. But they would come amazingly close to the boat, and we photographed many, both on the main channel and on the Linyanti, further east. We got some very good stuff, too, but the best would have been a motor-drive sequence I caught from what turned out to be exactly the correct angle. Unfortunately, Dick and I were using the technique called "bracketing" in which one camera is at a particular setting and the other at a different one. His was good but mine turned out somewhat better. One set was just too dark to reproduce. Luck of the draw. . . . It was mine. Despite very windy conditions at times, we were also able to take some beautiful water lily shots, the floating flowers a dazzle of color. I was as pleased with them as I was with the fishing.

Angels appear in strange places, but I never expected one on Etsatsa Island in the Okavango. There was a French couple staying at a makeshift camp some thousand yards downstream from us, the husband being a professional hunter and the wife—of all things—a registered nurse! The two were on their way out. Happily, though, we bumped into them and they learned of Dick's spider bite and condition. The wife was carrying more medical stuff than a mobile disaster unit,

Dick van Niekirk's superb shot of a fish eagle.

and she called early the next morning to give Dick a 5cc shot of Polaramine, a powerful antihistamine.

Dick has a hide like a piece of jerky and the injection really hurt him, besides affecting his motor reflexes. No way was I going to take him into the brain-frying sun that day, so we agreed that he would stay in camp. He decided to spend the day lying on his left side, having received the lance wound on the right, and drink beer through a straw. Actually, he was sound asleep fifteen minutes later and stayed that way the whole day, feeling much better at dusk. Just as well, since the un-named angel of mercy had given him final advice as she and her husband pulled out of the little aquatic enclave that formed the landing place on Estatsa: no alcohol for at least twelve hours or he would turn into a frog.

I was not present at the injection but I had hell's own fun that evening pointing out that he had spent the morning

Fish eagle.

running around a remote island in the Okavango with his pants lowered. I loved it! Dick, however, didn't think it was particularly funny. I was unable to record the name of that gracious lady who saved my friend from a great deal of pain, but should she chance upon these words, please accept our eternal gratitude. It was sufficient to make one believe in black magic!

Which reminds me . . .

While we were on Etsatsa, Bruce told me of the time he found a body in the Tuli Block, an area in eastern Botswana, bordering the Limpopo River. The hands had been chopped off to prevent identification through fingerprinting. The victim had been shot through the head, but before the murderer(s) could proceed with the usual removal of body parts for *muti,* that is "medicine" for black magic or *tagati* purposes, there must have been a disturbance, so the hands were removed and the person(s) responsible fled.

Ritual murder in Africa continues. Again, my files bulge with authenticated details concerning such matters in countries as far apart as Kenya and the southern Cape. The victims are always black but range in age from young children to the elderly. Bruce went on to tell of a particularly disturbing phenomenon that Wally Johnson had also known about in Botswana and, in fact, in Mozambique. This concerned the skinning *alive* of the victim for extra *power!* A great deal of *muti* killing goes on, and Bruce told us that one could, with the proper connections, obtain a human skin in such places as Maun and Gaberone.

The police have their hands full in trying to break up these unsavory practices and bring people to book. Both Wally and Bruce told us that these skinnings are performed for the benefit of certain local religious sects, the victim being *sold* by the family to a *naka* (witch doctor). According to Bruce, when a deal is struck for a victim, it is arranged so that the person disappears, often when going hunting with others. The person's disappearance is laid at the door of lion, leopard, and so forth, automatically implying no remains by the time word gets to the authorities.

Now don't go getting crazy ideas that you, as a foreign hunter and tourist, run any kind of danger from *tagati.* Don't go canceling your safaris and spreading alarm among others. You see, you just don't fit the menu. Just remember, though, that not everyone adheres to the same way of life and upholds the same kind of ideas you do. When you enter rural Africa, you enter a different world that must be respected as such.

Okavango water lilies, among the finest in the world.

Urban Africa has its surprises, too. The maid who works for us once a week—a thoroughly urbanized, very articulate, and delightful person—came to me rather furtively some time ago, knowing that I am a hunter. She asked if I could please obtain a vulture for her, dead or alive.

Asking why on earth she would be needing a vulture of any kind, I was advised that a friend of hers had told her she could get rich on the ponies if a vulture could be brought to a witch doctor they both knew. The witch doctor would consult the bird for the results of future horse races. Dead or alive, the bird would know.

Well, that's Africa—even *now*.

Dick van Niekerk, as a crime and news photographer for several major southern African newspapers at one time, was reminded of a baffling incident he had covered a few years before. It seems a white man had tried one day to enter the gate of his own home but had been floored by what felt like a mighty slap. He had tried again, with the same results. After calling in the police, who figured him for a nutcase, the man then summoned the local newspaper in desperation. Dick went along with his cameras and his cynicism to investigate.

Well, Dick reported that the guy certainly had had a resounding slap mark on his face, every finger outlined in lurid

The cocktail area (below) and dining area at Etsatsa.

scarlet. He had taken quite a few photographs of the man's face, using different exposures to be sure he "got it." Satisfied he had the pictures, he returned to have them processed, only to find that no kind of mark at all showed up. Nothing. Well, there was no explanation, but Dick swore they were there, and that he had gotten the pictures. Nobody was ever seen, and it was still light out when the photographs were taken. I guess we'll just have to call it the case of the phantom slap. And I suppose the chap had to use the back gate.

Dick was much better after the French angel of mercy's visit. He didn't feel quite up to going fishing the next morning, however, and, since I don't really like to fish alone, I decided to stay behind and spend some time at camp.

I was in the dining *kaia,* admiring the reed walls, reading, and listening to the continual *tink-tink-tink* of a fruit bat. At about eleven, a waiter came out, looked past me, and stifled a giggle. Expecting some lightly clad Tahitian maiden who had taken the wrong outrigger, I turned and found myself damned near face-to-face with a really big green, or vervet, monkey, of the type that had infested the island. The rascal was trying to sneak past my left shoulder to get at a bowl of fruit but fled at my bellow.

You could set your watch by the time the fish started feeding: five in the afternoon, sharp. Bruce was back, and with Dick still crashed in his tent, I decided to go out for an hour or so with Bruce and another gentleman. We ran upriver at full throttle and pulled in at the juncture of a feeder stream that had scoured a very deep hole in the bottom. It didn't take long to discover that the tigers were all the way down. In fact, I had to wait twenty seconds for the lure to sink before there was any hope of a hit on the retrieve. Nevertheless, just about every cast drew a strike. I had one especially heavy smash, but was unable to hook the bugger. Tigers will sometimes grab a lure so hard and hold it so tight with their savage teeth that it can't be torn loose to sink the ganghooks.

A few seconds later, the gentleman with us nailed a six-pounder and, after something resembling the battle of Jericho, managed to lead it into the net. It was by far the best of the trip. He was so kind as to make me a gift of the jaws, which are unique, at least as far as I know in freshwater fish. When a tiger breaks off a tooth—possibly by grabbing a crocodile, steamship, or submarine—a new one folds up to replace it, just as in sharks.

On the sort of hunches fishermen get, and considering that the current was easily six knots, we had to turn around and run past the deep hole every few minutes. Above it was a shallower area, and I started throwing for bream with the rod tip high so as to keep the Mepps from

Shot of tigerfish jaws, showing regenerative teeth.

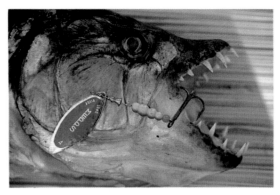

Head and teeth of a 6-pound tigerfish.

sinking too deeply. On that one drift, I took four bream, all good ones too, the best being about four pounds. The fight in these fish is unbelievable, even better than that of the tigers, I think. In that one run upriver, I caught the yellow-throated, the tilapia, and the thin-faced, all marvelous fighters and the world's best eating.

Tigerfish are damned funny creatures in their own way. Bruce told us on our last night that he had earlier had out a party that included a doctor, a man who was curious as hell to see what these fish were eating. Of forty tigers examined by him, however, not one of the fish had a single thing in its stomach. If they regurgitate like American bluefish, there was no evidence of it in the clear water. Of course, the fish were not wasted, even though they are a bit bony for the average American taste; the locals love them and were most pleased with the gift. Still, with so much natural food around, and considering their obvious lack of hunger, it's hard to figure why they would take a spinner or other lure yet not eat the baitfish around them. Probably, as I guessed earlier, the erratic behavior of the artificial lures just aroused their predatory instincts and they attacked out of sheer malice.

In all, the Okavango trip had been one of the most enjoyable legs of the combined safaris. We left extra early the next morning for the airstrip at Seronga so that we could have a crack at the African pike, which is actually not a pike at all. (Although it sure looks like a combination of pike and the American garfish). Weighing up to five pounds, *Hepsetus odöe* swarms the grassy fringes of the Okavango main channel only a few miles from Seronga. You almost have to work at *not* getting a strike with each cast. Sounds boring, but they are excellent jumpers and we had a ton of fun using light tackle.

But I had a reason above and beyond African pike for leaving early. I have been in Africa a fair amount of time, and I was aware that my gun permits were not in order and that my rifle and shotgun were locked up in Maun. I also knew that it was highly likely that somebody was going to throw his official weight

Results of a half-hour's fishing with light tackle on the Okavango main channel. Bream and tigerfish.

around in this matter if he got a chance.

I was not wrong.

However, I first had to *reach* Maun for the 1:00 P.M. flight to Johannesburg via Gaborone. That was quite an adventure in itself.

There was Dick, a couple from somewhere else, myself and all our luggage, as well as a great deal of stuff to do with the company. That's a lot of ballast. The wind was positively screeching from left to right at the Seronga dirt strip (such as it never would have screeched at Capstick International), and I started to wonder what kind of a time we were in for. The aircraft arrived, piloted by one of the rudest young fools I have ever had the displeasure to encounter. On takeoff, I shall never forget Dick and I looking at each other and figuring that we'd "had the course." We tried to lift off in the terrible crosswind and hit the ground three times before gaining enough altitude to clear the big trees at the far end of the strip. I really believed we'd had it. But somehow, probably scattering leaves from the treetops, we swung into flight and, foot by foot, gained altitude. I had no idea I could hold my breath *that* long.

(Before proceeding, I must point out that *I* had made the arrangements and that that particular charter had nothing whatsoever to do with the firm of Hunters Africa, the aircraft and the ill-mannered fellow who piloted it having belonged to a private charter company.)

Maun loomed ahead after an hour's flying time, looking something like a half-eaten dog biscuit. If I thought we had had problems on takeoff, I'd seen nothing yet.

No, we landed without incident, but the pilot, who sat in grim silence throughout, dumped us some four hundred yards from the main terminal and left, not so much as even muttering good-bye. I kept thinking he had gone to get somebody with a cart for the luggage, but we ended up carrying the *mpahla* ourselves.

After three trips, we finally hunched all the stuff into the main airport, where I noticed a small room with what were presumably indigenous officials of the Customs variety. Swell. It was only half-past nine in the morning, which gave us three and a half hours to sort things out before departure.

With meticulous politeness, I knocked on the door and produced my receipt certificate for the two guns. Twenty minutes later—let's be reasonable, they were playing cards—a gentleman dressed in civilian clothes with thick glasses, at least twenty ball-point pens, and an insolent gait, came out to the counter. I showed him the receipt again, and he advised me of two things:

1. The gentleman who had signed the receipt was not on duty that day;

2. There was no way in bleeding hell I was going to get my guns back.

This had a decided tendency to upset me, as we were speaking of quite a lot of loot in hardware. Being gifted, however, with the innate art of applied diplomacy, and being relatively Africa-proof when it comes to the unexpected, I made the mis-

Okavango water lilies.

take of trying to reason with the gentleman. Probably the Irish in me. . . .

"Ah, but, *Morena,*" said I, using the exhalted Tswana term of address for Respected Sir, God, or Customs Officer, "I was assured by *Morena Monare,* whose signature you will see on this receipt, that you gentlemen would be so kind as to promote international travel and the influx of foreign exchange to your lovely country and that you personally or, of course, one of your many assistants, would see that my guns were placed on the aircraft under your important direction."

Jaysus, if that ain't Oirish, what is? Dick was starting to twitch. Short fuse.

"No. You cannot have the guns."

Here we go again, I thought. I started to say something charming and probably equally effective, when he started to break loose.

An interjection is necessary here: nobody had ever seen this guy before. He didn't even have a uniform, so he went through great ceremony to imply his huge importance. As I said, I have spent a lot of years in Africa, but when officials start pulling wads of documents out and testifying that they are the Thirteenth Apostle, it's time to back away. Only, he wouldn't let me. Like blooming dawn, it suddenly hit me that this gentleman was brand new on the job, and that he wanted a gold star next to his name in the cafeteria by sticking Dick and me in jail for as long as he could after first provoking us into "action."

They have not yet made the solid-gold matched pair of Holland .470s that will entice me into that.

He shoved his very official face over the counter and said, "You foreign people are trying to take away my country!"

Actually, he didn't say it, he *shouted* it. Oh, my. I explained that we, as Americans, give millions of U.S. dollars in aid to his country in the name of friendship. I advised him that he could most happily keep his country, and that our countries were great friends.

"Now," he screeched, "you are being rude! Do not be *rude!*"

I made the appropriate gestures, realizing precisely what he was trying to do: arrest us.

Which he forthwith suggested with the marvelous comment that we were not only being rude to a high official of the Botswana government, but that we were breaking "international law" by asking for our guns to be returned to us. We had no valid permit, he explained with what some might call a certain lack of control.

I thought I'd give it one more try in hopes this chap was just another moron and really thought we were trying to get away with something. "But, *Morena,*" I said, "how can we be breaking your international law when we wish to *remove* the guns, not bring them in?"

He wasn't very pleased with the induction of any common sense, but was saved by a bit of very bad timing. The door opened behind us and the representative of Hunters Africa happened to arrive at that moment. "Mr. Capstick?" a voice rang out, and Dick and I naturally turned

around to see who might be calling me. Now, the fireworks . . .

"How dare you turn your back on me!" the man bellowed, loud enough to bring even his cohorts to the door of the card room.

I sighed and explained, *"Morena,* it is our custom to return a greeting, just as it is your custom. It would be poor manners not to do so, and the Tswana are experts on good manners. I'm sure you understand."

That seemed to slow him up a bit, and although he raged about my being insulting and potential jailbait for having broken his brand of "international law," he realized that we weren't about to fall for his tactics.

I motioned the Hunters Africa person away from the area, as he has to live there and I didn't want him having problems on my account. Then I advised the Customs man that I would make arrangements for his "international law" to be met. In the meantime, he was welcome to hold the firearms, presuming he was willing to take the responsibility.

"I am willing," he said, to my astonishment, letting us off the hook. Then, two things came to mind: (1) We had to go through this man on our way out and he could very easily delay us long enough to miss the aircraft, and (2) Dick van Niekerk was about to bust his face open, which meant that I would never open another Christmas stocking, at least not in the foreseeable future. I hate cutting cane, anyway.

I took Dick's arm and whispered, "Out. Now." I thanked the kind gentleman behind the counter for all his courtesy, and advised him that I would see to it that the embassy of the United States of America would see that Botswana's "international laws" were obeyed in future.

"Embassy" seemed to impress him. Anyway, we walked out and across the dirt road to the headquarters of Hunters Africa. I got Dick settled with a beer for the several hours wait for the flight and gave him a couple of the same pills I had given Fiona when she flipped out on the light aircraft in Zambia. I told Dick that they would help the lingering pain in his foot.

Well, the hour for our departure finally arrived, and after a beer at the Duck Inn bar at the edge of Maun Airport, where we saw Soren Lindstrom and chatted with him, noticing that he was much recovered from his lion mauling, we gritted our collective teeth and sallied forth righteously against the forces of evil.

To my astonishment, the man who had made the *original* arrangement to have the guns placed by Customs on the aircraft had been found! And, he was senior to my lightweight pal with the thick glasses and ball-point pens, the one so interested in "international law." I wonder if I have *ever* been so relieved.

The bad guy sulked, leaning in a corner, and we gave him not a glance. He almost glowed with malice when the guns and ammo boxes came through, especially when the senior man indicated him with a nod and said, "He's new. He doesn't know what he's doing yet."

Frankly, it did a great deal to restore my confidence in the officialdom of Botswana. Having been a previous resident and having held a full professional hunter's license there, I was most happy to see that the people of Botswana were most reasonable, fair, and fine people with whom to live and, certainly, with whom to enjoy a safari. There's always the oddball in any country in the world. They're outnumbered.

Botswana, despite its diamonds at Orapa and its other natural resources, seems to realize that game has an immense value in terms of foreign exchange. It fully understands the idea that Gordon Cundill, one of the greatest producers of foreign exchange in that country, put this way earlier: "Game is of immense value. It *must* be recognized as such."

....

One cannot go on four safaris in the Space Age—or is it really the Age of Terrorism—without indulging in a touch of retrospection.

Back in the first years of this century, respected and experienced writers were predicting that the game was almost gone, and that it surely would be by 1910.

They were wrong.

Now, I take pains to distinguish between "conservationists" and "preservationists," and the difference is vast. A conservationist, as typified by the legitimate hunter for sport, puts back as much as or more than he takes. And not just in game. Hunting isn't cheap these days, and the hunting economy is largely responsible for the survival of vast regions of unspoiled Africa where individual species can still breed. The safari industry is also responsible for the employment of huge numbers of indigenous people who depend on it for a living. In turn, these people support a great many other people. These are the cold facts.

The preservationist, on the other hand, believes that there is no conceivable logic in killing some game to save the rest. Often there are deeply held religious, moral, or personal reasons behind the preservationist's stance.

Hunting no longer needs a defense, since African people are much more aware of the importance of the economic implications concerning their fauna. (There are a few glowing exceptions, however, and they will be the losers. Correct utilization of game is the key to its survival *anywhere*.) I believe that preservationists are unexposed folk, people who will not recognize the facts behind wildlife survival and the key role of honorable sportsmen. The media are often to blame for much of the hysteria, bias, and ignorance. Preservationism is also big business.

So, if you're truly interested in the survival of wildlife, wherever you live, buy a hunting license. You don't have to actually go out and hunt, but your contribution will be pumped back into those coffers that keep wetlands wet and the wilderness areas wild.

The game *is* still there. You can still get eaten by a lion or mauled by a leopard. You can still be tusked by an elephant and collide with hippo. No doubt about that! Buffalo are still there and, in some areas, you can hunt elephant (which, as I've implied, have to be thinned out at times by officially sanc-

Puku *grazing on river bank. (A half hour after this photograph was taken they were attacked by wild dogs and a female slaughtered on the spot, although a male stood his ground.)*

tioned culling programs because of their damaging concentrations). Black rhino? Forget it. The horn is worth more than a eunuch in some Islamic countries, where dagger handles of rhino horn are a status symbol, and has long been viewed as a powerful aphrodisiac and medicine in many cultures. Blaming the safari industry for the black rhino situation today is a simplistic cop-out. The white rhino, however, may still be taken at considerable expense in much of southern Africa.

Where does all this lead?

Well, I don't think it's going the way

people told us it was going to go back in 1905. To be realistic, the problem is human overpopulation, and the resultant population explosion of cattle and other domestic stock. Only so many game animals can float on one shingle. Kenya is a prime example of the foregoing, with its astronomical birth rate and the tragic fate of game there once hunting was banned. The poachers have never looked back. Neither have the goats and cows.

After years in Africa—and I'm hardly an "old hand"—the following is apparent to me: unless the various governments wake up to the fact that they are depleting their only *renewable* natural resource, as Gordon Cundill so succinctly put it, things will slide even farther downhill.

If there is truly to be an end to the game, it will come from the express train, not the express rifle.

ACKNOWLEDGMENTS

In a book of this length, covering such enormous areas of yet-untamed Africa, it would be impossible to thank all those people who were of such help and value to me. That is why an attempt was made throughout the text to mention those people as they appeared.

I should like, however, to express my deep gratitude to all the members of Hunters Africa, who have been so incredibly efficient and courteous. I have made new friends in that organization. And I owe Gordon Cundill a special word of appreciation for his Foreword to this book; for his support, advice, and genial company; and for his solid friendship, which has meant a great deal to me.

Gordon's office staff in Pietermaritz-

burg will always be remembered, since they put the show together, from airline bookings to gun permits to a host of other details the outsider never sees. Thank you, Nora Chapman, Pam Maistrey, Angie Leaker, and Lynn Palmary.

Lew and Dale Games were stars, backed by their colleagues in Lusaka. And I remember here my old pals of so long ago, Joe Joubert and Daryll Dandridge, as well as newfound friends in Steve Liversedge, the Riggs brothers, and Andre de Kock.

The visit to Linyanti will always be rather special in my memories of these safaris. I remember John Northcote and, in particular, Daphne and Mike Hissey. I am sorry indeed Mike is no longer with us so that he could read these words. He will not be forgotten.

My friend of longest standing in Africa, Stuart Campbell, was a huge treat to see again, and I should like to thank him and Eric Wagner for their hospitality at Matetsi, where I literally dug into my past, enjoying grand bird shooting and the finest treatment.

Paul Kimble and Dick van Niekerk, my photographers on different segments of the safaris, were both reliable and skilled, taking their chances while they captured many special moments on film for the book. I only regret Dick's run-in with a dangerous spider, as it removed a great deal of the enjoyment of the jaunt for him.

To those of you who flew us, met us, smoothed out problems at Customs and elsewhere, transported us, and saw to our every need, know that you are remembered with gratitude, as are all my African bush friends whose bravery I shall never forget.

My files were invaluable in writing this book and it is here that I should like to thank Jessica Coughlan for her meticulous clipping service and ongoing interest in my work.

Finally, my wife, Fiona Claire Capstick, who not only typed the entire manuscript, but also used her literary talents in making suggestions along the way. She was there.

This book would have hardly been possible to produce without the valued cooperation of Contax-Yashica, courtesy of my good pal, Steven Erasmus, who provided a Duke's ransom in camera bodies, Zeiss lenses, tripods, and the rest of the paraphernalia for which all the above firms are so revered and, also, but not secondarily, the huge cooperation of Cecil Horowitz of Photo Agencies, distributors of Fuji Film in southern Africa. Gentlemen, I thank you and your firms much more than I can say. *Madoda, tina bonga wenazonke kakulu.*

While this is hardly a commercial book written on behalf of Gordon Cundill and his hearty band of archers, it seems less than fair not to let you know where to reach him should you wish to experience an African safari in expert hands. Cundill does not advertise; he does not have to. However, you can reach him at:

Gordon J. P. Cundill, Esq.
P.O. Box 2078
Pietermaritzburg, 3200
Republic of South Africa
Telex: SA 643335
Telephone: (International Code) + 0331-34317

I did not choose Gordon Cundill and his cohorts by accident. They have been directly responsible for a most significant year in my life, and I hope that as you read, you have savored some of the pleasures I experienced.

—Peter Hathaway Capstick

Outdoor Life Books offers the 7 x 35 binoculars
good for a wide range of outdoor activities. For
details on ordering, please write: Outdoor Life
Books, P.O. Box 2033, Latham, N.Y. 12111.